FOUR THOUSAND PAWS

FOUR THOUSAND PAWS

Caring for the
Dogs of the Iditarod:
A Veterinarian's Story

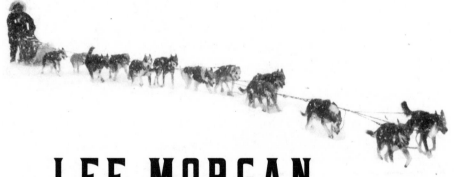

LEE MORGAN

Liveright Publishing Corporation

A Division of W. W. Norton & Company
Celebrating a Century of Independent Publishing

For information about permission to reproduce selections from this book,
write to Permissions, Liveright Publishing Corporation, a division of
W. W. Norton & Company, Inc., 500 Fifth Avenue, New York, NY 10110

For information about special discounts for bulk purchases, please
contact W. W. Norton Special Sales at specialsales@wwnorton.com or
800-233-4830

Manufacturing by Lakeside Book Company
Book design by Lovedog Studio
Production manager: Lauren Abbate

ISBN 978-1-324-09139-4

Liveright Publishing Corporation
500 Fifth Avenue, New York, N.Y. 10110
www.wwnorton.com

W. W. Norton & Company Ltd.
15 Carlisle Street, London W1D 3BS

1 2 3 4 5 6 7 8 9 0

Dedicated to Kristine Ann Morgan
and Spencer Ryan Morgan

For Nancy Ellen Rae and Norman Lee Morgan

Deep in the forest a call was sounding, and as often as he heard this call, mysteriously thrilling and luring, he felt compelled to turn his back upon the fire and the beaten earth around it, and to plunge into the forest, and on and on, he knew not where or why; nor did he wonder where or why, the call sounding imperiously, deep in the forest.

—Jack London, *The Call of the Wild*

When the Man waked up he said, "What is Wild Dog doing here?" And the Woman said, "His name is not Wild Dog any more, but the First Friend, because he will be our friend for always and always and always."

—Rudyard Kipling, *The Jungle Book*

CONTENTS

PART III

THE HARD PART

PART IV

ALMOST THERE

PART V

TO NOME

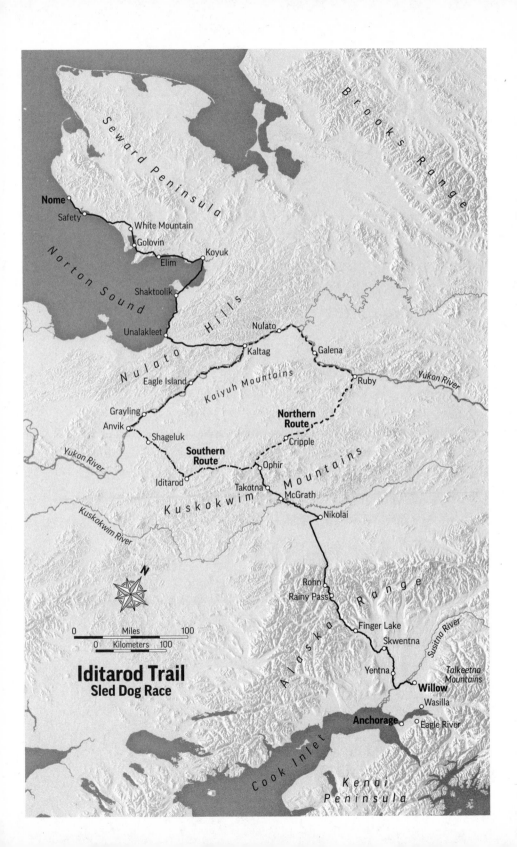

Iditarod Trail
Sled Dog Race

IS IT JUST A COUGH?

IT WAS WELL BEFORE SUNRISE AT UNALAKLEET WHEN WE HEARD the first cough.

Kim Henneman and I had volunteered for the overnight shift. While it was cold—as all nights in western Alaska are—it was not especially windy, and the snow had finally stopped falling. The landscape around Unalakleet reminded me, in some ways, of northern Norway, with its vast tundra, trees, and hills, though the fjords there are open water. The Norton Sound, on the other hand, is ice as hard as rock, a jumble of crags and cresting fissures the size of houses that had crashed into one another, creating a torturous landscape that was all but impassable.

Even with the bay frozen, a faint smell of saltwater hung in the air. Our checkpoint was on a beach that appeared smooth, but we knew that, under the mantle of wet, dense snow, there was a jagged array of boulders and smaller rocks with treacherous gaps between them. I'd learned this empirically, you might say; time and time again, I'd stumbled, fallen, and sunk to my waist in snowdrifts.

Kim and I had spent most of the evening talking, but as the night wore on, we had retreated into our own thoughts and spaces, me on my blue, plastic-covered straw bale; and Kim across from me, on hers. I liked working with her immensely. She was upbeat, almost always smiling, and a great veterinarian, the take-charge type who worked long, hard hours. When she wasn't attending sled races, she was a popular public speaker, and had been one of the first vets to advocate for the use of canine acupuncture. Like all trail veterinarians, including myself, her coat was spackled with patches from previous adventures all around the world.

We hadn't seen much activity so far. The checkpoint at Una-lakleet was two-thirds of the way into the race, so wide gaps had opened up between the competitors. Richard "Richie" Diehl had arrived at the checkpoint just a little while ago; two other teams had departed earlier in the day. Diehl's sled was parked over by an embankment, his dogs asleep on the beds of straw he'd laid down for them. Other than that, the dog lot was empty.

Aside from the incessant snoring of a particular black-and-white husky, the cough was the only sound that we'd heard from the dogs since they'd settled down. It was a dry hack, and not particularly loud. Kim and I watched as the apparent perpetrator got up off the straw, hacked a few times more, and then laid back down. I glanced at Kim, catching her eye. Neither of us spoke. There was no need to. A cough—even the soft, muffled variety such as this—was reason enough for concern, especially this deep into the race. We knew what it could mean: aspiration pneumonia.

There are specific things to watch out for in racing dogs. At the top of the list, or very close to it, is aspiration pneumonia. If a dog vomits during the run and then proceeds to inhale some of that material, the results can be devastating. Regurgitation can result from eating spoiled food, ingesting foreign material, or inadequate digestion time. Most of us have been warned to "wait half an hour after eating before you swim." It's the same for racing dogs resuming their run. Vomitus is laden with bacteria and viruses that are harmless if they stay in the digestive tract, but dangerous if they access the respiratory system. And aspiration pneumonia can develop in as little as forty-eight hours after a dog breathes in the offending material.

Instantly, I was on my feet. I grabbed my stethoscope and hurried over to the dog, Kim trailing closely behind. Our patient was asleep again, outstretched, with her arms in front of her. When I touched my stethoscope to her chest, she lifted her head slightly and gave me an irritated look. I listened quietly. Detecting aspiration pneumonia can be difficult at an early stage, as there are only ever-subtle differences in lung sounds. If it had developed a little, her lungs would sound like someone crinkling wax paper.

Relief. "Her lungs sound clear to me. Breathing normal." I turned to Kim.

A veteran of the Iditarod, Kim had a much deeper knowledge, at the time, of sled dog medicine, so I stood back to let her listen. After several moments, she looked at me and shook her head. She hadn't heard anything alarming either. We checked the dog's breathing again. It was neither too fast nor too shallow. If this were aspiration pneumonia, the dog would be visibly sicker, perhaps even running a fever, but her temperature was textbook. She gently sniffed my hand and, realizing that I had no treats to offer her, laid her head down again.

"She might have just snorted in a stray piece of straw."

Kim, usually so cheery, rocked on her heels, still looking intently at the husky. "It could be early pneumonia."

In truth, it could have been anything, including a reflex following an especially cold breath of air. I wondered whether the dog was fit to resume racing; and, in equal measure, *All this because of a cough*? Anyone who has owned a dog knows that they sometimes cough, and that it's usually nothing serious.

"She's just inhaled some dust," I suggested. "She's not coughed since her initial bout. Her physical exam checks out. She's back asleep, and looks just fine."

I could tell Kim was hesitant. We began to make our way back to our bales, discussing it as we walked, and I'd almost convinced her that it was nothing to worry about when another dog, far behind the first dog, started coughing. This cough was much louder, and he didn't simply lay down when he was done; he kept hacking until he expelled a large glob of sputum. My chest fell.

One dog coughing could be a singular event. Two dogs coughing was a pattern. I had been wrong. Obviously, we had more than a piece of dusty straw to reckon with.

By the time we got back to where the dogs were resting, a third dog, and then a fourth, were coughing. We worked our way around the whole team. None of them appeared sick. They all had normal temperatures. They readily ate the salmon snacks we offered. Whatever this was, it was affecting four dogs, all at the same time, with no other outward symptoms. The most likely explanation, then, was that a contagious respiratory condition, either viral or bacterial, had passed between them. They may have developed symptoms at the same time, but we knew they hadn't suddenly caught this. With respiratory diseases of this kind, there's always a latency period. Others on the team would be infected.

As Kim and I came to terms with this new development, the day-shift veterinarians began to trickle over from the bunkhouse, morning coffees still in hand. We discussed the dogs together, a research seminar there on the ice of Unalakleet. The dreaded aspiration pneumonia was still a possibility, but we all agreed that it would be highly unusual to see four dogs come down with it at the same time. Even the dogs who had coughed were alert and active. None of us could come up with a persuasive diagnosis. But we all understood what would have to happen next. The final third of the race was one of the toughest stretches, requiring sleds to power across the sea ice of Norton Sound, between those building-sized boulders of ice. This year had brought COVID-19, and a new complication: the elders of Shaktoolik, the next village on the course, had enforced strict quarantine and closed the town to outsiders. Gone was the usual, fully staffed checkpoint in the middle of Shaktoolik; instead, there was a far more rudimentary stop some miles away. At the stop after that, in Koyuk, there was a full team of vets, but that was eighty-five miles from here—at least fifteen hours' racing. In an emergency, there was no viable way for a veterinary team to reach the dogs between checkpoints.

Unalakleet had its own small airport. It served as a "hub" for the race, and if Richard Diehl's dogs dropped out here, it would be easy to get them back to Anchorage for treatment. We didn't know exactly what was wrong with them, but our decision was unanimous. The dogs couldn't carry on.

At some point during this discussion, I realized I would have to be the vet to tell Diehl. This is always a difficult discussion to have with a musher. They invest years of training—not to mention, at least $10,000—to enter and equip themselves for this one event. For most competitors, the Iditarod is not just a life-changing experience, but a life-defining experience. Diehl was in the upper echelons, someone in contention for at least a top-ten place.

It wasn't long before Diehl appeared in the doorway of the bunkhouse. Like the day-shift veterinarians, he was holding a cup of coffee. He'd had a few hours of rest but looked exhausted, as most of the mushers do after seven days on the ice. I still remember Richie's rookie year, 2013, when he placed thirty-sixth, with a completion time just under eleven days. (The next year, Diehl won the award for "Most Improved Musher.") By 2020, he was considered an Iditarod veteran. He had the slight build that a lot of mushers do; what made him stand out from the rest was his manicured beard, a stark contrast to the typical grizzly Alaskan look. He was still only thirty-six, and looked younger.

Diehl blithely scanned the horizon, sipping his coffee. It was only after a few minutes that he caught sight of us, down by his dogs. He scrambled down the hill.

"What's going on, guys?" He tried to sound relaxed, but I could hear the concern in his voice.

I described the coughing fits and explained that, at this stage, it's hard to tell whether the condition is viral, or even to determine how serious it is. He looked at me with bloodshot eyes. Already, tears were forming.

"I don't want to lose any dogs." His voice trailed off.

Diehl was in contention for serious prize money, and he was

within striking distance of the finish line. But his one and only concern was the health and welfare of his dogs.

I told him that none of us thought the dogs' lives were in danger, and that if he stopped here, the chances were high that his team would be alright. If he carried on, though, there were risks. I told him that it would be a long, long time before he'd reach another vet.

I pressed on. "Think about just stopping the race here. With this COVID thing going on, we don't know what's going to happen tomorrow, let alone the next few days. Call this year a wash. Everybody on your team is fine now."

He nodded. He was taking this better than I expected, which could only mean one thing. There was something he hadn't told me.

"I just called my wife," he said. "They've taken one of the dogs I dropped back at Kaltag to the emergency room in Anchorage."

The flight from Kaltag to Anchorage was over six hundred miles, and for that to have been arranged so quickly, the vets at Kaltag must have thought it was serious. That was eighty-two miles ago. I pictured the dog on an IV drip; getting antibiotics; being monitored in a veterinary hospital.

"It was just like we're seeing here," he said, waving his hand in the direction of his team. "But it was just him. It seemed minor, and none of the others showed any signs."

It was clear, now, that Diehl wouldn't just be leaving a few dogs behind and carrying on. He'd "scratch"—he'd drop out of the race entirely. The arrangements were made quickly, and Diehl made another phone call to his wife.

Diehl and his team had already traversed the Alaska Range of mountains; made it through the Burn, a wasteland left by a catastrophic forest fire; and raced up the frozen Yukon River, where the hazards are all but invisible—until your sled hits them. He'd spent many cold nights with only his dogs for company. Just a third of the course remained, and the terrain, while difficult, was eminently doable.

In the end, the dogs got the treatment they needed. The final consensus was that they had inhaled a fungus on bad straw back in Kaltag. They would be fine; even the one that had been airlifted from Kaltag to Anchorage would recover nicely. They'd be back again next year, yipping and yammering, ready to take on The Last Great Race on Earth once more.

For Diehl, dropping out of the race had been brutal, but it was the right thing to do. In this race, as in any elite race, this choice can mean life or death. But these are the choices we're called to make.

FOUR THOUSAND PAWS

Tongues wagging, these canine competitors are thrilled to race.

INTRODUCTION

THE LAST GREAT RACE ON EARTH

I N VETERINARY SCHOOL I WAS TAUGHT THAT DOGS ARE PHYSI- cally incapable of smiling—that they lack the facial muscles necessary to perform this basic action. The veterinarians who determined this clearly never witnessed the beginning of a sled dog race.

Year after year, dozens of canine competitors travel to Alaska to participate in the longest, most famous sled dog race in history, the Iditarod Trail Sled Dog Race. The start is always complete bedlam. Drunk on adrenaline, the dogs whip themselves into an almost insane state of anticipation. They strain at their harnesses; some jump and leap into the air, howling with excitement. Bark for bark, they match the enthusiasm of their human spectators, who cheer as if they're at a homecoming football game. While we wait for the start signal, I scan the sea of dogs. There's pure joy on each and every face—and absolutely no doubt in my mind that they're smiling. Of course, I'm smiling, too; I'm one of hundreds of volunteers who work to ensure that the race runs smoothly.

I first volunteered as a trail vet on the Iditarod Trail Sled Dog Race in 2012, and I've only missed a couple of years since. This book is the story of my time on the trail and the extraordinary canine athletes I've worked with—so far. There have been many brilliant books written about the history, origins, and running of the race, from Gary Paulsen's *Winterdance* to Gay Salisbury and

Laney Salisbury's *The Cruelest Miles*, and plenty of individual competitors have published their memoirs. But this is the first book written by a veterinarian of the Iditarod, someone who's volunteered to work behind the scenes. Naturally, my perspective differs from that of the mushers, out there on the ice with their dogs, but my time as a trail veterinarian has come with its own challenges. While I've seen extraordinary sights and met a lot of interesting people, I've also faced real dangers, from hypothermia and dehydration to snow squalls and fires, and I've made difficult calls about the lives and well-being of racers. I've worked nearly all of the checkpoints between the Ceremonial Start in Anchorage and the burled arch that marks the finish in Nome, more than a thousand miles away. I've slept in bunkhouses complete with showers and beds, and I've weathered bone-chilling nights in storm-tossed tents.

But this isn't a memoir or straightforward, year-by-year account of my time as an Iditarod veterinarian. This book centers the dogs themselves, and moves through the Iditarod checkpoint by checkpoint, matching the structure and rhythm of the race. Not all of the events in this book took place in a single year. Instead, they were drawn from my experiences at various races throughout the years. The events I describe in Unalakleet, for example, didn't occur in one year, but they all happened about a week into the race, when the field begins to spread out and, inevitably, teams are faced with tough decisions. As a veterinarian, I've met every type of person involved in the race: the mushers; the dog handlers; additional support staff; fans; and the pilots who graciously ferry all of us non-racers around. At the risk of sounding a little egotistical, the trail vet is one of the most critical roles, in large part because we're the ones who support the dogs themselves. With this book, I hope I can demonstrate just how much effort goes into ensuring the safety of the canine competitors—and how much the dogs themselves enjoy the race.

❊   ❊   ❊   ❊

IN THE STATE OF Alaska, few events attract as much attention, or create as much spectacle, as the Iditarod Trail Sled Dog Race. The event is held annually, during the first two weeks of March, when the conditions for sledding are optimal. Gone is the seemingly endless arctic night, when the sun is barely a smudge in the southern sky, and the windchill can drive temperatures below −50 degrees Fahrenheit. Still to come are the comparatively high temperatures of May, when the snow becomes thick and wet with the warm season approaching. In March, there's still a heavy mantle of snow on the ground, but it's cold and dry, so the sleds can glide effortlessly, their runners hissing along the trail. Days are broken up into an almost equal period of light and dark, with frigid nights and daytime highs that won't overly fatigue the dogs.

To say the Iditarod is "tough" is an understatement of the highest order; even to say it's "*infernally* tough" underplays it. In an age when summiting Mount Everest has become almost commonplace and there are four-star hotel resorts in deepest Amazonia, completing an Iditarod remains a signal achievement. I wouldn't dispute that the people who compete in ultramarathons in deserts or arduous cycling races like the Giro d'Italia are at the pinnacle of athletic performance. But the fact remains that the Iditarod Sled Dog Race is one of the hardest endurance events in the world. The length of the route is itself daunting, at 1,049 miles: a thousand miles, plus a symbolic forty-nine to honor Alaska as the forty-ninth state. Draw a line that long on a map of the lower 48 states, and it would take you from Washington, DC, to Miami; New York to Des Moines; Portland to San Diego; or Denver to Houston. It's a little less than half the length of the Tour de France. While the television coverage of that race lingers on aerial shots of green fields and chateaux, the audience understands that the cyclists are undergoing a grueling physical test. No one watching the riders heave themselves over the Pyrenees could possibly think otherwise. Yet even this does not compare to the Iditarod. The Alaskan wilderness is its own monster.

Like the cyclists, the mushers and dogs battle steep mountains, but they must also traverse freezing streams, treacherous snowdrifts, and deep spruce forests where headlamps are necessary even during periods of twilight. They face the Burn, with its burnt stumps and snags, and the Bering Sea, with its glare ice and gale-force winds, both forecast and unexpected, and they do it all in the hyperborean, bitter temperatures of the arctic. Competitors must also be prepared to go toe-to-toe with and even protect themselves against wild animals, including the occasional charging moose, which can hit a sled team side-on with the force of a pickup truck.

There are twenty-six checkpoints in the race, which can be thought of as twenty-six separate stages. Most begin at a town or similar settlement, some home to fewer than a dozen people. After crossing the Burn and the Norton Sound, the trail pushes northwest, becoming even colder and more remote. The human and canine participants face sleep deprivation, hunger, thirst, and aches and pains of every imaginable sort. Not only must dogs and mushers have a moment-by-moment awareness of their surroundings; they must also make difficult tactical decisions about how hard to push, and at what stage of the race; and crucially, where to take rests. And once a team sets out, it's on its own. There are no support vehicles to drop a spare sled or extra supplies. Mushers have to carry everything they'll need. At the time of this writing, mushers weren't allowed to have two-way communication—and it can be incredibly difficult to land a rescue plane in the wilderness. At most points on the trail, the fastest way to get to a team in trouble is to ride up the course in a snowmobile (or another dogsled). In an emergency, mushers either have to push on or go back to the last checkpoint. Despite the length of the race, it can be highly competitive. In 1978, it was decided like an Olympic sprint, with a photo finish.

❄ ❄ ❄ ❄

AN IDITAROD SLED DOG team typically consists of one musher and up to fourteen dogs, the dogs hooked together in pairs. Dogs are by nature pack animals, and even a team of untrained huskies attached to a sled will often instinctively bound in the direction of another team they see or smell in front of them. This, of course, is exactly what a musher wants them to do. It's the musher's job to seize that energy and channel it in the most effective way. A veteran musher once told me the story of how his dogs, upon seeing a competing team on a lakebed during the Yukon Quest—a 1,000-mile race from Fairbanks, Alaska, to Whitehorse, Yukon, in Canada—lasered in on them and began speeding along the ice with no instruction from him. The dogs on the other team, sensing that another sled was fast approaching, also kicked into high gear. Both mushers were left clinging to their sleds, desperately trying to slow their teams so they wouldn't overexert themselves so early in the race.

I'm often asked if the dogs taking part in the Iditarod are aware that they're racing against other teams. It's a fair question. Maybe they see it as an opportunity to run free, to release their seemingly infinite energy. (As any husky owner knows, the breed is prone to bouncing off walls if not exercised enough.) Huskies are also proud, intelligent creatures. Some of the most demoralizing cries I've heard in all my years as a veterinarian have come from dogs dropped from the race, watching their teammates leave without them. It may also be that these dogs share an inborn instinct as hunters to run; to work as a pack and pit themselves against rivals; and to strive to arrive first. But I have to wonder if it's more than that. I've observed the dogs as they prep for the race. When one begins to howl that canine kind of plaintive song, the other dogs join in until the din of the chorus is deafening. They leap and dance in their harnesses; sometimes only the snow anchor—a piece of iron about the size and shape of a handheld garden fork, set firmly in the ice—keeps them from rocketing away at the start of a run. I know the breed well, and it's not a stretch for me to say that huskies enjoy the thrill of competition, and that they want to win their race.

Mushers take great care in selecting and training their dogs. Today, only northern dog breeds like huskies are permitted to participate in the Iditarod; the rule was adopted in the early 1990s after musher John Suter entered the competition, on more than one occasion, with standard poodles on his dogsled team. (Race officials and veterinarians eventually pulled the poodles, citing, not unsurprisingly, health concerns.) Even so, very few purebred dogs are used on Iditarod teams. Most dogs are crosses, specially bred to contain husky genes. They practice like Olympic competitors; and like Olympic competitors, they practice for almost their whole competitive lives. During the summer months, the dogs pull wheeled carts along dirt tracks. They learn to work together, test their limits, and determine when it's safe to push through them. In short, they learn to trust each other, and, critically, the musher.

Dogs are assigned very specific roles on the team. There's no gender bias when it comes to selecting elite canines: racers can be male or female. The lead dogs are often the brightest and most capable. They're the two in front. The real captains. Lead dogs guide the sled and team through the wilderness, deciding how to surmount obstacles and obstructions like streams, hills, holes, and trees. To the other dogs, their call, right or wrong, is often final. Mushers may use different lead dogs during the race, choosing them based on terrain, weather conditions, stage of the race, or even dogs' attitudes on a given day. Directly behind the lead dogs are the swing dogs. Their job is to make sure that their teammates behind them work in unison. If the lead dogs go left, the swing dogs ensure that everyone else goes left, too. The wheel dogs are the pair directly in front of the sled. They're usually the biggest dogs on the team; they pivot the sled, making sure that when the lead dogs and swing dogs swerve around an obstacle, the sled is primed to change direction. The rest of the dogs—six to eight, between the lead and wheel dogs—are "team dogs," and they provide the heavy power. At every turn and obstacle, the huskies pass commands down the line, with the lead dogs yelping the way forward, and the swing, team, and wheel dogs following close behind, watching their swishing tails.

As the dogs push toward Nome, they perform an intricate choreography. This kind of training cannot be programmed; the dogs aren't machines. Even those who don't believe that dogs possess human-like emotions agree that dogs have quirks, habits, and personalities, huskies even more than most breeds. A successful musher must learn the strengths and weaknesses of each member of the team, strike a careful balance, and defuse often dramatic rivalries. True, dogs evolved as pack animals. But all packs, including sled dog teams, fundamentally consist of individual actors who display all the characteristics—and form all the dynamics—of human sports teams. They show loyalty, determination, and camaraderie. They also vie for dominance, and get angry, feisty, distracted, sullen, and jealous. The musher becomes the coach who not only takes the athletes to the peak of their individual potential, but ensures that they all cohere as a unit in time for the start of the race.

❄   ❄   ❄   ❄

FOR MANY YEARS, SLEDS set out from central Anchorage; then, the Municipality of Anchorage built a new state road that crisscrossed the trail. A large pedestrian bridge was built to accommodate passersby. On every other day, the bridge serves its purpose well. During the Iditarod, however, it created a bottleneck early in the race, even with timed interval starts. It wasn't what the dogs had been trained to expect. While some teams came to a screeching halt, others tried to navigate along the busy highway instead. This posed a problem for race organizers.

Some organizers suggested starting the race in a different city. This had already been done on a previous occasion, when a freak lack of snow on the southern part of the trail compelled organizers to move the start to Fairbanks, about 350 miles north of Anchorage. As an eleventh-hour alternative, starting the race in Fairbanks worked well. But it didn't offer a permanent solution. Fairbanks is much smaller than Anchorage, with a population of about 33,000 (compared to Anchorage's 290,000), and starting there would mean rerouting the entire first half of the course. Fortunately, there was an easier fix: just move the start up. Willow, a town approximately seventy miles north of Anchorage, would become the official start site. In pure sporting terms—that is, looking only at the course itself—this would be a minor change. But Willow is even smaller than Fairbanks, with a population of less than 2,000. There had always been solid, practical reasons for starting the Iditarod in the largest city in the state. For one, there's an international airport in Anchorage, and it's the only place with enough hotel rooms, bars, and eateries to service all the mushers, tourists, and journalists that the event attracts. The infrastructure of a large city not only makes it easier for people to arrive and congregate, but for competitors to pick up any last-minute equipment or supplies.

Thus, the "Two Start" solution was born. The first start, in Anchorage, would be purely for show. The teams would take off one by one, at two minute intervals, from Fourth Avenue. They would navigate through the side streets of Anchorage, following an eleven-mile course to Campbell Creek, where transport trucks would be waiting to take the dogs to Willow Lake for the official start of the Iditarod. The move turned out to be a great boon to the race. Once the teams set out, sled dog racing is not an ideal spectator sport. The Ceremonial Start created an opportunity for fans to see their favorite mushers and dogs. The hectic, colorful event has the character of a state fair: Alaskans who have been holed up for the winter appear to mingle with friends they may not have seen in months. There are pre-race festivities, including a ribbon-cutting and the Iditarod Musher's Banquet. Television networks and national newspapers send teams of broadcasters and photojournalists to cover the event. For many, it's a welcome departure from politics.

Race day brings people from around the world to Anchorage. Spectators line the streets two to three rows deep, everyone wearing thick winter jackets. Food trucks fill the streets behind them, offering Alaskan fare like moose chili and reindeer sausage, as well as traditional spectator-sport snacks like tacos and hot dogs. The aroma of fried meats carries through the cold, crisp air. Vendors do quick business with tourists, selling licensed and not-so-licensed Iditarod souvenirs. Individual conversations blend together, and as I walk by, I catch snippets of discussions, like changing stations on a radio.

In Alaska, the top competitors—competitors like Dan Seavey, John Baker, Jeff King, and four-time Iditarod winner Lance Mackey—are as idolized as Lebron James, Tom Brady, and A-Rod in the lower 48. Kids bring along virtually anything they hope to have autographed: photo albums of past races, homemade and professionally printed posters, plush toy huskies, single scraps of paper. Youngsters wait around like Little Leaguers loitering at the dugouts during Major League batting practice.

You may be wondering what exactly a musher does to earn this adoration. Even if all that was required of a musher was to stand on the sled while the dogs did all the work, they would have to have the strength and stamina to keep upright from morning to night in the face of arctic conditions. In reality, mushers play a far more physical role. To help propel the sled up steep inclines or steer around sharp bends, they place one foot on the runner and push into the snow with the other, exerting almost Herculean force. In the whiteout conditions of an unexpected blizzard, when the dogs can sink up to their bellies in snow, the musher will jump off the sled and forge ahead of the pack, breaking trail for the dogs to follow. At rest stops, mushers spend hours tending to their dogs, hauling heavy sacks of food and nursing portable stoves as they slowly melt ice to make drinking water. The number one rule of sledding, I've been told, is *Never let go of the sled.* If you fall off making a turn, or while driving your foot into the snow, you must keep hold of the handlebar, because the dogs will not notice. They'll continue to power away.

Many mushers have waxed poetic about their experiences on the course—describing the natural beauty, the spiritual awakening that comes with often total isolation from other human beings—but their job is deeply challenging. An oversight during race preparation, a bad call, or even a moment's lack of concentration can prove disastrous. Still, it's the dogs who are far and away the most important participants in the race. They provide the forward motion as the sled powers more than a thousand miles through what can be brutal conditions. Even the mushers who are household names in Alaska admit that the real stars are the dogs.

The dogs, too, enjoy the attention at the Ceremonial Start. They grin at the camera in a way that only huskies can, their eyes radiating excitement, their mouths open, and their tongues—all bright and pink—wiggling back and forth. Some appear to pose for photos, standing up straight and proud, with their tails curved over their back. Other dogs are aloof, eschewing the admiring crowd to hang out alone or with their canine companions, not venturing out to the fans.

❄ ❄ ❄ ❄

ESTABLISHING A STRETCH OF trail that isn't part of the official race also created a new commercial opportunity: the Idita-Rider program. Months before the race, people of all backgrounds and ages bid on a chance to ride in the sled of their favorite team. For about the price of an airline ticket from Washington, DC, to Alaska, a lucky few riders ride eleven miles with the teams, from the downtown all the way to the Campbell Creek Science Center. They sit low in the basket at the front of the sled, where the team supplies will be stored during the race; in other words, they sit closer to the ground and the dogs than the mushers themselves. It's fast, terrifying, and exhilarating all at the same time, and many Idita-Riders say afterward that riding with an actual team on the Iditarod Trail was the best experience of their life.

The dogs are just as eager to start as the mushers and the Idita-Riders, but of course, they have no idea what a "Ceremonial Start" is. They think this is the real deal, so when a team enters the chute, the dogs begin to strain at their harnesses, and mushers have to firmly anchor their sleds to prevent a false start. Yips and sharp, pointed barks fill the air as the teams anticipate the start. When the signal is finally given, the musher pulls up the snow anchor and yells "Go!" (Despite movie stereotypes, rarely does the person driving the dogs yell "Mush!" to signal a start; in fact, the word "musher" derives from *marche*, the command a *French* musher would traditionally give.) The dogs know exactly what the command means. The bottled-up anticipation explodes as soon as they're free to run. They bolt out, oblivious to anything but the trail ahead. The sled bounds forward with the motive power of fourteen dogs. Now, they're in a state of unbridled exuberance. It is a wild, barely controlled melee.

And it's incredible to watch. In two-minute intervals, the sleds snake down Fourth Avenue, past stores and office buildings. They skid sideways as the route breaks sharply off Fourth and turns onto one of the back roads. Balanced at the end of their sleds, the mushers are elated. The runners, sheathed in sturdy plastic, *whoosh* as they glide over snow, ice, and asphalt. Some spectators try to

Iditarod veteran Mitch Seavey races with an Idita-Rider during the Ceremonial Start.

follow the sleds through the narrow city streets, but they soon fall away as the dogs outstrip them. After a hundred yards of a full-on sprint, the mushers shout, "Good dogs, good dogs!" and the dogs drop off the pace, falling into an organized trot. Both man and dog share a moment of glee. All of Alaska is ahead of them.

PART I

A LESS CEREMONIAL START

CHAPTER 1

IDITAROD VET

EVERY DECEMBER, FOR MANY YEARS BEFORE I FIRST VOLUN-
teered, an advertisement in the *Journal of the American Veterinary Medical Association* caught my eye. It was a call to apply for
a week-long workshop on sled dog medicine, held in Anchorage,
Alaska. The ad promised attendees an introduction to the various
conditions and therapies unique to canine athletes. It would take
place just before the Iditarod, and if you passed the course, you
might be offered the chance to volunteer as a trail veterinarian.

All my life, I've enjoyed fishing, camping, hiking, and kayaking. Despite increasing industrialization and deforestation across
America and the world, Alaska has remained wild and untamed,
and I'd quietly always wanted to have my own Jack London wilderness adventure: to stay in a tent in subzero conditions, cooking my meals over an open campfire. I loved the idea of playing
a part, an integral part, of an iconic and storied event like the
Iditarod. Every year, though, I told myself that I didn't have the
time (or money) to pursue such bold undertakings, and even if I
did, they were looking for someone with specific experience that
I just didn't have. Applicants to the workshop in Alaska were
expected to come in with a working knowledge of sled dogs,
and to have had experience working smaller sled dog races—
even to have raced dogs themselves. While most of the volunteer veterinarians come from Alaska and the lower 48, the event
attracted vets from Australia, Norway, South Africa, Germany,

France, and the United Kingdom. They are all at the top of their field—the experts' experts. At my veterinary practice in central Washington, DC, I hadn't exactly seen many sled dogs as clients.

Since 2002, I've run the Georgetown Veterinary Hospital with my wife, Kris, who handles the office management, allowing me to focus on the medicine. We cater mainly to domestic pets; it's the kind of place you'd take your cat when her litter box habits change, or your dog when she gets stung by a bee. To my credit, though, I'd been voted among the "Best Vets in DC" by the *Washingtonian* and "Veterinarian of the Year" by *Veterinary Practice News*, and I'd been recognized by organizations such as the Westminster Kennel Club Dog Show; The Seeing Eye, a foundation for guide dogs; NASA; the National Geographic Society; the Smithsonian Institution; the US Navy; and the US Marine Corps. Still, when I finally *did* apply, I found it hard to explain why I should be considered for the course instead of one of the hundreds of other applicants. On the application form, I stressed that since the 9/11 attacks, veterinarians working in big cities have become increasingly interested in the treatment of working dogs. There's an awareness that police dogs, search dogs, and sniffer dogs, for example, have unique medical needs, and in fact I'd given specialized treatment to these hardworking dogs at my practice. I had also worked with dogs who competed in agility competitions—not exactly running a thousand-mile race, but those dogs were athletes, right? As I filled out the form, I worried that my main qualification was that I'd once adopted a three-legged Siberian Husky. We named him Sabo, after Chris Sabo, a third baseman for the Cincinnati Reds, because his facial patterning resembled the goggles Chris wore. He'd been our family pet, but also the clinic's official "Greeter Dog."

While researching, I read up on the longtime head veterinarian, Stuart "Stu" Nelson. He had a reputation for being meticulous in selecting not only top-notch practitioners, but also people who were generally easy to work with; eager to work long, unpaid hours; and could persevere in the extreme weather that forms the basis of an Alaskan winter. The common theme, I gathered, was that he didn't want anyone in the veterinary corps who'd waste time complaining. He seemed more interested in the attitude of veterinarians applying than in narrow, hands-on experience with sled dogs, so I stressed my work ethic when I threw my hat in the ring. I was pleasantly surprised to be accepted, at least to the training program.

❄ ❄ ❄ *GEORGETOWN, DC. 3,783 miles to Nome. Ten weeks before the race. 54°F. Fair.*

ALL WANNABE IDITAROD VETERINARIANS are mailed a hefty preparation manual months before the race. The packet that arrived included a book on the systems in place for treating the dogs before, during, and after the race. Reading it, I was struck by the number of provisions in the rule book designed solely for the welfare of the dogs themselves. No risks were to be taken with injured dogs; the rule is that they have to be transported to the next checkpoint along the route—or the previous one, if closer—and surrendered to the care of the veterinarians stationed there.

This hasn't always been the case. The Iditarod began in its modern form in 1973. The inaugural race was said to have been 1,049 miles long; using modern measuring techniques, it has been determined that the route was closer to 975 miles. It followed part of the old Iditarod Trail, which, in turn, was based on a network of trade routes that the Athabascan, Inupiat, and Yupik peoples had developed over centuries. Before 1908, Alaska had barely been surveyed by US authorities; then, a gold rush brought thousands of prospectors to the area. As they spread up the trail to the north, a string of settlements grew along the route to support them. Within ten years, whatever meager amounts of gold existed to be found *had* been found. The rush came to an end, and the trail fell into disuse and disarray. Not even the adoption of Alaska as the forty-ninth state in 1959 could renew interest in the region. In 1973,

great swaths of the Iditarod Trail were still impassable; even the
US Army's toughest snow-clearing vehicles couldn't advance more
than a few miles. It was unclear whether teams would even be able
to reach the finish line. Participants in the race would be more
than just competitors; they would be trailblazers and explorers.
In the end, thirty-four teams agreed to compete. Their incentive
was a then-enormous prize of $55,000—about $300,000 today,
adjusting for inflation. The winner, Dick Wilmarth—a miner and
trapper from Red Devil, Alaska—completed the course in twenty
days. (Today, most competitors finish in eight to eleven days.) Just
twenty-two teams finished; the others were forced to drop out.

That first year, there was only one veterinarian in attendance,
covering no less than thirty-four teams and the entire thousand-
mile course. Dr. Terry Adkins was a twenty-eight-year-old veterinarian serving at Elmendorf Air Force Base, a US military facility
in Anchorage. He was given two hours on the day the race started
to inspect every dog. After that, he hopped from one checkpoint
to another in race organizer Joe Redington's bush plane. At each
stop, he treated the dogs that needed aid. There were no protocols
yet in place, so Adkins would simply approach each musher and
ask if they had any problems with their huskies, or if any of them
needed veterinary care. If a serious injury occurred away from a
checkpoint, or while Adkins was at another checkpoint, the nearest ham radio operator would call it in; Redington would then fly
the veterinarian to wherever he was needed. As Adkins later told
reporters, he volunteered his time because he loved mushing and
the dogs who participated in the sport. The next year, in 1974,
Adkins competed in the race for the first of twenty-two times; he
rounded out his Iditarod career in 2006.

Despite Adkins's best efforts, the mushers and dogs who competed in the 1973 race were left largely to their own devices.
Mushers cared for their canine counterparts as best as they could,
instituting routine checks at each leg. Still, between sixteen and

Veterinarian Major Dr. Terry Adkins examines a dog for heartworm at Francis E. Warren Air Force Base in Wyoming. Adkins was singularly responsible for the care of dogs competing in the 1973 Iditarod.

thirty dogs died that first year, with most succumbing to aspiration pneumonia or dehydration. No musher wants to see their dogs die, let alone in pain; many raise them from puppies and form real bonds with them over the years. The dogs that competed in the inaugural race were all working dogs, rather than pet or companion dogs, but they were just as valued. Until the early 1900s, dogsleds were just about the only way into—or out of—the Alaskan interior. Mail, medicine, food, and other supplies were all hauled by sled. With the introduction of air travel in 1923, Alaskans began to carry out these tasks via small aircraft, but the service was hazardous, and there are places in Alaska, then as now, where landing a plane is a practical impossibility. Although less technologically advanced, dogsleds offered stability and consistency, and today, many Alaskans continue to use sleds recreationally.

Like farm dogs, military dogs, and police dogs, sled dogs risk injury and death. The mushers who entered the inaugural race understood these risks and had, in fact, been warned by race organizers that the course could prove fatal for *humans*, too. (By fortune, skill, or sheer dumb luck, no human lives were lost on the trail that year.) What the race organizers really failed to forecast was the amount of attention, both positive and negative, that the first Iditarod would attract. This proved to be a double-edged sword. On the one hand, the race had sparked the public's imagination, and there was a clear appetite to make it an annual event; on the other, the race and its organizers were now subject to intense scrutiny. The animal rights movement was then in its infancy, but it wasn't hard to persuade the public that the Iditarod had been a disaster for the dogs. Concern poured in from around the world, and not just from people who had never experienced the harsh realities of the Alaskan wilderness. Race organizers were criticized for their "callous disregard" for animal life. The bad publicity ultimately led then-Governor Bill Egan to write to Redington condemning the treatment of the dogs. No sooner than it began, the Iditarod took on a reputation for animal cruelty.

It was clear—to mushers, spectators, commentators, and other veterinarians alike—that the organizers could have done more to ensure the safety of the dogs, and that things would have to change if the event was to run again. The Iditarod Trail Committee wasted no time, promptly rewriting the rules to include mandatory eight- and twenty-four-hour rest stops and other measures that wouldn't penalize mushers who allowed their dogs to rest. Later Iditarods would employ not one but a small army of veterinary medical volunteers, about forty to sixty in all, and a head veterinarian to oversee them. There would be a team at each checkpoint, and as the competitors cleared the early stages of the race, the teams would "leapfrog" up the trail. When these and other changes were implemented in 1975, the death rate dropped dramatically. Just two official deaths were reported. Still, two is two, and the race organizers, committed to minimizing harm, continued to push the race in a positive direction. Rules evolved and expanded. New measures were instituted. Within a few years, procedures like mandatory drug testing were introduced.

To this day, the Iditarod continues to draw ire from animal rights activists, making many companies wary of sponsoring the event. Much of the activists' rhetoric is based on the idea that every year hundreds of dogs are dropped due to injury, illness, or exhaustion, with the strong implication that countless dogs are driven to the verge of death by cruel mushers, then abandoned in the wilderness or left behind at checkpoints to starve. I hope this book shows, in many examples and great detail, the infrastructure in place to care for the dogs, and how the organizers have spent decades striving to ensure and improve animal welfare. Dogs are dropped at the earliest potential sign of a problem—precisely because that minimizes animal suffering— then cared for until they are reunited with their owners. This happened before my time, but those who were there tell me that there was another revolution in the quality of care following the arrival of Stuart Nelson Jr. as head veterinarian in 1996. Stu lives in northern Idaho, but since 1983, he's spent three weeks each year on solo kayak explorations of the Alaskan Northwest. He first volunteered as a trail vet in the mid-1980s, answering a magazine ad just like I did. By all accounts, mushers seemed to instantly warm to him; his medical expertise and innate outdoorsmanship meant that they listened to him, trusted him almost instinctively. Before Stu took charge, the veterinary staff played a relatively passive role in the race. They were there if needed—to patch up dogs who'd been injured or become sick— but were otherwise inactive. Stu encouraged them to take a more participatory, even proactive, role. Beginning in 1996, there was a new emphasis on preventing injuries in the first place, and volunteers were expected to be up to speed with the latest developments in veterinary medicine.

The standard of care has now evolved beyond anything the first competitors could have imagined, and only continues to improve.

Today, every dog is examined carefully before the start of the race. In order to participate, mushers must present bloodwork demonstrating that their dogs have no unseen physiological diseases. The veterinary staff now includes two program managers, a veterinary pathologist, and an electrocardiogram (ECG) consultant who oversees a team of fifteen veterinary technicians; before the race, these technicians check the hearts of all the dogs, looking for cardiological irregularities and other signs of danger. During the race itself, teams are required to stop at all checkpoints for at least a brief inspection of the dogs. At major "hubs"—checkpoints like McGrath and Unalakleet, where teams tend to take longer rests—a permanent team of three veterinarians performs an extensive examination of each dog. All this information is logged, so there's a comprehensive record of each dog's condition before and during the race.

Most importantly, Iditarod veterinarians *always* get the final say. If a veterinarian deems a dog unfit to race, the dog must be dropped then and there, no questions asked. Dropped dogs are promptly flown back to Anchorage and looked after until they can be reunited with their owners; this is a central part of their care. These dogs are not, as some say, merely "dumped." No veterinarian would volunteer to oversee an event in which dogs are pushed to and beyond the limits of their endurance, patched up, and sent out to face new hazards. A veterinarian's responsibility is to the animal, above all, and when it comes to that animal's health, the vet must always err on the side of caution. Most of a trail vet's day-to-day work consists of monitoring for often minor signs of distress and confirming, at every turn, that dogs are fit to continue. As a matter of course, volunteers for the Iditarod must have a uniquely high level of commitment.

There will always be risks, but the systems in place at the modern Iditarod take those risks seriously. This is not to say that the Alaskan wilderness is not a dangerous place; the orientation packet, with its massive winter gear checklist, clearly stated otherwise.

While the mushers and dogs would bear the brunt of the arctic conditions, I wouldn't be working in pockets of warmth and luxury. There were no hotel rooms or fancy lodges for veterinarians along the Iditarod Trail; more often than not, I would sleep in tents that I'd help set up. I quickly realized that even working as a trail vet who never ventured, say, more than a hundred yards from the vets' station would carry its own risks.

By far the biggest threat to the volunteer staff is the cold. Blizzard conditions; heavy, whiteout winds; and subzero temperatures are the norm in Alaska during race season. While the canine competitors are naturally adapted to cold conditions, human beings are not. Our core temperature is usually about 98.6°F; most of the dogs run at about 101.5°F. There are myriad reasons for this: for one, humans lose internal water at a prodigious rate; we also lack a double layer of fur (some of us are starting to lack even a single layer); and we have limited circulation to our feet relative to a dog. The manual provided by race organizers went into great depth outlining the risks of hypothermia and frostbite, and how to combat them.

I had read enough books on mountaineering to know that with frostbite comes the risk of sequela, like gangrene, as well as amputation and even death. I knew that I'd need a warm coat and good boots, and the list had other items I assumed would be there: special socks, ski pants, sleeping gear. I had predicted that I would need basic camping gear like a knife, a single-burner stove, cooking utensils, a breathable sleeping bag ("polar-rated"), a ground cloth, and an inflatable mattress. But it hit me just how isolated I would be when I saw the personal survival gear that I would be expected to carry: a first-aid kit, a bivouac tent, a signal mirror, a folding pack saw for cutting firewood. To me, at that point, it seemed a little extreme, but the manual made it clear: I had to be ready to survive in the event that a plane crash left me stranded between checkpoints, fifty miles away from safety, at night and in a blizzard.

❄ ❄ ❄ ❄

IF SELECTED FROM AMONG the vets who passed the course, I would be traveling from checkpoint to checkpoint in small bush planes, so I would be restricted to two bags: a backpack and a duffel bag. Those two bags would have to hold everything I'd need for weeks in the field. As you might imagine, Washington, DC, is not the best place to equip yourself for the Alaskan winter. After some uninspired searching, I ended up at The North Face, a national chain with a branch just down the street from my clinic. The store window featured a mannequin standing in a pile of wool and Styrofoam bubbles, dressed in a bright-red, one-piece arctic jumpsuit. The racks inside the store were full of high-end ski jackets, hats, and boots for the relatively mild East Coast winters.

I talked to the twentysomething salesman behind the counter. When I mentioned the Iditarod, he smiled approvingly and said he'd just returned from hiking across Peru, where he'd summited one of the peaks in the Andes, where temperatures can range from 95°F to −40°F. I soon learned that most people working at The North Face were serious hikers and climbers who took the job mainly for the generous employee discount and flexible hours.

"I'll need something heavy-duty. I saw a jumpsuit in the window, the red one, and—" I'd already pictured myself in it, striding courageously through a blizzard.

"You're going to be bending over a lot, having to move quickly from one spot to the next," he said. "You can't do that in a jumpsuit."

Defeat.

"Those jumpsuits don't breathe well, and you're going to build up a sweat. You want a good, cold-weather parka as an outer shell and layered clothes so if you do overheat, you can shed something. You can't do that with these jumpsuits. We don't have everything you need in stock here, but let me research what we have at the warehouse."

I returned a few days later. My Virgil led me down a flight of stairs to where he'd laid out a vast array of outdoor gear: gauntlet-style mitts; heavy-duty gloves and snow boots; wool socks; an Alaskan aviator's hat; several shirts of varying material and thickness; and a chunky, down-insulated parka. None of it matched, but I didn't care. It looked warm.

He proudly explained the function of each garment.

"Keeping your feet warm will be most important," he told me. "Once your toes get cold, you are pretty much done."

First, lightweight socks, to absorb the sweat. Then, heavy socks, to help my feet retain heat. Next, the boots. Many Iditarod volunteers wear mukluks, a type of heavily insulated footwear that's warm yet lightweight and flexible. For all future Iditarods, I would wear mukluks, but the first time I went, I chose a pair of Timberline boots, cumbersome but rated to −30°F. These Frankenstein boots, I would later find out, are not good near dog feet. More than once I accidentally stepped on a husky's paw, which resulted in a loud yip and several turned heads. With mukluks, you could feel the ground, and even if a misstep was taken, the soles were soft and pliable enough that it wouldn't cause an injury to a stray paw.

In addition to socks, boots, mitts, gloves, and hats, I bought ski pants, ski goggles, a face mask, and piles of fleece-based clothing for layering. The knowledgeable outdoorsmen all swore by fleece. I was told to *never wear cotton*; it only adds weight and retains moisture, like a sponge. The parka I bought, an arctic-rated North Face model, had dozens of pockets for tools and dog treats. During my first Iditarod, I ordered a large commemorative patch which I sewed on the back. Over the years, my patch collection grew until the entire back—and part of the front—was covered. Veterinarians are usually easy to spot at the Iditarod because they have the coats with the most patches. That, and we wear a fluorescent armband that says "VET."

As I suspected, the gear was monstrously expensive, especially so since I hadn't even confirmed that I'd be among the veterinarians selected to head out on the trail. But I was ready for the challenge. Well, at least, I was dressed for the part.

CHAPTER 2

JOURNEY TO THE CENTER OF THE LAST FRONTIER

THE IDITAROD BEGINS IN ANCHORAGE. GETTING THERE FROM Washington, DC, is as simple as a single plane change in Seattle. The headquarters of the Iditarod—the Lakefront Anchorage Hotel, also known as the "Millennium"*—is only a short taxi ride from the Ted Stevens Anchorage International Airport. It was a particularly snowy year; in 2012, Anchorage received more snowfall than it had in the past decade. (This being Alaska, that says something.) As the taxi meandered through canyons of snow and ice with walls more than a few feet high, I felt the car swerve with the wind. It was like we were driving through a mountain crevasse.

This is my first memory of Alaska. Deep, deep snow, and gale-force winds pushing that snow across roads and up over low buildings. The night air was freezing; where precious sunlight had thawed, ponds of black ice now formed. I saw the hotel in the distance, squat like an igloo oasis in the middle of all that snow. Taking care not to slip, I made my way into the foyer, where I was greeted by a stuffed musk ox sealed in a glass sarcophagus. The hotel, that is to say, is decorated exactly as you might expect a hotel in the American Northwest to be decorated. The walls

* The hotel opened in 1986 as the Clarion. From 2001 through 2015, it was known as The Millennium Alaska Hotel. Since then, the official name has been changed to Lakefront Anchorage Hotel—but many Iditarod competitors and volunteers still call it the "Millennium."

are lined with massive cedar logs; where the logs meet, a fireplace roars. Mounts of truly gigantic salmon and trout vie for wall space with yellowing photographs of the anglers who caught them. The glassy eyes of taxidermied animals—wolves, bears, stags, and mountain goats—follow guests around the lobby. The hotel, I thought, was showing its age and badly in need of a facelift, but somehow this added to the romance of it all.

From the check-in desk, I was sent to Room 101, where the Iditarod Task Force had set up shop. The banquet hall had been converted into an operations center for the race; it was now crammed with groups of people, all huddled around computers, evidently trying to divine something from the spreadsheets and maps on the monitors. The conversations merged into an all-encompassing hum, and the smell of coffee and body odor—not yet defrosted, we all had our coats on—hung in the air.

It was during this noisy, smelly chaos that I first met Joanne Potts. Stu Nelson may have been head veterinarian, but Joanne's reputation preceded her. She was the person who "got things done," who, when the inevitable Big Problem™ occurred (and they always do, with events of this size), would save the day, time and time again.

We'd spoken a few times on the phone, and that was enough to earn me a hug. She was cradling a blue-eyed, twenty-week-old husky who was all too aware of his own cuteness.

"Arctic," she told the dog, "this is Dr. Morgan."

I shook Arctic's paw, but even before our introduction was done, I could tell that he had tired of me; he wriggled away to seduce more admirers. Joanne handed me a cap and volunteer-only shirt, both emblazoned with the Iditarod logo. When she handed me the keys to my room, she told me that I'd be sharing it with four other vets. I thanked her for taking a chance on me this year and, like Arctic, took my leave. Being on the move since the early morning had worn on me, and fatigue was beginning to set in. But there was one very, very important mission

Huskies are cute—and they know it.

that I still needed to complete. The winter-gear checklist hadn't included snowshoes. In fact, it actively discouraged veterinarians from bringing them; they're bulky and awkwardly shaped, and thus take up valuable space on a bush plane. But they certainly aren't illegal, and selfishly—desperately—I wanted to try them, just once.

I took off my sneakers and pulled on my Timberline boots. I retrieved the contraband from my duffel and snapped them on. Within twenty seconds, I was outside, flopping like an overgrown penguin on the dense snow around the Millennium. I loped over hillocks and across fields, the snowshoes easily supporting my 220-pound weight. I climbed embankments over ten feet high. This, I thought, is what the astronauts who bounded across the Sea of Tranquility must have felt—although they, from the footage I've seen, didn't fall over quite as often. I ended up fairly far from the hotel. As I made my way back, I saw something I never imagined I would see anywhere, let alone in downtown Anchorage. Under the dim light of a streetlamp, the hulking frame of an adult bull Alaskan moose heaved. He must have seen my snowshoe display, and he regarded me somewhat lazily, clearly not seeing me as a threat—thankfully, because he was much, much larger than me, larger than I'd ever expected a moose to be. We watched each other for another beat or two before he turned and continued down the sidewalk, slowly fading from the soft light.

❋ ❋ ❋ *ANCHORAGE, AK. 975 miles to Nome. Tuesday before the race. 21°F. Light snow.*

THE LECTURES BEGAN THE next morning. Everyone in attendance was a veterinarian with at least five years' experience of clinical practice. We had all treated a lot of dogs in our time; we were here to learn about what made sled dogs different from your ordinary hound. These lectures were not the protracted, dry discussions of current laboratory research that I'd become accustomed to. Discussion here was pragmatic and focused. The talks were based on empirical wisdom—about what works, and what doesn't—that can only come from dealing with the same issues repeatedly. Simply put, the lectures were different because our patients were different. The sled dogs that compete in long-distance races are endurance athletes. Just as a person who exercises by walking to the fridge would not be prepared to run the Boston Marathon, the average dog, taken from the comfort of their favorite sofa, would not be able to compete in the Iditarod. Sled dogs must be able to maintain an extraordinarily high level of work output, in deep snow and on thick ice, for long periods of time on many consecutive days.

While the dogs that run the Iditarod tend to be Alaskan huskies, they're in no way American Kennel Club–certified. In a way, this is fitting; the word "husky" was coined by English-speaking sailors to describe the dogs the Indigenous peoples used. It was a shortened form of "Huskimo," a catch-all term used to lump together all of the peoples already living in the region when the Europeans docked. (The more familiar English spelling is "Eskimo.") The "Huskimos" or "Huskis" had distinctive "Huskimo dogs." Many sailors reported being startled by the dogs' "impressive" stamina. By the 1850s, "husky" had come to signify the dog, rather than the person. These "husky" dogs resembled the modern breed in some ways; they were relatively small and had already evolved various adaptations for living and working in polar conditions, including webbed feet. (Husky paws aren't just tough pads; their webbing, like my snowshoes, spreads their weight and prevents ice from building up between their toes.) Huskies also have an all-important insulating double coat of fur that not only keeps the dogs dry, but is also an effective insulator against the cold. The inner layer keeps the dog warm by trapping air; the outer layer (or guard hair) is slick and helps to shed ice and snow.

When Europeans began exploring the northern polar region in the nineteenth century, they were (literally) out of their element. None of them, not even the Russians and Scandinavians, had experienced such frigid temperatures. Sailors wore standard cotton uniforms. Although they noted with appreciation the efficient, warm garb of the Native peoples of Alaska—which included fur parkas and mukluks—the explorers refused to adopt this form of clothing. Never mind the fact that these clothes had been developed by peoples who had lived in the region for millennia; it was beneath them to dress in this "archaic" fashion. As a direct result of their hubris and xenophobia, many of them died of exposure.

Europeans took a similarly disdainful view of the use of dogs for travel and carrying loads. They relied, instead, on "man-hauling," or lashing teams of three to five men to great carriages of food

Nineteenth-century Europeans used the term "Huskimo" to
describe the Native peoples of Alaska. Their dogs were known as
"Huskimo dogs."

and equipment, which they would then pull, or attempt to pull,
over miles of rough ice and deep snow. Needless to say, this practice was exhausting, inefficient, and burned too many necessary
calories. While teams of huskies could pull people over hundreds
of miles in a single day, European men strapped to one of these
contraptions could expect to make, in the same time, between ten
and fifteen miles. When in dire need of supplies, savvy Europeans employed Native "runners," with their dog-powered sleds, to
move between far-flung camps.

To European eyes, the dogs used by the Native Alaskans
looked more like small wolves than the domesticated elkhounds
and sheepdogs of their homelands. It was widely assumed that
Indigenous populations, in Alaska and elsewhere, were vestiges
of a more "primitive" branch of the human race; it followed that
their dogs represented some ancient, isolated, or otherwise "pure"
lineage native to the region. Yet we have many photographs

of early Alaskan life, and even in those faded black-and-white images, it's obvious that the dogs pictured have a variety of coat patterns and builds, suggesting that they were not at all "pure." The visual evidence was ignored, and Europeans, demonstrating their imperial arrogance and naïveté, continued to maintain that the Native peoples simply acquired their sled dogs by venturing out into the Alaskan wilderness and taming any lone wolves they discovered there.

Recent DNA studies of dog remains found at archaeological sites reveal that the reality is precisely the opposite. Huskies share more DNA with wolf breeds native to Siberia than with wolf breeds native to North America, which suggests that huskies were brought to Alaska as sled dogs by some of the earliest humans to migrate to the Americas. Archaeologists working in Siberia have uncovered evidence of 9,500-year-old sleds and harnesses; other studies have shown that the process of breeding sled dogs may have been underway as early as 13,000 BCE. These findings are contested, but if accurate, they indicate that the ancestors of modern Native Alaskans were among the first humans to domesticate dogs anywhere in the world. DNA from North Asian breeds like Shar-Peis began to appear in the lineage of huskies between 3,000 and 5,000 years ago, which suggests that by then, at the latest, there was already an extensive intercontinental interchange of working dogs, signifying trade, barter, or some other form of contact.

European explorers eventually came to appreciate the breed. To an extent, that is: Norwegian Roald Amundsen's bid for the South Pole in 1910–12 demonstrated just how little some Europeans cared for animal (and particularly husky) life. On June 3, 1910, Amundsen left Oslo for the South Pole; six months later, his expedition arrived at the Ross Ice Shelf—so named for Sir James Clark Ross, who discovered "The Barrier" in 1841—where Amundsen, relying heavily on huskies for transportation, set up a

A dog team pulls a sled through a snow-covered field, circa early 1900s.

base camp and various supply depots. At the same time, an expedition led by Captain Robert Falcon Scott, a British Royal Navy officer, was making its way toward the South Pole. The Brits, however, scorned the use of dogsleds for transportation. (In fact, the British establishment saw Amundsen's use of dogs as evidence of his dishonorable character.) Instead, Scott's team employed ponies, makeshift caterpillar tracks, and even man-hauling. While Amundsen's team cruised to its goal in a matter of weeks, Scott and his companions, vainly trying to man-haul sledges to the bottom of the world, died in a frozen wasteland. Upon hearing of the Norwegians' accomplishment and Scott's demise, one Briton—in some accounts Prime Minister H. H. Asquith himself—is said to have raised a glass and proclaimed, "Three cheers for the dogs, then." But Amundsen's dogs had by then died; as planned, they had been butchered and eaten, some of them fed to other huskies before those huskies, too, were eaten. Despite their loyal service, Amundsen from the outset saw them as nothing more than expendable machines.

Following Amundsen, the British polar explorer Sir Ernest Henry Shackleton also (and much less horrifically) relied on husky power for his expedition to the South Pole in 1914. Frank Hurley, who joined Shackleton on the expedition, marveled at the huskies as he took them out for runs in the summer of 1915. He was particularly impressed with one of the lead dogs, writing in his diary that he was a "magnificent animal," a "noble creature, dignified in gait, master of the team." He added, "A good leader will ferret out the best track through rough and broken country, will not allow fighting among the team or indulge in capricious activity. A good team of 9 dogs will haul about 1000 lbs."

While there has never been one "historic" husky breed, the American Kennel Club has recognized a competition breed, the Siberian Husky, since the early 1930s. There are some mushers who use only purebred Siberian Huskies on their teams, but much more for aesthetic than competitive reasons. To see a full team of fourteen black-and-white Siberian Huskies going full speed—with their pink tongues hanging and their fierce blue eyes gleaming—is truly a marvelous sight. But as handsome as they are, they won't win you the Iditarod. The truly competitive mushers use dogs that have been bred for endurance; they prioritize stamina over speed and strength. An Alaskan husky, the most common husky you see pulling a sled, is essentially a mutt, and its lineage can include a variety of dogs, often with border collies and setters in the mix. As a consequence, a lot of dogs running the Iditarod look more like Labradors or pointers than true huskies. But since they have at least some husky in them, they have a husky's webbed feet—and that all-important double coat.

The rules of the Iditarod haven't always included breed requirements. As I mentioned, in 1990, the American musher John Suter entered the race with a team consisting of eight standard European poodles and eight huskies. He'd attempted a more modest version of this in 1988, with three standard poodles on his team: Umiat, Ulu, and Toto. About a mile from the finish line, Suter stopped and replaced his lead husky with Umiat. He thus became the first musher in the history of the Iditarod to cross the finish line with a poodle as his lead dog. The story received a lot of press; Suter and Umiat even appeared on Johnny Carson's *The Tonight Show*. None of this endeared Suter to his fellow mushers.

The 1990 Iditarod was a different story. Not only were there eight poodles on the team, but the air was unusually warm that year. The poodles' fur had gotten wet and then frozen into clumps of ice that all but engulfed the dogs. When they slept, they froze to the ground, and by the time they reached the first major checkpoint, at McGrath, they were shivering uncontrollably. Ice balls had formed in-between the toe webs, and some dogs were on the verge of hypothermia. Several had frostbite. After inspecting the dogs, veterinarians forced Suter to drop the poodles. Already, they were 300 miles into the race; Suter maintained that they had fared well through the previous checkpoint, at Nikolai, and only faded "really bad" in the subsequent fifty miles to McGrath.

Health concerns and other incongruities aside, it's worth asking whether the poodles were ever truly pulling, or even able to pull, their share of the weight. A team of eight huskies can easily pull a sled—in fact, a strategy that many top mushers employ involves whittling down the number of dogs in the later stages of the race, dropping even healthy dogs, so that the team becomes lighter, more efficient, and easier to manage. Suter did not object to leaving his poodles in McGrath and ultimately finished the race. Since 1992, almost certainly as a response to Suter's poodles, the race committee has banned dogs without at least *some* husky genes from competing.

While genetics play a significant role, so too, does experience, for running (and especially running long distances) has a high metabolic cost. The dogs' muscles must be strong, but most of all, they must be efficient. The ability to run fast and consistently for long periods of time depends on the body's ability to provide adequate energy to working muscles and to efficiently remove waste products such as carbon dioxide and lactic acid. In both humans and dogs, only about a quarter of the energy from the breakdown of fats and carbohydrates in food is converted into mechanical energy; the rest is dissipated as heat. The primary focus of training for a race—for both humans and canines—is teaching the body to get better at converting available energy from glucose, carbohydrates, fats, and proteins into energy. This can only really be achieved through regular exercise.

Endurance exercise not only augments skeletal muscle but also increases heart size. A study of racing sled dogs conducted by Dr. Kenneth Hinchcliff at the University of Melbourne has shown that sled dogs have larger cardiac dimensions relative to their body size than their sedentary peers. Whereas a sled dog's heart accounts for nearly 1 percent of its overall body weight, the heart of a sedentary lap dog, on average, accounts for about 0.8 percent of its body weight. The larger size of the heart in sled dogs is a direct result of endurance training. Echocardiographic studies have shown that, during a typical training season, both the muscle mass of a sled dog's heart *and* the size of the ventricular cavity increase, meaning that the heart becomes stronger and can pump more blood. The faster the cardiovascular system can deliver blood to muscles, the more oxygen that will be available to those muscles—and the faster that metabolic wastes will be carried away. Thus, the resting heart rate of sled dogs, like that of many human endurance athletes, is much slower than their non-athlete counterparts. An average Labrador has a resting heart rate of about ninety beats per minute; a typical sled dog, on the other hand, has a resting heart rate closer to forty beats per minute.

Modern huskies are small animals, weighing no more than forty-five pounds.

During exercise, however, its heart rate may climb to well over 300 beats per minute.

Naturally, sled dogs competing in endurance events like the Iditarod have enormous caloric demands. It's not at all unusual for a husky to burn 10,000 to 12,000 kilocalories in a single day—five times the recommended human level of 2,000 kilocalories. (Mushers, by contrast, burn about 6,000 calories in twelve hours of mushing.) Because fat is a good source of caloric energy, sled dogs are often fed high-fat diets, both during the competition and in training. For a domestic dog, say, a French bulldog, a high-fat diet not only promotes obesity but puts the animal at risk for a painful, potentially fatal disease called pancreatitis. This is fairly common in the domestic dogs I see at my Georgetown practice. And yet, despite their high-fat diets, pancreatitis in sled dogs is extremely rare. While it's unknown why Alaskan huskies can digest such high-fat meals without developing pancreatitis, I have to imagine that it's at least partly because their digestive systems have been trained, like those of human diabetic patients on a ketogenic diet, to break down fats more readily, just as exercising trains the muscles to perform more efficiently.

❋ ❋ ❋ ❋

While this would be my first time working with racing dogs, I had had some experience with Siberian huskies, and I knew, even then, that they were very different from other dog breeds. For one, like Arctic, they're all keenly aware of their own beauty—to the point of being vain. They're also extremely intelligent and independent. These last two qualities can make for a dog that's difficult to train, especially in a household environment. I grew up around dogs. Labs, collies, mutts; these are the kind of dogs that will do whatever you ask. If you want them to fetch you a ball or a stick, they'll fetch you that ball or stick. This is not the way of the Siberian husky.

As I said, early in our marriage, my wife, Kris, surprised me with a three-legged Siberian: Sabo, manipulator extraordinaire. Although not yet a year old, this small dog, with his teary, aqua-blue eyes, had already learned to elicit sympathy by offering to shake hands with his stump, wearing an oh-so-pitiful expression as he did. As I later determined, Sabo could, when he wanted to, shake hands by balancing on his haunches and extending his good "arm."

Sabo was loving, kind, and an absolute devil. By all measures—except, perhaps, in the number of limbs—Sabo was a typical husky. As a breed, they tend not to buy into our notions of human-dog hierarchy; as far as they're concerned, humans and huskies are on the same plane. If you ask them to do something they want to do, they'll do it with unmatched enthusiasm. If, on the other hand, it doesn't seem like a good idea to them, they won't do it at all, ever. Siberian Huskies can also be entirely without shame. Once, while we were having friends over for pizza, we noted Sabo's absence.

Most of the time, he wanted to be where everyone else was. I went into the kitchen to find him standing on the table, eating the still-steaming pizza straight out of the box (and before anyone else had had a chance to grab a slice). A Lab might hang its head low, draw its ears back, and peer up at you pitifully. A husky won't.

Huskies, in other words, are not good "starter" dogs for people. If someone told me they were looking to adopt a dog for the first time, huskies would be just about the last breed I'd recommend. One thing huskies—and for that matter, all Arctic breeds—love to do is run. Sabo ran with the local dogs at the end of the street. In those days, Kris and I lived by the York River in Virginia. There were no cars and plenty of open spaces, so dogs were free to roam pretty much wherever they wanted to. Sabo, I remember, had his own version of the game "fetch." I would throw a stick, and all the dogs would run after it. Sabo would burst out with the group, then stop about halfway and wait. One of the Labs would retrieve the stick and, smiling, begin to make his way back toward me. Sabo would then intercept him, wrestle the stick away, and drop it at my feet. He had essentially outsourced the game of fetch: I wondered if he'd been some mid-level executive in a previous life.

The desire to pull seemed almost innate: Sabo was constantly pulling me around, sometimes by leash, sometimes with teeth. Once, I hooked his lead around my belt, balanced myself on a pair of cross-country skis, and tried "skijoring" with him. He sprinted as fast as he could, putting his whole weight into the makeshift harness. I spent almost all this time about to fall over, falling over, or having fallen. Neither of us was strong enough to go uphill, so we ambled up those slopes side by side; and when downhill slopes proved too steep, I had to slow down for fear of running him over. I was surprised by the functionality of our little "sled" and even more so by Sabo's willingness to listen, to work with me as we navigated the slopes. Huskies, I realized, may be fiercely independent of mind and spirit, but when they are put in a harness in

Huskies are proud, intelligent creatures. Some huskies will pose for photos by sitting up straight.

front of a sled, they're team players. They cooperate; they run in rhythm; they don't (always) steal sticks.

❊   ❊   ❊   ❊

Of the many lectures I listened to, only occasionally tuning out to reminiscence about Sabo, the one that most piqued my interest was delivered by Stu Nelson. Supplementing his talk with images of brightly painted towns, Stu walked us through the checkpoints one by one, from Rainy Pass, with its mountaintop vistas; to the remote Alaskan villages of Nikolai and McGrath; to Unalakleet, with its abundant caribou and *oogruk* (bearded seal); all the way to Nome, where the race terminates. A map of the old Iditarod Trail—a sprawling system with smaller trails branching out in all directions—flashed on the screen. Beginning in the ice-free port of Seward, the trail stretches over 950 miles to Nome; if you counted all its side branches, it measures about 2,200 miles.

There was one phrase that Stu objected to at any point on the trail, no matter the circumstance: "That's not my job." Our primary concern as veterinarians would be caring for the dogs, but everyone would be expected to pitch in and make sure that each checkpoint ran as smoothly as possible. In essence, we would be part of a larger support team consisting of countless communication personnel, pilots, dog handlers, cooks, competition judges, and other volunteers, each with their own responsibilities but who may, at some point, need help completing some of their tasks. In addition to organizing medical supplies and treating dogs, veterinarians could expect to be called upon to cook, build tents, move straw bales, and burn rubbish after teams departed from checkpoints.

Stu insisted that volunteers carry a survival kit at all times. He described a narrow escape of his own, several years ago, in the Alaskan wilderness. Late in the kayaking season, Stu, on a solo float trip down a remote northern river, came upon a sandbar in the middle of a bend. The bar split the river into two parts: a fast, deep section on one side, and a shallow arm on the other. He tried to make for the shallow part, but failed; the boat shot around the bend, right into a low-hanging branch that unseated him. Thrown headfirst into the river, Stu was left to scramble to the relative safety of the shore as the river carried the kayak out of sight. Fortunately, Stu had managed to keep hold of his backpack, which contained his survival equipment. For two weeks, he lived off the land, until a canoe—the last that had been given a permit to travel the river that season—appeared. From this incident came his mantra, *It is not survival gear unless it is on you.* I didn't plan to do any kayaking, solo or otherwise, but I took his point.

Whether focused on the dangers of the Arctic, the dogs, the trail, or veterinarian conduct,[*] the lectures only whet my appetite for the wild. I was desperate to get out there, to be among the

* The Iditarod has a strict code of conduct. Veterinarians are expected to be professional, courteous, and abstain from both alcohol and sex. These last recommendations are pragmatic, not puritanical—a trail vet needs to be focused on the job, not making or, worse, fending off advances.

chosen veterinarians to head out on the trail. And somehow, I was. Some students elected not to participate; they had attended in the hope of securing a spot next year. Others realized it wasn't for them, or Stu Nelson made a determination on their behalf. (Later, I would be told I was "one of the lucky few.")

That night, just a few days before the Iditarod was set to start, those of us who had been selected to head out on the trail went to the Millennium Hotel's bar, the aptly named Fancy Moose Lounge, for a last drink. The bar had a panoramic window overlooking the frozen lakefront, where half a dozen bush planes—de Havilland Beavers, Cessna 206s, and a Piper Super Cub—were parked on the ice. They were tiny, fragile-looking things. We didn't yet know which checkpoints we'd been assigned to. But we were giddy with excitement, unabashed and unknowing.

Chapter 3

EXAM DAY

T HE FIRST TASK OF AN IDITAROD VETERINARIAN IS TO PER-
form the mandatory pre-race physical exam. On the Thurs-
day before the race, the day after the lectures finish, each
musher surrenders their dogs to the veterinarians for a thorough
physical exam, blood test, and ECG.

There are two rules that fundamentally determine how the
Iditarod is run. All sled dog races, including the Iditarod, have
regulations stating the maximum number of dogs that can start
for a team as well as the minimum number of dogs that must
still be running when the sled crosses the finish line. While the
maximum number has varied over the years—in 2019, it dropped
from sixteen to fourteen dogs—the minimum has held firm at
five. Once a sick, injured, or tired dog is dropped from the race, it
cannot return later, even if it has fully recovered; and it cannot be
substituted. There's no way for mushers to simply "ship in" sub-
stitute dogs. This means that mushers, both before and during the
race, must closely monitor and care for each and every dog that
they hope to proceed with. At any given point in the race, mushers must make tactical decisions about the number of dogs they
run. The more dogs there are, the more mouths there are to feed;
the more supplies they must carry; and the more complicated the
team dynamics. For the top flight of mushers, races like the Iditarod typically involve strategic management of lead dogs; opti-
mizing dog drops; and factoring in conditions like the weather,

the state of the trail, and the strategies and progress of other front-runners. These mushers have a specific plan for the number of dogs they'd like to have at each stage of the race and drop dogs strategically to gain advantage.* Less experienced mushers or mushers who want only to finish, rather than win, often opt to start with a smaller team, which is easier to manage, and conserve it throughout the race.

Mushers typically bring between twenty and twenty-five dogs, more than will start, to the pre-race check. This gives them options for team selection as well as backups, should the inspection uncover any problems with their preferred huskies. Even experienced mushers with elaborate plans will make some last-minute decisions about which dogs make the team. In any case, vets have to examine every *potential* team member. With between sixty and eighty teams competing in the Iditarod each year, the vets have at least a thousand dogs to examine. Every available vet is drafted to help with this process. It's the one time, after the lectures, that all the vets are in the same place at the same time—and it requires waking up very, very early. Many hours before dawn, the veterinary team piled into a school bus to ride to Wasilla, where the official headquarters for the Iditarod National Historic Trail are located. Guarding the door is the moonlit statue of Balto, the heroic lead husky of the 1925 diphtheria serum run. It was beginning to snow again; inside, a cheerful staff greeted us with donuts and hot coffee.

The inspections take place in the parking lot behind the museum. We set up our stations and medical equipment, readying ourselves for the onslaught of huskies. The first time I prepared my examination kit, I felt a pang of nervousness. My clients were famous mushers who had known and trained

* Many competitive mushers will dramatically streamline the sled at the last checkpoint before the finish line, planning to increase their speed by reducing the weight as much as possible. This can involve dropping dogs and any remaining unnecessary supplies alike.

Race judge Karen Ramstead was once a competitor. Here, Karen is pictured racing with a full team of huskies (and an Idita-Rider) near Goose Lake, during the Ceremonial Start.

with their dogs for years, and whose primary responsibility, as a musher, is to understand their abilities and limits. I had been practicing veterinary medicine for many years, but the sum total of my experience with sled dogs, then, was four days of lectures. My mind raced. Who was I to tell an experienced musher that they could or couldn't race a particular dog? What if I told a musher to drop a dog and I was wrong, and there was no reason the dog couldn't go on? What if I passed a dog that developed problems on the trail? And what of the dogs themselves? Would they be vicious? Squirrelly? Mean? They're working animals, after all. Were they more wolf than dog? Would I even be able to examine them?

I calmed myself down by repeating the mantra I reserved for such situations: *The mushers may know their dogs better than me, but I knew medicine better than them.* I was good at my job; I had learned to pick up on the subtle cues that signal deeper and potentially serious problems. I needed to trust in my training and my instincts, and act decisively. As for the physical risk, well, that's why they invented muzzles—and I'd learned through bitter experience treating domestic dogs that there is often less trouble to be had examining large dogs than fractious purse dogs. At least I could bear-hug a large dog.

The teams began arriving at daybreak. Mushers transport their dogs in modified pickup trucks. Each dog gets its own cubbyhole, with a window hatch so they can stick their head out to see where they're going. Most dogs use this opportunity to curl up and sleep. My first year, I was paired with veteran Iditarod veterinarian Vern Otte, which infinitely eased my pre-exam anxiety, since Vern was on a first-name basis with all of the mushers. Each team was given a scheduled time slot; the mushers seemed to understand that these were approximations, and when they would actually be seen depended entirely on how smoothly things went for the team or teams before them. The attitude, overall, was relaxed. Everyone knew that the vets were working hard, and that their turn would come, sooner or later. Mushers and staff who had not seen each other since the previous year caught up on gossip. Stories were traded, memories shared.

I had spent the last four days learning about husky anatomy and physiology, but I was still shocked to see how small they are. No dog weighed more than forty-five pounds. As for the idea that Alaskan huskies are a vicious breed, this notion was dispelled forever by my first patient, who ran over to lick my face. He was promptly followed by his teammates, who crowded around to get their share of pets and hugs. I realized that these dogs were just as used to being handled and interacting with humans as any other dog. Not once did I have to resort to muzzles or bear hugs.

When Vern and I took a break, I noticed a large Norwegian flag hanging from a nearby truck. Since part of my family hails from Norway, I walked over to introduce myself. The musher,

Sometimes, my patients are a little too *friendly.*

Sigrid Ekran, was a petite woman with an easy smile. She was world-famous, a sporting icon in Norway—yet friendly, with the excitement of a teenager. Sled dogs, she told me, had been part of her life since she started racing at the age of eight. This was her second Iditarod, but she had competed all over Europe, and had already won the Norwegian *Femundløpet* and *Finnmarksløpet.** I immediately volunteered to inspect her team.

And what a team it was. They were all like happy puppies at a dog park. As I knelt to examine a dog that looked more like a Labrador than a husky, I felt his whole body shake with excitement. Tail wagging, tongue hanging, he looked at me with smiling eyes. As I leaned in to press my stethoscope to his heart, he licked my face from chin to forehead. I laughed, wiped the dog spittle from my cheek, and tried again. But again, as soon as I bent toward him, he planted a big, sloppy kiss. After my third try, with no foreseeable end to the kisses in sight, Sigrid stepped in to help.

* All mushers participating in the Iditarod must have successfully completed at least one other qualifying long-distance race.

After I finished with him, I proceeded to the second dog in line. She was a gentle, small girl, and sat patiently as I examined her. But I was still within kissing range of the first dog, and he was far from done with me. As I listened to the second dog's heart, I felt a warm splash across the back of my neck. I turned around to see him wide-eyed, tail spinning like a propeller. So again, Sigrid had to assist.

Now finally out of his reach, I moved down the line and completed my inspection of the team. Finding nothing wrong with any of the dogs, I crouched beside the first dog and signed off on my report. As I did, I kissed the top of his head, to let him know that we were still pals. With Sigrid's permission, I reached into my pocket to give him a treat, but instead of finding a biscuit, I found the second dog's snout. No biscuits, only snout. She had sniffed out my stash and, while I was distracted by paperwork, helped herself to the contents of my pocket. Her long, narrow muzzle fit perfectly inside, leaving her eyes exposed to watch me. She'd hoovered up all my treats like an aardvark sucking down termites. When I looked down to confront her, she didn't remove her snout but turned her gaze up at me as if to say, "Oh? Was I not supposed to eat all the treats?"

After I finished with Sigrid, I moved on to the next team. Again, I found the dogs to be content, friendly, and in great shape—that is, until I got to the fourth dog in line. Something was off. At a glance, she seemed fine. She was just as happy as the rest of her team, wagging her tail and yapping along with the other pups, but on closer inspection, her gums were slightly too pale, paler than I'd expect to see in a healthy dog. I checked her heart rate, which was normal. I checked her breathing rate, which was also normal. Still, there was something that troubled me about those gums. I compared her gums against those of the dog beside her; sure enough, his were a slightly less pallid shade of pink. I inspected a few other mouths, just to be certain. By this time, Vern had arrived with coffee. Gratefully accepting the hot cup, I told him about my concerns. The musher, too, joined our conversation.

I reasoned with myself. It could be a normal variation in gum color and mean nothing at all. But it could *also* mean that the dog is anemic, that she has an abnormally low percentage of red blood cells. This could indicate several things; what worried me most was the possibility of a gastric ulcer. But the musher reported that there had been no change in her appetite, and no episodes of vomiting or diarrhea. All in all, she seemed normal.

"Let's see what the bloodwork says," Vern suggested. He grabbed the dog's file—every dog has one—and examined the results.

"There it is." She had a low packed cell volume (PCV), a measure of her red blood cells; not quite low enough to count as anemic by laboratory standards, but low enough for me to make a decision. I turned to the musher. This was it, the first time I had to tell a musher to drop a dog.

"My concern here is that if you race her, this PCV will drop. If there is in fact an ulcer present, racing her will make it worse and she will get very sick. I recommend you replace her with another dog if you can." I chewed my lip as I said this. The musher was a veteran competitor; he'd know that rookie vets often performed the pre-race physicals.

"You really think it would be for the best?" he asked. I could tell that this was a dog he particularly hoped to race.

"I do," I responded, trying to sound as decisive as I could.

The musher mulled it over.

"Okay. Yes, if it's for the best, I won't race her." He gently caressed her head, and I felt a wave of relief.

Later, the dog I examined was given an endoscopy. She was found to have some small lesions in her stomach. She was placed on medication and recovered within a matter of days. If she had run the race, she could have suffered serious complications.

I had successfully picked up on a subtle sign, diagnosed a problem, and taken action, and the musher had accepted my judgment.

By the end of the day I had examined or helped examine over seven hundred dogs. I slept soundly on the bus ride back to Anchorage. I was dropped off at the Millennium, at what felt like the furthest possible point from my room. My four roommates were already there and fast asleep; I collapsed on my cot without bothering to get undressed. But I didn't care. I was part of this now. I had done my job, and done it well.

CHAPTER 4

THE WINNER AIN'T THE ONE WITH THE FASTEST SLED

O N THE FIRST SUNDAY OF MARCH, WITH THE PRE-RACE CHECK-ups complete and the Ceremonial Start out of the way, the teams line up along the shore of Willow Lake, for the true start of the Iditarod.

This is an emotional time for the mushers. Today is when reality hits. Soon, they'll be heading out into the wilderness, and for long stretches of the next few weeks, they'll be as alone as anyone can be. There's an element of danger involved. Granted, no musher has died while competing in the race, but there have been close calls and serious injuries. The mushers know that there are risks—and few ways to be rescued. If you compete in the Iditarod, you've accepted the possibility that you may not walk away from it; indeed, the whole point is that you want an extreme physical challenge. The mushers may be anxious about the challenges to come, but at the start line, they're gracious. What seems to hit them is an overwhelming sense of appreciation for the family and friends who helped them reach this point. A commitment to the Iditarod is more than a commitment to a week-and-a-half of racing; competitors (and volunteers) typically spend weeks away from home and work. Mushers begin training with their dogs in the late summer. Their loved ones will often pitch in, driving to pick up equipment; lugging supplies; feeding and caring for the dogs, when

necessary; and even sewing outerwear. Every musher understands the sacrifices that have been made on his or her behalf.
The contrast between this outpouring of love and support and
the isolation ahead is sharp.

A temporary camp, mostly consisting of pickup trucks and
other support vehicles, is set up near the lake. As the teams make
their final preparations, noise fills the air. Willow may be a town
of less than 2,000 people, but a few times that number show up
at Willow Lake each year for the official start of the race. The
dogs are barking, the organizers are shouting. There are television crews and documentary filmmakers. Everyone seems to
be looking for someone or something. At the center of all this
activity is the start line, marked by a banner strung between aluminum poles. Behind the line volunteers orient the teams in
the right direction; beyond the line, there's safety fencing—the
kind of orange plastic mesh you might see around a construction
site or a parking lot—for about a hundred yards. The spectators, all clad in thick, brightly colored coats, take up positions
behind the fences.

❊ ❊ ❊ *WILLOW, AK. 964 miles to Nome. 10°F. Cloudy.*

WHILE ON THE COURSE, the dogs wear booties, not to keep their
feet warm, but to protect them from cuts and prevent snow and
ice from building up between their paw pads. These booties aren't
particularly difficult to make. Typically, they're sewn together
using nylon, polypropylene (a thermoplastic polymer), and occasionally canvas, and secured in place with Velcro. If a bootie isn't
tight enough, it will quickly fly off; if it's too tight, it can cut off
circulation. Generally, by the time a musher qualifies for the Iditarod, they have mastered the art of fitting booties.

There can be up to fourteen dogs on a full sled team, and

Veteran mushers know how to quickly and efficiently put on dog booties.

each dog has four feet. A musher will change their dogs' booties once or twice per day, meaning that each team can plausibly go through a few thousand booties during an Iditarod. After feeding the dogs, it's the most time-consuming task at a rest stop. Some mushers hold on to used booties, employing them as spares over rough terrain. But most mushers just discard them at checkpoints, alongside other detritus. This crop of booties is quickly harvested by volunteers, especially by veterinarians. (They make great handouts if you're invited to speak at a school group.) Other mushers will simply hand them over, if you're polite: I once asked DeeDee Jonrowe, a three-time Iditarod runner-up, if I could have a couple of her old booties and she gave me an entire bag of them, all in her trademark pink color. While team colors may vary, all teams use essentially the same equipment. The dogs pull a lightweight sled, typically made of either spruce or fiberglass. Mushers may build sleds themselves or buy one, adapting it for endurance racing by stripping some parts from the frame and reinforcing others. These are not complex, over-engineered machines, and they all follow the same basic design: a light (but not too light, or it will tip over) boxy frame, with a sturdy, U-shaped "brush bow" at the front to deflect objects like tree branches. The sleds are smaller than you might imagine; the frame is five feet long, and the main body is about two feet wide and two feet tall. A handlebar adds another foot in height.

The two runners—the "skis"—are metal and about seven-and-a-half-feet long, so they stick out a few feet behind the body of the sled. The skis are about two inches wide and sit twenty inches apart. A strip of plastic slides onto the runner, and it's that plastic that makes contact with the ice, not the metal. The strip wears down and is replaced every couple of days, or more often if the trail surface is more abrasive.

The musher stands on the back of the sled, legs apart, on "footboards," which are often covered with slip-resistant rubber. The handlebar rises from this structure. Mushers keep a tight grip on the handlebar at all times, and will often use it as a rest. Most sleds come with a large claw brake, consisting of iron spikes attached to a plank by a hinge; if a musher wants to stop, they just step on the plank. The best way to secure a sled is a snow anchor, a multipronged hook attached to a line. The mushers keep these anchors close at hand and, at a scheduled stop or in the event of an emergency, throw them out into the packed snow and ice to hold the sled in place. Volunteers at rest stops keep a close eye on the snow anchors. If they aren't careful, they can be hit by a thrown anchor or, more commonly—and speaking from experience—can trip over the line securing the sled.

In front of the stage is the cargo bed or "basket," a high-sided holding area with a heavy-duty nylon bag fitted to a flat, solid base. For the Ceremonial Start, the Idita-Riders sit snugly in there, feet tucked safely behind the brush bar. (Again, this should give you a good idea of the basket's size and sturdiness.) During the race, the basket holds food and other supplies that the mushers might use between checkpoints, and if necessary, serves as a bed for injured dogs. The whole sled, unloaded, weighs about thirty pounds, but even with the musher, harnesses, equipment, and supplies added, it won't add up to even half the weight of the dogs. A full team of fourteen sled dogs weighs approximately 600 pounds, about as much as four refrigerators. Or half of one Alaskan moose.

The dogs are paired, two by two, along a centrally running "gangline," to which they're connected by an intricate system of nylon tuglines. The tuglines attach to harnesses that the dogs wear around their chests, rather than their collars. This design not only maximizes pulling force but provides comfort, obviating pressure on the dogs' necks and ensuring that they can continue to breathe unimpeded as they lunge forward. As a simple matter of physics, the dogs aren't straining under the yoke. They're not hurtling

Injured dogs may sit in a special compartment on the sled.

along the course at full speed, like a pack of wolves chasing their prey. For most of the race, their pace is actually quite a dainty trot.

Through this system of lines and harnesses, the motive strength of the huskies is channeled into a single pulling force. If the dogs are trained well, the musher can control this force using only his voice. Yell the word "Gee" and the entire team turns right; "Haw" brings the team left. The choreography of a well-seasoned team of dogs is stunning. Together, the dogs, sled, and musher function as an integrated unit, each dependent on the other as they traverse the Iditarod Trail to Nome.

TEAMS TAKE OFF IN two-minute intervals beginning at 2 p.m. The last sled leaves about four hours after the first. Two nights ago, at the Mushers' Banquet, each competitor pulled a number from a mukluk boot. That number determines their starting position, and their starting position can make a significant difference in their experience of the race. The first sleds have to break trail, expending energy to flatten the snow; plus, they're the first to encounter obstacles like fallen tree branches, snow-buried rocks, and, one year, a discarded washing machine. Those in the middle of the field can take advantage of the packed snow, but they run the risk of having their experience dictated by the leaders. The teams bringing up the rear, then, are left to negotiate the deep ruts left by the leaders and the "midfielders." No musher would choose to be the first out; nor would they choose to be among the last. But the middle of the pack has plenty of challenges, too. Sled dog racing is not some great strategic exercise like a game of chess—too much depends on moment-to-moment conditions on the course—but every competitor has a plan, and has spent the last two days thinking about how their place in the running order might affect that plan.

About a quarter of the mushers competing in the Iditarod each year are competing for the first time. They're officially classed as "rookies," and newscasters will often play up the idea that they're naïve or inexperienced, that they barely know one end of a husky from the other and have no idea what they're about to encounter. This is pure journalistic license. All competitors, even those who are appearing for the first time, have not "wound up" in Willow by sheer fortune or accident. They are not rich people who have bought themselves a place, or who palled around with the organizers. The *only* way to qualify for the Iditarod is by performing well in events like the Klondike 300, a 300-mile race across Minnesota, or in international events on a similar scale: the Norwegian *Femundløpet* and *Finnmarksløpet*, for example, where Sigrid Ekran cut her teeth. Experience counts, as does familiarity with the Iditarod Trail. But it's a matter of record that most of the mushers who "scratch," or fail to complete the race, have competed in the race before. *No one* is guaranteed to finish.

While they wait for their allotted start time, the mushers chat nervously with friends and family. They fuss with equipment they've checked a dozen times and make sure, just one more time, that all harnesses and lines are secure, and that all supplies are in the sled. They then say their goodbyes and make their way to the line, where they'll wait for a short while, the dogs working themselves into a frenzy. When the countdown ends, the sleds burst into a tunnel of color and noise before plunging out onto the trail. That's it; the human world is already behind them. There's only crisp white snow below, a slate-grey sky above, and an unbroken line of dull, bare trees on the horizon. The teams ahead have already been reduced to small black dots. The dogs give chase, taking advantage of the freshly cut path in the snow. Within seconds, there are no sounds except the hissing of the sled and the panting of sixteen dogs. The sled powers across the ice plain toward the trees, where a few clumps of hardy spectators stand, waiting for the dogs to pass into the forest. After that, until the first checkpoint, it's just the musher, the dogs, and the sled.

✷ ✷ ✷ ✷

FROM THIS POINT FORWARD, all teams have the same basic task. Get to the first checkpoint, and then the next, and then the next, and so on until Nome. There are twenty-six checkpoints on the course, each about fifty miles from the last, and three mandatory breaks. Mushers must take an eight-hour rest at one of the checkpoints on the Yukon River, and another eight-hour rest near White Mountain, about seventy-seven miles from the finish line in Nome; they must also take at least one twenty-four-hour break. When and where is up to the musher. But competitors can make additional stops as often as they like, or they can be forced into a longer stop if, say, their sled is damaged.

At the major checkpoints, the competitors will restock with provisions. Before the race, each musher supplies carefully packed and labeled packets of consumables: batteries, toilet paper (used as kindling for camping stoves, as well as for the obvious purpose), underwear, spare parts for the sled, and so on. These items are flown up the trail and made available to mushers at select checkpoints. Make no mistake, checkpoints are not like pit stops for race cars or rest stops on the freeway. There are no crews waiting to help refit the sled and hand the musher whatever they need. In fact, there are strict rules banning outside assistance during the race. At checkpoints, mushers must hitch up their own dogs and haul all food and other supplies, often in the form of fifty-pound bags, themselves.

In the early years of the Iditarod, many mushers believed that the best way to win was to race the dogs as fast as they'll go, for as long as they're able, and to keep the time spent at checkpoints to a minimum. Most now take a vastly different approach, one that reflects our increased knowledge of canine medicine and the unique demands of the Iditarod: they stop frequently and stay at stops as long as possible. The dogs eat, drink, and get plenty of rest; instead of wearing out early, they're fresh to the fight each day and finish strong.

While no team today takes just the three required breaks, different mushers have different strategies for resting. Some elite competitors try to gain the upper hand by figuring out when and for how long their rivals will stop; they may also camp between checkpoints to keep rivals guessing about the state of their team. Generally speaking, sled dog racing isn't a sport that requires mastering game theory, but mushers do play mind games. Their subterfuge is hardly Machiavellian, though, and only as sinister as casually mentioning to a rival, usually at a checkpoint, that you're planning to stop for the night, then watching that rival relax and settle in—as your sled speeds off into the dark.

At every checkpoint, from Willow to McGrath and from McGrath to Nome, veterinarians are made available for inspections. A team of veterinarians even attends to the dogs at the start line. Most of us, however, remain at the Millennium Hotel, waiting to find out which checkpoints we've been posted to.* By now, we've been told that we'll be divided into teams of no more than six people; that we'll be flown to a checkpoint, where we'll set up a vet station; and that after we've finished at that checkpoint, we'll be flown back to Anchorage and posted to a new checkpoint farther up the trail.

Traditionally, then, my Iditarod begins at the Millennium. While the sleds power away from Willow, I pace the lobby in slippers, loitering with rest of the vets. We perk up when a member of the communications staff appears. A few names are called. The message is the same each time: *The plane is warming up outside. You have fifteen minutes to get to it with your gear.* The veterinarians then

---

* That is, unless you're posted to Skwentna, the second checkpoint. Veterinarians typically set up a checkpoint the day before the teams start to arrive. Since most teams arrive at Skwentna on the first day, vets set up the day before the race.

race to their rooms, cram as much as they can into their packs, and, with approval from Rebecca, who oversees the thirty-pilot "Iditarod Air Force," board a bush plane to their destination.

My first year, it wasn't until late Sunday that I was told to report to the airfield. When I stepped onto the landing strip I had no idea where I was heading. But it didn't matter. I was finally going out on the Iditarod.

PART II

THE
FIRST
QUARTER

CHAPTER 5

GO!

EVERY PART OF THE IDITAROD IS DEMANDING. RELATIVE TO
what's to come, though, the first few hours *do* allow the
teams to ease into the race. The first stage is a relatively flat,
forty-three-mile course through the birch and spruce woods of
the Susitna Valley. Yentna Station is located about eighteen miles
from the confluence of the Susitna River and the Yentna River.
It takes teams about five hours to get from Willow to Yentna.
The trees have been cleared from the trail for most of this stage.
I've seen it from the air, and it's a long, straight line of white
cut through the forest. For the mushers, it's like driving along a
long, wide road with trees on either side. The trail isn't packed
snow or a flat surface like a skating rink—standing on the back
of a racing sled, the smoothest sections feel more like riding on a
badly maintained dirt track. There are no actual roads. Even this
close to Anchorage, the race is already deep in the wilderness.
The only traffic noise is the dull buzz of an occasional distant
snowmobile, or a light aircraft. There is no glow of city lights to
the southeast.

This stage of the race is not completely straightforward. Side
trails crisscross the main trail, and mushers have been known to
head down one of those, disorientated by a blizzard, or after dark,
or (most often) when the lead dog smells something really interesting and decides the trail must be *that* way. If one team heads off
in the wrong direction, the next one often follows, either because

the musher sees another team going that way and assumes they know where they're going, or because the scent of the first team *is* the really interesting thing that the team of dogs want to investigate. The trail is not always clearly marked, and there are precious few landmarks. Even the most experienced Iditarod mushers have moments—sometimes hours—riding with the nagging sense they're on the wrong route, or should have reached the checkpoint by now. At this stage, though, the teams are close enough together that everyone except the leader has fresh sled tracks to follow.

From a spectator's perspective, Yentna is perhaps the best checkpoint of the whole Iditarod, despite having an official population of eight people. It's early in the race, so the field hasn't yet spread out and spectators can see more teams simultaneously (or near simultaneously) than at any other checkpoint in the race. The race leader will reach Yentna shortly after 7 p.m. on Sunday, and all but a couple of stragglers will have reached the checkpoint by 10 p.m. It's also an extremely practical place for spectators because, with a little bit of planning, they can get there on snowmobiles, and stay the night at the Yentna Station Roadhouse, a bed-and-breakfast lodge run by Dan and Jean Gabryszak.

Almost every musher aims to reach Skwentna, the checkpoint after Yentna, before the end of the first day. Although the distance from Willow to Yentna is only forty-two miles, teams are still expected to stop at Yentna Station for a quick veterinary inspection. The objective, for most mushers, is to pass through as quickly as possible, as the dogs are still fresh and raring to go. This early in the race, and so soon after the pre-race inspections, very few dogs will have any issues. Working in pairs, the veterinarians at Yentna ask mushers if there are any issues, quickly check the dogs, and often sign the logbook, or "Vet Book," within two to three minutes of a team's arrival. Of course, this begs the question: Can a pair of veterinarians really examine an entire team that quickly? While the full examinations that occur when a team stops to eat or rest at a checkpoint *do* yield the most data, the shorter exams are still immensely useful. I can often determine just by watching the dogs whether one has an issue with its feet, for example, or its breathing. Like a choreographer studying a chorus line, I can see simple breaks in the rhythm that point to a problem. It doesn't take a vet three minutes to work out if a dog is arriving in a distressed state. Some teams feed their dogs at Yentna, and these teams will get a full veterinary inspection. But the inspection won't slow them down as much as the process of preparing food. Whether the musher carries it with them or has it shipped to the checkpoint in advance, the dogs' food will be frozen. Feeding time necessitates setting up a gas burner, melting some snow, retrieving heavy sacks of food, and then defrosting enough food for fourteen dogs in the boiling water. The musher does all of this without any help, and the whole process takes at least an hour. The only common reason for a stop longer than this at the first checkpoint is if there's an equipment failure and the musher needs to repair their sled, or for weather conditions—a musher might, for example, choose to wait out a storm ahead if they're convinced they can make up the time the next day.

The distance from Yentna to Skwentna is thirty miles. Getting from one to the other usually takes between three and four hours. Fortunately for the sleds, the terrain is flat, and the route mostly follows the course of the river.

❄ ❄ ❄ *SKWENTNA, AK. 892 miles to Nome. 21°F. Fair.*

I'VE BEEN POSTED TO that second checkpoint, Skwentna, a few times. Skwentna is not a "town." The Alaskan government calls it a Census Designated Place, or CDP. Basically, it's a statistical anomaly—a few buildings that happen to be more or less in proximity to each other. There's not much to the place.

On a high embankment overlooking the convergence of the Yentna and Skwentna rivers, there's a two-story community center, a handful of houses, a small log cabin post office, a firewood shed, and a couple of outhouses. Its official population of ninety includes the hunters and trappers who live up and down the river, off the grid, eking out a living from the wilderness. The US Department of Agriculture has another designation for this area: a "Plant Hardiness Zone." The coldest temperatures of the year are typically in the −40°F to −30°F range. In early March, when the Iditarod rolls through, the temperature rarely rises above freezing, and on an average night, it falls to about 10°F.

Skwentna is the first overnight stop for many of the teams. Here, the veterinarians really get down in the snow, performing a comprehensive physical exam on each dog. I say "get down in the snow" because, truthfully, the vet station at Skwentna can hardly be called a station; it's really just a tent down by the river, close to where the sleds arrive. The tent is usually assembled for us before we reach the checkpoint, but we still have plenty to do before the competitors show up. We go through the contents of the medical chest, first, to ensure that what is supposed to be there is actually there. This also allows us to familiarize ourselves with the equipment, so we aren't frantically searching for things during an emergency.

While the tent is the center of activity for veterinarians, the center of activity for the mushers who stop at Skwentna is a cabin, one of a handful sat atop the embankment overlooking the checkpoint. For the rest of the year, this cabin serves as the local post office. But in 1973, for the inaugural Iditarod, it was opened up as a "checkpoint headquarters." Its owners, Joe and Norma Delia, moved cabins shortly after the race, but generously allowed race organizers to continue to use their home; for twenty-five years, they have volunteered to cook meals for hundreds of mushers and staff. To get to the cabin, mushers have to trek four

Tents are an essential part of the Iditarod for volunteers. We eat in them, sleep in them, and even practice veterinary care in them.

hundred feet up a slippery path, one that can be treacherous in the dark. It's worth the risk, though, to reach the domain of the "Skwentna Sweeties."

The scattered locals of Skwentna get together only a few times a year, and the Iditarod, especially, provides a good excuse to light a bonfire, drink a beer or two (or three), and coerce someone into playing their guitar into a microphone. Everyone involved with the race looks forward to the hospitality of the fun-loving "Sweeties," who spend weeks before the race preparing mountains of food. Inside the cabin, piled high on tables, you'll find moose chili, moose sausage, bacon, pasta of all kinds, fried chicken, salads, vegetables, and great platters of biscuits and gravy. The smell of fresh coffee and cocoa waft; day and night, the Sweeties hand out steaming mugfuls. Somehow, they're always all smiles, and if they know you, they'll greet you by your first name. Most of the Sweeties are women, but there are one or two men, and they all wear garish feather boas, paper tiaras, Mardi Gras bead necklaces, and fluorescent yellow T-shirts that say "Sweeties." It's warm in the cabin, and there are multicolored Christmas lights strung through the rafters, which gives the interior a festive feel.

I can hear the local festivities through the thin canvas of the vet station. Once we finish setting up, we head up the path to the cabin, where we devour bowls of chili and discuss strategy: Who should pair up with whom? What meds should we have close by? Which one of us will meet the sleds at the entry point? The idea is to develop an efficient, close-knit system that enables us to examine the dogs in a timely fashion, but still provide thorough, thoughtful care. We agree in advance how to deal with any major problems and sculpt an emergency plan. The vets will hold a variation of this meeting at every checkpoint, although rarely in an environment as cozy as the log cabin at Skwentna.

Each checkpoint comes with its own challenges. But as in any race that's been run dozens of times, there's also a store of solid institutional wisdom and hard data. Old Iditarod hands chip in with advice and anecdotes for rookie vets:

"The challenge at Skwentna is that the teams arrive in quick succession: one sled coming in every few minutes."

"We know from past Iditarods that the first team could reach us as early as 8 p.m., and the rest will stream in one right after another steadily until about 9 a.m."

"About half the teams push on to the next checkpoint at Finger Lake; we won't know who'll do that until they arrive and declare. Obviously they don't want to be delayed."

"It's going to be a busy night."

We agreed not to take shifts; we'd all be on duty all night. While this meant that we'd be outside for many hours, the workload, at least, would be spread evenly among us. On the first day, we don't expect the dogs to show any real attrition or exhaustion, but injuries can happen at any time, and it's our duty to spot them and spot them quickly. At this stage in the race, we only expect one or two dogs—out of the entire field—to be dropped, but we still need to prepare for them. Once dogs are officially dropped, they become the responsibility of the veterinarians. We make sure that they're comfortable, fed, and cared for until they're flown to Anchorage. At checkpoints close to the start, the dogs are flown directly to Anchorage in groups of four or five; if they're farther away, the dogs may make a pit stop at the nearest "hub." Later in the race, the "line" of dropped dogs at checkpoints can become crowded, with up to forty dogs waiting to be flown out; accordingly, most major hubs have separate veterinary teams to care for dropped dogs.

❄   ❄   ❄   ❄

WITH OUR PLAN IN PLACE, we shuffled back down the steep path to the river. The receding light from the cabin, with its promises of hot coffee, chili, and conversation, tantalized us.

The vets are never the only volunteers at a checkpoint. As we made our way toward the vets' station, small teams of fellow volunteers busied themselves with last-minute chores: setting up straw-bale dividers along "chutes" to divert teams into one of two slots; filling bowls of fresh water from the ice well in the river; laying out straw beds; and attending to myriad other details. About forty teams will stay the night at Skwentna, so the volunteers have to find room for more than five hundred dogs to bed down, far enough apart to prevent rival dogs from stealing other teams' food, sniffing out potential mates, starting scraps, or devising some inventive combination of the above.

I gripped the cup of coffee in my hand, feeling the heat dissipate in real time. It went cold before I even reached the riverbank, and almost as soon as I set foot on the ice, I slipped. A few precious drops of caffeine splattered onto the snow and drained away—an omen, I thought, that tonight would be a long night, indeed. Nearby, a bonfire blazed. The local festivities had picked up. Bottles passed between old friends, and a small, makeshift stage, assembled from bits and pieces of wood and canvas, now hosted "musicians." What they lacked in talent, the huge amplifiers flanking the stage more than made up for in decibels.

Soon, the dogs racing toward Skwentna would detect this activity. The smell of woodsmoke and meat carries for miles, and pools of electric light cast their glow into the wild. By the time the first teams reach Skwentna, it's dark. There are hazards when running at night, sure—poor visibility being the most obvious—but on bright days, the glare from the snow and ice can quickly become painful, and can leave a musher riding just as blind as they would be at night. The lower temperatures at night typically make for better race conditions. The harder the ice on the surface of the trail, the faster the sled goes. Not to mention, the dogs get hot when they run; the cold night air cools them down.

It isn't long before the first cry announcing an approaching musher is raised. "Dog-team on the river!" echoes along the bank. Most of us can't see the team; the river has a bend in it, about a hundred yards before the checkpoint line, that breaks our line of sight. Consequently, we don't have much time between the first glimpse of the team and its arrival. In the distance, I can just barely make out the flicker of the driver's headlamp and his silhouette moving through the rows of trees. Then, the sled made the turn at the bend, and the entire team came into sight. First, the glow of the dogs' eyes, followed by the outline of sixteen huskies pulling in unison, and finally the sled. The huskies were trotting, keeping an even, rhythmic pace. They cast a barely audible shushing sound over the ice.

When the cry went up, the other volunteers at the checkpoint had scurried to their positions. They now guided the dogs and sled through to where we, the vets, were stationed. A race official took down the basic details: the name of the musher; whether they intended to stop; any problems? Once this information had been recorded, the official pressed a pen into the musher's still-mittened hand, asking him to approximate a signature. We stood close by, waiting for word on whether the team would be stopping. I surveyed the dogs. Their expressions were placid yet sleepy. As far as I could tell, they weren't exhausted, though, and I got the sense that they would carry on without complaint if the musher wanted to—but he thought it would be prudent to rest them here. The dogs, then, would get a full examination, and that meant it was time for me to step up.

After introducing myself, I started the examination with a cursory look over the dogs; as they trotted toward the rest site, I scanned for obvious abnormalities. Satisfied that they all *looked* good, I began to assess the lead dogs. I always enjoy working with leads. They're the team captains, with all the self-confidence and pride of a high school quarterback. The first of the leads, a young female husky, was still smiling from the run. Her eyes sparkled and shone with exhilaration. She'd just run over eighty miles at a 7 mph pace, with a few minutes' break thirty miles ago, but already her breathing had come down from a pant to a regular, even *resting* rate. The race was young, and the weather, nice and cold; still, she'd recovered faster than an Olympic marathon runner. As I knelt in the snow, I ran my hands through her coat, let her smell my stethoscope, and then proceeded, gingerly, with the inspection, using my headlamp to see. When performing a checkup, it's crucial to be both quick and thorough, and these two goals often conflict. Taking a few moments to let a dog relax around you pays large dividends. No one, not even a dog, wants to be manhandled during a physical.

The husky's heart beat normally. She didn't have as much as a sinus arrhythmia, a common heart irregularity among human long-distance athletes, and one we find on occasion in competition dogs as well.* She had a healthy frame, with no signs of muscle

* It's easy to confuse a benign sinus arrhythmia with a more serious disturbance.

Working at night can be difficult, with often only our headlamps to guide us.

loss. Dogs competing in the Iditarod burn, on average, 10,000 calories per day and so have to maintain an appetite. If a dog showed signs of muscle loss this early in the race, it would be a clear indication that they're not ingesting enough calories—and that, in turn, would be a signal to drop the dog from the race. I finished examining her, gave her a quick rub behind the ears, and proceeded down the line to the next dog, and then the next, and so on until I had checked all the dogs. The musher had begun to feed them, tossing small, frozen fish fillets as quick treats to keep them happy while the more substantial meal—a gloopy mix of ground-up offal and biscuit—thawed and warmed over his camper stove. The examination, in all, took about fifteen to twenty minutes. In the meantime, several other teams had arrived; their exams were underway nearby. After finishing with the first team, I moved to another, nearby. All the dogs were curled up, fast asleep, on nests of straw.

Veterinary training courses always include special units on cardiac problems; we spend a lot of time learning how to detect and distinguish among them.

All except one. She sat bolt upright and eyed me suspiciously as I approached.

I had been told that even on a busy night, one or two dogs always stand out. The musher introduced her as Amy. During the race, Amy's place had been in the middle of the line, where she had kept her head down and provided power. If I'd seen the whole team in action on the trail, I doubt I would've paid much attention to her. But now, with a gentle snow falling on her face, I studied her closely. She appeared so dignified, so noble.

"This is her third Iditarod," the musher said.

Amy didn't seem aggressive or anxious, but you can never be sure, so I approached her with caution. I lightly patted her head and spoke in a soft whisper—nothing to frighten her. She stood up when I checked her belly for signs of pain, lifted her paws when I needed to look them over, and sat still while I shone a penlight in her eyes. When I was done, she laid down, stretching her body to its fullest extent, letting the lactic acids dissolve away from her muscles. She held that position, enjoying the delicious feeling we all get when we retire from a long day's haul. Before I even finished my notes, she was fast asleep. I watched her a little longer, my headlamp lighting the ice crystals forming and swirling around us. For a moment, it felt like we were in a snow globe.

As I moved from team to team, competitors began to blur together. I recognized a few familiar faces, but aside from a quick hello and a post-exam debrief, I said very little. I scribbled my name on Vet Book after Vet Book, with short notes if I felt that any of the dogs needed to be examined more closely at the next stop. Four hours passed like this; the last of the dog teams until dawn passed through around 2 a.m. As agreed, all the veterinarians worked all night. There was an outdoor thermometer in the tent, showing a bracing −20°F, but the air was humid, heavily laden with moisture from the river and the breath of a hundred humans and many more dogs. The metabolic heat from the work had kept me fairly warm, but now that there was a lull, a chill set in. I had worked up a sweat, soaking my undershirt, and the warmth of my body now finally met the arctic air.

❖ ❖ ❖ *SKWENTNA, AK. 892 miles to Nome. −24°F. Fair.*

Late that night—or early the next morning, depending on how you look at it—I meandered through rows of sleeping huskies, all curled up in balls on their straw nests. Huskies like to work themselves into this position when they sleep, and will often keep their wet nose warm by covering it with their tail, like a fluffy ouroboros. The scene reminded me of Sabo, who slept in the same position. During snowstorms, it was near-impossible to get him inside. He preferred to be out in the elements, letting the snow fall over him until he was completely covered. Once, I'd been horrified to look out and see only a mound of snow where Sabo had been laying. I raced out in bare feet looking for him. When he heard me call, he erupted from the drift, calmly shook off the remaining snow, and glowered at me for waking him up.

Occasionally, a dog lifted its head groggily, but for the most part, the dogs remained fast asleep. While they tend to fall asleep quickly and deeply, the mushers often pace about, taking only short naps. They'd spent far longer than I had out in the freezing temperatures, exerting themselves; if I was tired, they must be on the verge of collapse. There were still plenty of tasks—loading supplies, checking equipment, feeding the dogs, clearing up, getting the next meal ready—to be completed, but I suspect what was really keeping them awake was a combination of adrenaline, stress, excitement, stubbornness, and an almost single-minded focus on the race. In a competition with such enormous physical hardships, it can be easy to overlook the psychological toll, but the Iditarod is far from an adventure holiday. Many competitors have written books about their experience of the race. In

A husky rests on straw.

This Much Country, Kristin Knight Pace describes how the Iditarod changed her perspective on the world, introducing her to a new, welcoming community and giving her a renewed sense of purpose following her divorce. In *Fast into the Night*, Debbie Clarke Moderow explores the connection between people and nature; while the Alaskan landscape inspires awe, it's the intimate bond with her dogs that is the heart of Debbie's connection to the natural world. Neither Kristin nor Debbie—nor any other musher who has competed in the Iditarod—has characterized the race as "easy" or "relaxing." This isn't some "Eat, Pray, Love" exotic vacation. Theirs is the kind of hard-earned spiritual enlightenment that comes with climbing a treacherous mountain and wondering, all the while, if you'll make it back.

Entry requirements for the race today are stricter than ever; still, there are competitors who "blow out" even before they reach Skwentna, becoming so overwhelmed with the task ahead that they suffer a kind of nervous breakdown. Just about every competitor has had moments where they've considered what's to come and doubted their ability to make it to even the next checkpoint. Mushers have also been known to hallucinate or become delirious. This is hardly surprising, given how sleep-deprived they are, and how the light, shining through thick branches, plays tricks on their eyes. While my job is to ensure the safety and health of the dogs, I also keep a watchful eye on the human competitors, knowing that any misstep, mishap, or particularly vivid hallucination can be fatal.

There's a mental toll for volunteers at checkpoints, too, particularly in the more isolated locations like Skwentna. On my way back from the dog lot, I overheard veterinarian Dr. Gretchen Love conversing with Ann, one of the older "rookie" veterinarians. Gretchen, as always, was upbeat and alert. But Ann seemed extremely fatigued; she slumped over as she stood. As I drew near, my headlamp illuminated her face, and I could see that her lips had turned a deep shade of purple. Gretchen was urging her to get some sleep, pointing out that only four or five teams had yet to arrive. This had clearly been the topic of conversation for some time. Gretchen turned to me, pleading for help.

"We can manage it by ourselves, right, Lee?"

I nodded vigorously. Ann had been performing physical exams, without a break, for about five hours. Although adequately dressed for the arctic weather, Ann is naturally very thin; if I, with my layer of insulating fat, was feeling chilled, she must be near-frozen. The temperature was below zero; frostbite wasn't out of the question. I remembered that this was her first night on the trail. The Iditarod is an endurance event for volunteers, too, and it's not at all unusual for a rookie veterinarian to make the same mistake some of the mushers do by physically expending themselves too early, so that they never really recover. I prodded her, too, but Ann remained resolute. She would not be the first one to call it quits for the night. Just then, another veterinarian, Gayle Tate, newly freed from the whisky-soaked clutches of a haggler at the bonfire, marched straight past us, shaking his head and mumbling as he went.

"Man, I need to get some rest. I think I'm finished for the night." He cast a sideways glance at us, and, assessing the situation, added, "Ann, do you want to turn in?"

Finally, Ann relented, agreeing to get some rest now that she wouldn't be the first veterinarian to turn in. While Gayle and Ann climbed up the hill toward the cabins, Gretchen and I remained on the river, waiting for the stragglers to arrive. We took turns dozing on a bale of straw until the final team appeared, just before dawn. We checked them in and examined the dogs—all looked good—before we, too, trudged toward the cabins. I looked forward to my nice, warm sleeping bag.

CHAPTER 6

JUST SMUDGES

TEAMS LEAVING SKWENTNA FACE A GRUELING, FORTY-FIVE-mile trek to the next checkpoint, Finger Lake. The route is deceptively uphill, passing through thick forests and swamplands. The horizon is marked by a belt of tall, dark-green pine trees, behind which loom mountains that look like the pyramids children draw when they're told to draw mountains. This is the Alaska Range—not just the tallest peaks in the continental United States, but the third-highest range above sea level in the world, after the Himalayas and the Andes. The teams are heading directly toward the mountains, but for hours and hours, they won't seem to get any closer. (The route to Finger Lake is uphill because the teams are in the foothills of the mountains.) As they approach the checkpoint, the teams will power over a section of frozen, snow-covered Finger Lake itself.

My first assignment on my first Iditarod was to Finger Lake. At the time, I thought it was the best possible posting. I was thrilled to be stationed at one of the "wilderness" checkpoints. The word "wilderness," for me, evoked images of being deep in the mountains, far from civilization, where I could pitch a tent, cook meals, and live life as if I were in a Jack London novel. It wasn't until later that I discovered why so many of the old-timers tried to avoid the checkpoint.

The night before I left for Finger Lake, I was told that I needed to be in the lobby, ready to go, by 5 a.m. at the latest. I arrived

The Alaska Range, seen from above.

early; my pilot was already there, waiting for me. He was a lean man wearing a baseball cap and mirrored sunglasses.

"I'm eager to get going," he told me.

"It's exciting, isn't it? The race?" I replied.

"I mean, I have a lot of people to fly a lot of different places today, so I want to get started as soon as possible," he said. We agreed to head out right away. Most of the bush pilots, I soon learned, have flown in this region for many years. They've learned the nuances of Arctic and mountain flight: they know how to navigate using natural landmarks such as rivers; how to fly under, over, and around weather; and how to avoid mountain downdrafts that can easily snag and crash planes. The occasional "mishap," as they call it, still happens, but I try not to dwell on that.

A sliver of red sun appeared on the horizon as we walked toward the Cessna 180 parked on the lake outside the hotel. The plane had a proud and purposeful look to it, as tail-dragger airplanes often do. It was painted red and white, for visibility; its various dings and dents testified to the countless hours it had spent in the air. I helped the pilot peel off the partially frozen engine cover, then stowed my bags in the back. The leather upholstery was dry and cracked—another indication that the plane was a veteran of Alaskan air travel. Like most bush planes, the Cessna was equipped with superheated engines and skis. The skis, although useful for landing and takeoff, make the plane difficult to maneuver on the ground. The two of us had to manually lift the tail and swing the nose around until it faced down the lake.

With all my gear on, I barely fit in the copilot's seat. (The pilot had removed the control yoke from my side. Whether for lack of space or trust, this struck me as a wise decision.) Since I had limited mobility, the pilot assisted with my harness. This wasn't just a regular seatbelt; it was a whole restraint system, comprising two straps and two lap belts that converged to a point where they clasped together. After securing his cargo—me—the pilot slammed the passenger-side door, giving it a thump with his fist for good measure. Moments later, he leapt into the pilot's seat and began reading through a pre-flight checklist. I was briefed on emergency procedures and asked for my flight certificate, a small, blue slip of paper that indicated I had signed away my right to sue in the event of injury or death.

I hadn't been terrified by the prospect of this flight—in fact, I knew how to fly and had flown planes myself—but it's always sobering to sign a risk waiver that mentions "your death." I knew the statistics; flying in Alaska is about twice as hazardous as it is anywhere else in the United States. Over the last decade, about 40 percent of all fatal accidents on commercial flights have been in Alaska. Most of the state is "uncontrolled airspace," meaning that there's no one in a control tower keeping an eye on you. In areas with radar coverage, smaller planes fly low enough that they can disappear from monitors. It wasn't statistically likely that I'd crash, but it was statistically *more* likely. Fortunately, both the takeoff and initial ascent went smoothly. Almost immediately, we were over the two-mile-wide arm of Cook Inlet, an ice-choked

Me and one of the bush planes we use to get between checkpoints.

bay with water the color of gun metal—an ominous, cold gray. I wondered how long I would last if our engine suddenly stalled, and the plane plummeted into the bay. Could I swim a mile to the safety of shore? I doubted it.

A field of white, lily-pad-like objects bobbed in the water. I had read about pancake ice, but I had never seen it before. The flat discs, rounded by countless collisions with other bits of ice, ranged from one to ten feet in diameter. No sooner had I spotted them than they were gone; the Alaskan wilderness now unfurled beneath me like some grand, panoramic map. I was mesmerized by the endless tiny details. I felt as if only the ground were moving, and we were stationary. I marveled at wildlife—king eiders and long-tailed ducks, Arctic foxes running through the underbrush, a couple of moose drinking from ponds—and the vast expanse of tundra, with its snowfields, rivers, and leaf-stripped trees. Up here, 1,500 feet in the air, I could trace the meandering paths of dark streams that had only just begun to melt, the worst of the winter finally giving way to the barest glimmer of spring.

The flight from Anchorage to Finger Lake is only about an hour. Looking out my window, I could see the soaring, snow-covered mountains of the Alaska Range. We were heading straight for them; I craned my neck to see the summits.

Finger Lake sits surrounded by mountains, at the entrance to a pass through the peaks, which the competitors would soon take. The pilot overflew the campsite to let them know we were here and planning to land. People waved up at us in acknowledgment. I saw someone jump on a snowmobile, presumably to meet us. I realized, then, that we would not be landing at an airfield. There were no control towers out here. The airstrip, as it was, was located less than a mile from the camp, on the lake itself. In March, the ice is solid to a depth of four feet, but the surface isn't flat. Ice and snow have formed crests and troughs that make crossing the lake on a snowmobile or dogsled as choppy as a rough sea. There was no way a plane could land on that; we needed some-thing smoother. The pilot told me that we'd be landing on a part packed flat by snow machines (Alaskan vernacular for snowmo-biles). As we came in for the final approach, I looked to see if we were lined up with the "strip," but it was difficult for me tell where the packed snow ended and the loose snow began. Orange pen-nants had been set out to mark the outline of the landing strip, but again, I could only make out a few of those.

The pilot leaned over and shouted, "No screaming!"

I thought he was joking. "No screaming?! What's there to scream about?"

"Just no screaming, okay?"

Before we could land, the pilot had to pump the skis into posi-tion using a large lever that sat between us. It took at least fifty pumps for the skis to lock into place. If that sounds primitive, it gets worse: the skis have no brakes, so once you touch down, you are at the mercy of aerodynamics. The plane stops only when it runs out of momentum. If the snowmobiler who packed the snow didn't make that runway long enough, or if the pilot landed long, the plane might slide off the end, into the unpacked snow, and travel until it encountered a relatively immovable object. When a plane is sliding like this, a gust of wind can easily flip it or throw it sideways.

The pilot artfully swung the Cessna into a nice downwind turn. The snowmobiler that had been dispatched from the camp to fetch me and my gear caught up with us before we had even come to a stop. He gave us a little room, and I found out why when the pilot gunned the engine, causing the Cessna to skid 180 degrees until it was upwind again. When the skis finally touched the ice, the plane was still traveling about 70 miles per hour. For the first quarter of a mile, it barely lost any speed, but it was moving in a straight line, and the ride was as smooth as any landing in a small plane could be. After that, the plane began to slow: a textbook landing. No screaming.

I clawed at my seat buckle to extract myself from the complicated restraint. I thanked the pilot and jumped onto the ice to collect my kit. Both the duffel bag and backpack had already been

"Hallelujah." A fitting song for this view.

loaded onto a sled attached to the back of the snowmobile, and I deduced that that sled was also my seat. Before my "taxi" had even reached the checkpoint, the pilot was airborne again, a tiny red dot in a cobalt blue sky, off to ferry another volunteer.

❋ ❋ ❋ *FINGER LAKE, AK. 852 miles to Nome. Dawn.*
−12°F. Mostly cloudy.

Like the runway, the checkpoint at Finger Lake was set up on the frozen lake. The location, no doubt, had not been selected because it's an oasis of warmth. The mountains do nothing to protect the area from the wind, which comes down, pummeling and bitter, across hundreds of miles of ice fields. Temperatures are almost always subzero, and one year, I was there when it plummeted below −30°F. (When I removed my inner glove for an instant, the wind left my fingers frost-nipped.) The cold makes even moderate work more tiring, and the weather is some of the harshest on the course. This is part of the reason why veteran volunteers think of Finger Lake as a hard-luck posting—but after multiple postings there, I still can't shake the feeling that this place, especially, embodies the romance of the wild. The surroundings are breathtaking. Up close, I can see waves of crystalline snow, sculpted by the wind, on the lakebed. Deep, fragrant pine forests surround the lake, and at twilight, the mountain peaks shimmer in red, gold, and pink hues. Nightfall brings clear skies; without clouds or light pollution, the stars seem to shine brighter. Great Horned Owls hoot in branches.

Finger Lake is one of the few checkpoints located on private land. It sits on the grounds of the Winterlake Lodge, a four-star hotel that caters to an affluent crowd. Tourists pay about $8,000 each for three days of personalized Alaskan adventures. The lodge offers a range of activities, including helicopter and ski-plane tours; hiking, snowmobiling, and mountain biking;

birdwatching; whitewater rafting and kayaking; and even dog-sledding. A gourmet chef prepares high-end meals on-site, often using fresh-caught fish from the lake. The lodge itself, half-hidden in the thick pine forest that goes up to the lakeshore, has a large, log-cabin-style main building and a dozen or so private log cabins. All of this is owned by Carl Dixon, who has been running the resort with his wife, Kirsten, for nearly thirty years. Carl's cherry-red helicopter is always parked right outside the lodge, ready to fly guests to the next spot on their holiday itinerary.

The Winterlake Lodge doesn't shy away from advertising the fact that it's on the Iditarod Trail. (One of the most popular activities at the resort is actually a guided walk along the trail.) While this has *become* a selling point, the relationship between the Dixons and the race organizers hasn't always been so peaceable, and fairly so; the race literally bisects Carl's property. Every large sporting event, from the Boston Marathon to the Indy 500, leaves its detritus. Carl knows his guests come to the resort to relax and enjoy the solitude and primeval grandeur of the woods, and he is fastidious about keeping the area clean. As long as the Iditarod Committee ensures that the place is left exactly as it was found, Carl allows the race to continue operating through his property. Volunteers are told to clean up after themselves at every checkpoint, but at Finger Lake, we were told to be especially diligent. Once the competitors pass through, everything is disassembled. The straw used for bedding is raked up and transported to a ditch, where it's burned. Every last piece of trash and waste is collected and taken off-site with the personnel and their equipment. While flying overhead, I had seen the resort and surrounding buildings. But I had yet to see the actual checkpoint.

"Where's the camp?!" I yelled over the sound of the snowmobile's motor.

"That's it!" the driver yelled back, pointing to a mass of spruce trees ahead. I could just barely make out a clearing in there. As we approached, I clocked a large tent, a few straw bales, and a small,

makeshift folding table. I clambered out of the sled and introduced myself to the volunteers standing at the table, who were
frying some bacon on a two-burner stove. The only other piece of
equipment I could see was a coffee machine. Otherwise, the tent
was empty.

"Where is everyone else?" I asked.

"We're it, so far," came the reply. One of the two men offered
me some burnt bacon and coffee for breakfast. We sat on the straw
bales and chatted. They weren't veterinarians, I learned, but members of the communications team.

At a checkpoint like the next one, Rainy Pass, volunteers are
shown to a cozy, preheated cabin upon arrival. All we really have
to do is unfurl our sleeping bags. Many of the checkpoints in the
second half of the race are based in towns or villages, and the volunteers are housed in a community center or similar public building. Despite being on the grounds of the Winterlake Lodge, the
Finger Lake checkpoint is totally removed from that world. The
volunteers assigned to this checkpoint must set up everything
themselves. They erect all tents; assemble the wood-burning
stove; drill a well into the lake for water; and prepare the parking
area for the sled teams. As I recounted all these tasks in my head,
the reality began to sink in.

"Are we going to be the ones setting everything up?" I asked
my colleagues.

They both smirked and nodded.

I was all for the adventure of living in the wild for a few days, but
I had imagined that there would be a dozen or so people here, and
at least some hardened, world-weary Alaskans. These two didn't
look at all outdoorsy. If I was the expert here, we were screwed.

"We've been working on this since it got light," one said.

"All the tents and poles were laid out for us, but it snowed last
night, and they got buried and frozen together. We had to find
them and thaw them out. Then we had to put together the tent *and*
the stove that heats it," the other added.

In the hours since they'd arrived, they'd managed to set up one folding table and one tent for the communications team. Don't get me wrong, putting up one of these tents is no easy feat. They're large, white structures, each measuring about twenty-four feet by ten feet and supported by heavy steel rods. The outside walls are water-repellent, and the inside is lined with a reflective, NASA-like fabric designed to retain heat. Once erected, they provide about as much warmth and protection from the elements as can be expected in polar conditions—and I was now part of the team responsible for assembling them, plus some smaller two- or three-person tents. Begrudgingly, I collected the metal tubing for the second tent and carried them like firewood to where we'd be setting up. It was so cold that even with my heavy mitts on I could feel the freezing metal against my palms; if I had touched them barehanded, my flesh would have peeled off. The tent coverings were, indeed, frozen together. Even the lining was laden with hoar frost.

Every half hour or so, a bush plane arrived bearing volunteers. The members of the veterinary team—Ann and Tate, plus Betsy King, a veteran of the Iditarod, and two German veterinarians, Tanja and Ruth—trickled in, and by midday, there were six veterinarians stationed at Finger Lake. (At first, I thought this excessive; only later did I find out why Stu Nelson always staffs this checkpoint with as many veterinarians as possible.) More members of the communications team arrived, too. Each new arrival brought some new fragment of tent-building expertise with them, and by lunchtime we'd set up all four of the main tents, as well as some of the smaller tents for storing supplies. The later arrivals also brought food; unfortunately, it turned out that the only cooking equipment allocated to Finger Lake was that single two-burner Coleman stove, the one my colleagues had used to burn bacon. We'd have to use that stove to provide breakfast, lunch, and dinner for everyone.

The logistics of feeding volunteers varies wildly from

Volunteers prepare hearty meals in the camp "kitchen."

checkpoint to checkpoint. At the first two checkpoints, Yentna and Skwentna, all the teams show up within a few hours of each other, so we can work through them in a single shift. This makes sit-down meals possible. Later in the race, we have set mealtimes again; by this time, huge gaps have opened up in the field and we can take breaks with some regularity. When the checkpoint is in a town, the locals often supply the food, and I've enjoyed a variety of delicious if (for my taste!) somewhat outlandish dishes, including caribou, moose, seal, and whale blubber. At Finger Lake, however, it's impossible to make elaborate dining plans. At this point, a few days into the race, competitors are beginning to spread out, but erratically so. When they will arrive—or how they'll be grouped together—is impossible to predict.

In the end, we set up a grab-and-go station with granola bars, M&M's, potato chips, carrots, and cold coffee. We had the stove, too, but it would be a full-time task to attend to the burners. One of the volunteers, Alan, offered his services as a camp cook, provided that he wouldn't be held responsible for any other chores.

We all quickly agreed. A friendly, hardworking man in his early thirties, Alan proved to be able to blacken *any* food beyond recognition. He doled out burnt pancakes, charred bacon, and cremated sausages. In all honesty, these didn't taste too bad relative to the frozen-solid candy bars, fruit, and snacks at the picnic tables, which I had to hold in my mouth until they were malleable enough to chew. These crimes against cuisine were, of course, taking place almost literally in the shadow of a world-renowned luxury hotel with a banquet room and gourmet chef.

That night, the night before the first teams were set to arrive, Carl invited us up to the resort for a dessert course. The whole team accepted Carl's invitation, except for me. I'd volunteered for the first shift, and I knew that the lead mushers were expected early. I needed my sleep. But in truth, I didn't sleep much at all. That night, I remember, was especially frigid, and by complete chance, I would witness, for the first time, the aurora borealis.

❄   ❄   ❄   ❄

MY FOURTH-GRADE TEACHER, MRS. Divens, was something of an adventurer, and she often put on slideshows for our class. One of the slideshows documented a cruise to Alaska, and among the photos of glaciers calving into aqua-blue waters was an underexposed shot of the northern lights. She explained that the picture didn't capture what she saw that night, not at all. Her excitement about what she had seen but couldn't describe stayed with me for decades.

I hate to admit it, but I was seriously underwhelmed when I first saw the lights. Later that night, long after the veterinarians had returned from the lodge, I coaxed my body out of my warm sleeping bag and went out into the bitter cold to use the euphemistically named "honey bucket." Afterward, sprinting back as fast as I could, I caught sight of a faint glow on the horizon. It was a peculiar green; I knew it couldn't be light from a city, given the

This photo from the Bureau of Land Management makes the northern lights seem a little less smudge-like.

fact that we were out in the middle of nowhere. Almost as fast as the light appeared, it vanished. I pondered the aberration a bit, wondering if I'd seen a spaceship. I quickly realized that it could only have been one thing: the northern lights.

The next day, I mentioned what I'd seen to my colleagues. To my surprise, they were totally irate. How could I have seen the lights and not woken everyone else up to come see them, too? I muttered that I was a rookie, that I thought seeing the aurora borealis was commonplace around here, that it would be like waking people up because it's snowing. Anyway, I said, they hadn't been all that impressive. Just kind of green smudges.

❋   ❋   ❋   ❋

THE LIGHTS FORM when charged particles from the sun react with elements at high altitudes in the earth's atmosphere. Ironically, that year witnessed a massive increase in solar activity—I got the benefit of this a little later on in the race. By the time I was in McGrath, 158 miles up the trail, every night saw a display starting early in the evening on the western horizon, then taking over the whole sky. The colors could wave banner-like in a gentle wind or huge pulses of green could swiftly expand and contract as if the sky itself was breathing. There were dramatic color changes, with deep reds and purples in the mix.

Native Alaskan cultures have many legends that incorporate the northern lights, and they generally characterize them as living, frolicsome beings. One legend is that the lights were the spirits of the dead playing a game, kicking around a ball that was really a walrus skull. The early peoples of Nunivak Island in the Bering Sea told a similar legend, but instead of playing with a walrus skull, the spirits kicked around a human head. Other groups in Alaska said the lights were spirits of the animals they had hunted for food, most notably the beluga whale, caribou, and salmon. The hunters in these tribes saw the aurora borealis as proof the prey had successfully crossed over to the heavens, and were now happy.

CHAPTER 7

FIRE AT FINGER LAKE

ONE YEAR, THE VETERINARIANS' TENT AT FINGER LAKE HAD AN innovation: a real camp kitchen, complete with a stove and a full-time cook. There was a stove in our tent, too. Naturally, it was up to the volunteers to assemble it. The instructions read like a list of warnings. The stove had to be placed near the far wall of the tent to prevent carbon monoxide poisoning. The fuel drum was to be kept outside, with a fuel line running underneath the tent flap. Even by Alaskan standards, this stove was difficult to operate. It was big, old, and made from clunky pieces of cast iron, none of which fitted together correctly. Once the oven was in place, it was nearly impossible to move—and extremely temperamental, often cutting out for no apparent reason.

I staked out a position for my sleeping bag close to the door. I hated the idea of having to crawl over everyone else to get out of the tent. Although I was as far away from the stove as possible, I could still feel its heat. *This*, I thought, *is what passes for luxury on the trail*. At exactly 3 a.m. the night before the sled teams were due to arrive, I woke to the sight of fellow veterinarian Bill Sampson inches from my face.

"The goddamn stove is out."

That got me up. Or maybe it was the sudden realization that I was freezing. The stove must have been out for a while; frost had already formed on the sides of the tent. Seeing that, and hearing the wind howling outside, I realized how seriously we needed to take this. I felt around for my headlamp, and by the time I turned it on, everyone else was already up. There were several vets looking over the stove, trying to figure out how to get it started again. I knew nothing about how the stove operated, only this: if you turned the knob to "On," then hit an ignition button, it was meant to go "poof!" and there would be warmth. Stoves, obviously, weren't on the syllabus at vet school; no one in the tent knew much more about them than I did. One of my colleagues had the presence of mind to head outside to check on the fuel tank and line, and reported back almost immediately that both were fine.

Someone suggested that we could relight the stove with a match. As it turned out, we didn't have any matches, but we did have a BIC grill lighter. The veterinarian nearest the stove turned the gas up and sparked the lighter. Nothing. The dial was spun to its max and allowed to run for a while. I could tell I wasn't the only person who thought there was a potential hazard, here. A consensus that the veterinarian should "be careful" emerged, and someone crafted a long safety match from a marshmallow stick and toilet paper. All this time, the gas was running. The crude torch was held up, someone flicked the lighter, and I swear I felt the heat before I saw the explosion. The initial ball of flame cleared fast, but then fire leapt from the stove and climbed up the outside of the aluminum chimney. The clumps of straw surrounding the stove were alight. Someone at the opposite end of the tent called out to make sure that we were all okay. Thankfully, no one was injured in the initial blast. But now we had a real crisis on our hands. Dense smoke, coming mainly from the straw, began to fill the tent. The flames gushing from the oven were dangerously close to the tent fabric, licking, already, at the inner lining. People scrambled about yelling and coughing, throwing snow on the fire, and beating the flames with blankets.

My instinct was to run. I was right by the exit, and departing quickly could be the best way to help. If I took a seat on the lifeboat of a sinking ship, I reasoned, that'd be one fewer person for the captain to worry about. There wasn't a captain, though, just an urgent need to bring the fire under control. Hacking up smoke, I poured water from my canteen onto the blaze, then started scooping snow as fast as I could. Everyone else was doing the same, and together we brought the inferno down to a small fire. Those closest to the chest containing the vital medical supplies carried it outside, and between us we somehow managed to salvage all of our equipment. No more than fifteen minutes after Bill woke me, the fire was out, and the emergency was over—but now everyone in the camp was awake. We ran a quick check to make sure all the veterinarians were present and intact; the only "injury" was some singed facial hair. Later, when other volunteers asked what had happened, we told the story as though we were characters in a thriller, all of us heroes, acting valiantly— even selflessly—to put out the blazing fire. (When head vet Stu Nelson arrived the next day, we changed our tune, and he learned that there had been a "small mishap.")

One of the volunteers knew how to operate a stove, and they fixed ours with an almost embarrassing amount of ease. The tent began to warm through, but we wouldn't be returning any time soon. When straw is on fire, it smolders more than it burns, producing a thick, rancid smoke. The fumes still lingered in the tent, and we desperately needed to air out our lungs and belongings, not to mention our medical supplies. After some debate, our benighted crew moved into what was supposed to be the mushers' tent. It was 4 a.m., four hours before sunrise. Most of my colleagues settled back down to sleep. I had barely slept, but I knew I wasn't going to, not with all that adrenaline running through my veins. I had prepared for this, though; one of the skills you pick up on the course is the ability to manage tiredness. I got up and quietly put on my thermal underwear, overclothes, and parka. I'd need a coffee, sure, but otherwise, I was ready for my shift.

I wandered over to the communications center, where wires and cables of all sizes and colors snaked the walls and floors. The volunteers there, I learned, had been up all night monitoring the sleds. The mushers aren't allowed radios, but each sled has a GPS tracker. Sipping lukewarm coffee, I watched the glowing blips move across the screens. An experienced eye could discern what was happening: more snow had fallen than was forecast, so the trail was fresh, soft, and much harder to pass over. I was told that Nicolas Petit's sled was in front, with a chasing group close behind, then a long, strung-out line. Petit was one of the younger mushers, and his strategy seemed to involve pushing harder than his rivals during the early stages of the race to build up a lead. He was five miles away from us now, and we estimated that he'd arrive at the edge of the lake in about an hour. After his sled arrived, there would be a short respite, followed by a rush of competitors arriving in quick succession, all before dawn. No dogs had been dropped; each team had all sixteen dogs, and every dog would need to be examined. Even with six veterinarians, we were in for a busy morning.

The tables in the communications center were covered with

Tables inside the communications center.

faxes and hastily scribbled notes. While I waited for Petit, I brought myself up to speed on the goings-on of the race. Most of the faxes had been sent from the previous checkpoint, Skwentna, and detailed the positions of competitors, but there were some general messages for the veterinary staff, too. I read one from Stu Nelson reminding us to make sure that mushers' veterinary handbooks were signed, as some teams had left Yentna without verification that their dogs had been cleared. (Not good.) As Petit approached, the other veterinarians filtered into the communications center. We watched the blip grow closer; when he was two miles away, we bundled up and, bracing for the cold, exited the center.

The "entrance" to the checkpoint was brightly lit for the television cameras. Field lamps on giant stands towered over us, acting as a lighthouse for the racers. For us, down on the ground, it was difficult to see anything beyond the ring of light. All around us it was pitch-black, so much so that I needed help orienting myself in the direction of the lake—which, as it turned out, was in the opposite direction of the spruce trees I was walking toward. We looked out across the icefield and—yes!—there it was, the tiny glimmer of Petit's headlamp. We watched it, transfixed, trading theories about how far away it was. Before long, we began to hear the yipping and yelping of Petit's dogs. Then came the huskies' eyes, blue-green flecks bobbing up and down on the lake in a distinctive, wave-like motion. A familiar nervousness set in. These were race conditions, and I didn't want to be responsible for delaying anyone or, worse, rushing an examination and missing a serious problem. But there was no time to dwell. The dogs were upon us. I glanced at my wristwatch. It was 4:55 a.m.

The musher stepped off his sled. Within seconds, he had anchored his team and was signing the logbook. Cameras flashed. People congratulated him on taking an early lead. Journalists asked about the state of the course, the weather, his progress, and so on, their voices melding together into a cacophonous chorus. The sudden press of human contact must have been disorienting for him; for the last several hours, he had been powering through the night, the only person for an hour in any direction. Before he became a competitor himself, Nicholas Petit worked with Jim Lanier, a tried-and-true veteran of the Iditarod, and helped him train for the 2011 Iditarod. Lanier first competed in the Iditarod in 1979, six years after the running of the first modern race—while Petit was still in diapers. In 2012, Lanier missed the race because of hip surgery, and he let Petit take his place. Now, they were competing against each other, and—at this very early stage—Petit was beating his mentor. It's the sort of story that journalists love.

Petit had chosen to stop at Finger Lake rather than proceed to the next checkpoint, Rainy Pass, so his sled was ushered to an assigned "parking spot." It glided to a halt as the team dogs followed the example of the leads. The young musher and his dogs, I noticed, resembled one another, all covered in snow and ice: Petit's beard was frozen, as was the fur around the dogs' mouths. They looked wild but happy. After laying down straw for the dogs to rest on, Petit fed them frozen cubes of beef and kibble. To defrost additional meat, he boiled some water from the lake over a small gas stove. The dogs have no problem chewing the frozen beef, but hot meals help keep them hydrated.

While Petit boiled the food, I set to work. One patient at a time, I told myself. After the first, there would be fifteen more dogs to examine, but the first would be my priority now. I worked down a mental checklist: pulse, breathing rate, gum color. I palpated her limbs, her spine, her chest; simply touching a dog in these places can reveal any potentially problematic lumps or masses. Despite their reputation for resilience, huskies are not particularly stoic dogs, and they'll often vocalize when you touch an area that is sore. Generally, this vocalization allows me to pinpoint a source of pain. If the pressure hurts a lot, they'll try to get away. This, of course, is an indication that I need to look at that area more closely.

These are the same basic tests that I'd run on a family pet in Georgetown. The difference between a sled dog and a domestic dog, of course, is that a sled dog is pushing itself to its physical limits. Even a seemingly trivial issue can have serious consequences for these canine athletes, and once they're past the checkpoint they'll be a long way from emergency assistance if they need it. So I inspected her paws carefully, and I pressed my stethoscope a little closer to her chest than usual. Her heart, I thought, was thumping along nicely, and her breathing was crisp and unburdened. Both the husky and I were satisfied with my exam; as I made my way toward the next dog in line, she settled down peacefully on her bed of straw.

On the other side of the gangline, Betsy King was doing the same thing. Generally speaking, it's good to have at least two vets working on each sled dog team. It's an efficient, effective approach that in theory means that teams can be checked in in half the time it might otherwise take a single vet to check a team. (This is a race, after all.) More importantly, from a strictly medical perspective, it allows each of us to examine individual dogs more thoroughly. If one of us finds a problem, we can quickly get assistance, and if there's a question or decision to be made, a second opinion is close at hand. Betsy and I worked well together and, I was gratified to see, at the same pace. It wasn't long before we'd checked all sixteen dogs and were able to clear the team. I told Petit that his dogs were in good shape and—I nearly forgot, despite Stu's fax— had him sign the official log. Petit's team rested for another four hours, then took their leave of Finger Lake.

❄   ❄   ❄   ❄

THE NEXT FEW TEAMS arrived in quick succession. It was early, and the dogs, I could tell, were ready to curl up and catch some shut-eye on their beds of straw. But as race protocol dictated, I had to examine each and every dog before clearing them, sleepy ones included. I knelt beside the next team and patted one of the two lead dogs. It was easy to tell which dogs were Iditarod veterans. As

Out on the course, rest is key. This husky is catching up on shut-eye in his nest.

I finished examining my first patient, the small, black-and-white husky behind her opened a tired eye and stood, albeit groggily, without prompting. She knew the drill; I imagined she had been through this many, many times. I used my stethoscope to listen to her heartbeat and lungs.

While I pressed on with the exams, I was becoming aware of a problem developing around me. The previous night, long before the fire roused us from our slumber, we set up parking spaces for the sleds, carefully positioning them so as to prevent entanglements (of any kind) between competing teams. We knew that, even after the forty-mile trek from Skwentna, there would be dogs on almost every team rowdy enough to try to scrap with a dog or dogs from a competing team. No competitor has ever died from fight-inflicted wounds, but bite lacerations can be deep and serious, and fights are most prevalent in these early stages, when energy levels are at their highest. Sometimes, fights break out among teammates; female dogs in estrus are particularly feisty. A good musher knows who gets along with whom, and which of their dogs may cause trouble. Usually, they too have strategies for where to place dogs when resting. This wasn't the problem. All had gone to plan today, and we had put enough distance between teams to prevent fighting. The problem was that the parking lot was beginning to overflow. We were quickly running out of space. There were just too many teams, coming in too fast and too close together, and many of them were staying. Some teams, as expected, had powered straight through Finger Lake toward Rainy Pass. Lance Mackey, Aliy Zirkle, and Petit's mentor Lanier—all big names expected to do well—arrived within a few minutes of each other, around 6 a.m., and immediately signaled that they wouldn't be stopping, that they'd be using this opportunity to overtake Petit. The teams stopped only as long as they needed to get our sign-off. We conducted quick visual inspections and sent them on their way within minutes. But these competitors, the ones "blowing through," were the exceptions; many more teams decided to stay and rest for at least a few hours. By 7:45 a.m., about four hours after Petit arrived, we had parked twenty sleds and over three hundred dogs, all of whom needed to be inspected. We abandoned our rosters and predetermined plans; individual vets now leapfrogged from team to team as they were needed. If Betsy started with the lead and swing dogs at the front, I started with the dogs closest to the sled, the wheel dogs. Fundamentally, our task remained the same. Working as quickly as we could, we examined dog after dog, intermittently palpating and listening to heartbeats until the late morning.

With all the attention on the dogs, it can be easy to forget about the mushers, whose health is also of vital concern. (The mushers often forget about this, too.) When I approach a team for an exam, the very first question I ask is about how the musher is doing: Are they eating and drinking enough? Are they feeling the effects of the cold? While I *am* concerned about their health, I do have an ulterior motive. Mushers spend months, even years, building a rapport with their dogs. They know them better than anyone else, and are extremely adept at identifying even the subtlest abnormalities. Nine times out of ten, the most important thing for a vet to know when examining a dog is whether the *musher* thinks there's a problem. It's crucial, then, for the veterinarian to earn the musher's trust, to let them know that you're on their side. Whatever you do, you should never alienate the musher by ignoring them; for this reason, I often explain my methodology in advance.

If there's a problem with a dog, though, mushers rarely wait for me to ask. One of the mushers who stopped at Finger Lake told me without prompting that the third dog on her team, a female husky, was not pulling as strongly as she was at the start of the race. She added that there were no visible signs of lameness or problems with her appetite. I began to work my way down my checklist. No vomiting? No vomiting. No diarrhea? No diarrhea. I could sense her impatience—wasn't I listening? Why wasn't I concentrating on the problem she just alerted me to? There are many reasons, the first being that I still needed to assess the dog's general condition. Operating under pressure without a mental checklist is risky; it's easy to forget to check something. There's a good diagnostic reason, too. If I'm told a dog is limping on one leg, examining the dog's good legs first gives me a sense of the normal flexion and extension in each joint, which I can then compare to the problem leg and get a better idea of where and how severe the injury is.

In this case, I could see that the husky was not putting all her weight on her left foreleg. After carefully explaining to the musher why I would be starting with her right foreleg, I began my examination. As expected, the dog showed no discomfort when I flexed the right leg. When I touched her left shoulder, however, she didn't yelp, bark, or nip at me, but there was an instant change of expression. Now she was looking at me with pleading eyes. Clearly, something was causing her pain. I'd been expecting to see injuries like this; earlier, in the communications center, there had been talk of heavy snowfall. Racing conditions are

At each checkpoint, the dogs receive individual veterinary care.

ideal when the trail is flattest, and the dogs are running on packed snow. Deep snow can be tough to slog through, especially when it's heavy with water. Most of the time, a dog running in deep snow isn't "injured," per se, just tired to the point that they need to be dropped. But it *is* possible to sustain an injury in deep snow. This tends to happen when the dogs are going at a steady pace and one of them hits a "pocket," or hole in the ground disguised by snow. The inertia of their forward progress in combination with the abrupt stop places considerable strain on the joints. This typically results in a shoulder pull or bicipital strain—and that's what I seemed to be looking at.

Canine competitors train rigorously and extensively for up to nine months before the race. They're more than prepared for the task ahead. In fact, during the race, the fastest teams can travel up to 110 miles per day. But in the Iditarod, as in any other sport, injuries can and do happen. Shoulder and wrist injuries account for the vast majority of orthopedic problems. These can occur in deep snow, as with this dog, or when dogs take sharp turns, especially when running fast. It was once thought that the likelihood of injury positively correlates to a sled dog's average speed—that the faster a given dog runs, the more likely they are to sustain a shoulder injury. A recent study conducted by Dr. Dirsko von Pfeil found that the fastest teams were actually *less* likely to incur shoulder problems, though it's not clear why. It's possible that teams traveling over deep ruts left by leading teams are exposed to poorer trail conditions, resulting in more stress on the ligaments and muscles of the shoulder. Or it could be that slower dogs are simply spending more time on the course, and so are exposed to the risks for longer periods of time.

"I have bad news," I told the musher. "We need to drop this one."

"The limping's not bad. Isn't it the sort of thing that heals itself?"

"It's her shoulder."

"Oh."

If this had been a minor wrist problem, the musher would have been right. A mild carpus pull might resolve itself. This isn't the case for shoulder injuries. Following a course of rest and anti-inflammatories, the husky would be fine in a matter of days, but no shoulder injury was going to heal itself while she was still in the race. The musher knew this, and she quickly accepted it.

The husky seemed to know what was being discussed, and I watched her expression change from pleading to plaintive, as if to say, "It's not that bad. I can continue." The noises made by dogs when they realize they're being dropped are heartrending; they can and sometimes do howl all night. Dogs are by nature pack animals, and they don't like it when their pack moves on without them. I've heard stories, over the years, about dropped dogs breaking free from their handlers and racing off to look for their team. These dogs are typically found by other teams, bundled up, and brought to the next checkpoint. Bearing this in mind, I gingerly fastened a slip lead over the husky's head. As I led her away from her teammates, I felt her turn to look back. Once in a while, a dog will put on the brakes and force you to carry them to the dropped-dog line. But she never stopped walking; she just moped forward, head down.

There's a color code—based on the severity of the illness or injury, as well as the level of additional care required—assigned to each dropped dog. This husky was definitely "white," since her injury wasn't life-threatening. White dogs are usually cared for by veterinarians and other volunteers at the checkpoint, and after the checkpoint is taken down, they ride back with us to Anchorage. "Red" dogs, by contrast, are in critical condition. For red dogs, race organizers send a bush plane to the checkpoint for immediate transport. "Blue" dogs fall somewhere between red and white dogs. They're in stable condition, but they don't wait with us to fly back to Anchorage; instead, they're put on the first flight back. Since she would be staying with us for a while, I hooked the injured husky far down the dropped-dog line, where she curled up in a ball and buried her snout in a pile of straw. I administered the medications needed and wrote out a prescription for the vets back in Anchorage. Soon, they'd be handed a file that recorded exactly what I'd done and when.

The husky was not the only dog to be dropped that morning. Most injuries at this early stage weren't serious: strained muscles, sore legs, chafing from the gangline. Occasionally, I treated exercise-induced diarrhea, or paw-pad abrasions. I saw a few split toenails. When I pointed these injuries out to the mushers, I told them that I'd give the okay for the dog to continue—that the problem would resolve after a brief rest—but almost every time, the musher elected to leave the dog with us. Mushers, when it comes down to it, not only have a great deal of financial investment in their dogs but emotional investment, too. As a practical consideration, a dog with a muscle ache will not be able to pull its fair share, and any injury increases the risk of a more serious injury. If I think it's a serious problem, I don't give them a choice. But given the choice, mushers almost always err on the side of caution.

CHAPTER 8

HOW ACCIDENTS HAPPEN

A FEW YEARS AGO, I TOOK ADVANTAGE OF A LULL IN THE ACTIV-
ity to hike a little way up the trail with Bill Roth, a photojournalist from the *Anchorage Daily News*. Bill wanted to get
some good action shots. He loved being out here, photographing
the dogs. He had covered the Iditarod for many years and was on
a first-name basis with many of the mushers. Once, he'd taken a
photo of me kissing a husky that made the newspaper.

Our plan was to catch the teams just after they'd left the

Smooch!

checkpoint. As we walked along the trail, glancing back to make sure that there weren't any racers coming out of the chutes, Bill described how to find the best angles.

"Here," I suggested, eager to impress him. I pointed to a small knoll right beside the trail. "Right at the side of the course. From on top of that, you'll get some shots as they come up over the rise."

"But if I stand at the bottom of that hill, I'll see anyone who wipes out," he replied. Bill motioned to the trail. There was a sharp left-hand turn just before a hill. While veterans of the race know to take this stretch slowly, rookies, he explained, often charge down the embankment and wind up buried in a snow-bank in a tangle of dogs and harnesses. Thankfully, the only injuries sustained here have been to mushers' egos. Regardless, to a sports photographer like Bill, it's a front-page picture waiting to happen.

As Bill clambered down the hill, I stepped off the hard-packed snow on the course to stand atop the knoll I had spotted. Unfortunately, it was not a knoll; it was a bush covered with snow. I immediately sank up to my waist. I flapped around for something to grab, something to use as leverage to pull myself out. There was nothing. I heard the distant sound of cheers back at the camp, and the unmistakable yips of huskies leaving a checkpoint. It hit me, then, that I might actually be in the path of the approaching teams. Feeling through the snow with my foot, I found a branch that I thought would support my weight. It did not. The branch cracked, and I fell back, away from the trail, to be swallowed up to my neck in a snowdrift. I was trapped.

It is a universal law that when you do something embarrassing— that when you are at your most awkward—the person who witnesses it will be someone you know, perhaps even someone you had hoped to impress. The musher coming up the trail could have been any one of the forty people yet to leave the checkpoint, but of course it was a musher I had chatted with extensively. As she approached, I saw her look quizzically in my direction, evidently trying to understand how a disembodied head might have ended up in a field of snow. Then, recognizing me, she broke into a broad smile.

"You fell in the snow!" she yelled, laughing as she sped by. I thought I could make out smiles of merriment among her huskies, too.

I had a bigger problem: at any moment, Bill, the esteemed photojournalist, keen on snapping photos of Iditarod mishaps for the papers, would be making his way up the hill. But, like the quicksand in an old Western, the more I struggled to free myself, the deeper I sank. If I moved one arm out of the hole, the other side of my body sloped down. I dimly remembered that the way out of quicksand is to swim. I attempted a breaststroke, but only succeeded in getting a mouthful of snow. I could hear Bill's snowshoes crunching toward me. In a panic, I decided that the snow on my left side was firm enough to support my leg. I put all my strength in my left leg, which meant, of course, that my right leg plunged down into the snow. Suddenly, I was staring up at my left ankle, doing the splits.

Bill now stood in front of me, a look of bewilderment on his face.

"Hi," I said, sheepishly.

"Hi. What the hell are you doing?" He didn't seem all that worried for me.

"You might need to give me a hand here. Please don't take any pictures."

Click click click. He was laughing so hard I thought he would burst into tears. "My God, all I can see of you are your head and foot!" *Click click click.* "I mean you look absolutely ridiculous. You're not hurt, are you?" *Click click click.*

If you're from Alaska, or you've lived there long enough, you know what to do in this situation almost instinctively. Bill put his camera down, laid flat on the snow like someone inching over thin ice to save a person who has fallen through, held out his hand, and pulled me out.

"I don't suppose we could keep this little incident to ourselves?" I pleaded.

"Not a chance," he laughed. "Not a chance at all."

❀ ❀ ❀ *FINGER LAKE, AK. 852 miles to Nome. Midday. 16°F. Cloudy.*

AROUND MIDDAY, I was approached by Hank DeBruin, a lanky Canadian musher, one of the very few driving a team composed of Siberian Huskies. Their elegance and disposition captivated him. As he once told me, there's "nothing prettier than a Siberian Husky running for all it's worth through the snow."

Hank was anxious about Andy, a rust- and cream-colored husky on his team. Andy was a veteran of no less than seven Iditarods, a true denizen of the course who had earned his place at the front of the sled. (It was obvious, too, that he was Hank's favorite.) Although still a young dog by most standards, grayness had crept into the hair around his muzzle. I could tell that the other dogs looked up to Andy, as they seemed to match his every move on and off the trail. Even now, while the team rested, Andy struck a pose of strict, redoubtable discipline. Hank may have been the musher, but this was clearly Andy's team.

"I can't put my finger on it," Hank told me, "but something doesn't seem right. I thought I saw him limping a few times, maybe."

A musher's intuition, as I've said, is rarely far off the mark. They know their dogs better than I ever will, and it's not uncommon for them to sense problems, even invisible ones, almost clairvoyantly. As I settled down next to him, Andy fixed his slate-blue eyes on me. He wasn't snarling or raising his lip, but his poise was disdainful, and his expression odious. I'm careful not to ascribe too many human emotions to dogs, but I got the sense that Andy saw the veterinarians as just another obstacle to overcome on his journey to Nome. Kneeling, I ran my hands up and down his torso and limbs, concentrating, especially, on his legs. But Andy was unflinching. I couldn't elicit any discomfort whatsoever. He knew why I was here: I was here to determine whether he could continue the race or not. If Andy could talk, he would never tell me where it hurt. Why give me the ammunition? He wanted to race.

Still, Andy was a professional. He knew that dealing with me was part of the game. Hank had already removed his booties, and Andy allowed me to examine him thoroughly, raising each leg voluntarily as I checked his paws for cuts and abrasions. His feet were clean and dry. His heart and lungs sounded normal, and he had just eaten a frozen salmon snack, so his appetite was clearly unaffected. In short, I couldn't find anything wrong. I waved Betsy King over for a second opinion, but she wasn't able to find anything either. After our exam, Andy settled back into his straw nest and slowly, consciously, licked his feet, as if to rid himself of any trace of our scent. Hank, Betsy, and I conferred.

"I couldn't detect any problems, but the absence of evidence is not evidence of absence," I offered, hesitant.

"Could he be sick?" he asked.

"You know better than I do that there are a dozen ways he could've been injured on the trail. Or maybe he was just a bit off for this one leg of the race. Hard to say."

Hank interjected. "What are you recommending?"

"The conservative approach would be to keep Andy here, but..." I trailed off. I knew that Hank relied on Andy as his lead, and Andy himself clearly felt that he was fine. Weighing against this was the knowledge that Rainy Pass, up in the mountains, was one of the toughest sections of the course. I had to make a snap judgment call.

"Keep an eye on him," I told Hank. "Trust your instincts, and if they tell you he's not right, or he stops pulling, then get him into the sled basket and drop him at the next stop."

Hank agreed. To make sure that the veterinarians at the next checkpoint were aware of our recommendation, I sent a note ahead to Rainy Pass, instructing them to pay particular attention to Andy when he arrived. Later, at McGrath, I caught up with Hank's team; Andy was doing just fine. In fact, he went all the way to Nome, finishing his eighth Iditarod.

❄   ❄   ❄   ❄

IT WAS LATE IN the afternoon when Newton Marshall arrived. As he anchored his sled, I began my physical examinations of the dogs. Newton had a happy, healthy lot, and despite running over a hundred miles in less than forty-eight hours, they all looked fresh; each dog greeted me with a smile as I walked past. At the front of the sled, I bent down to examine the lead dog, and she

The dogs have distinct personalities; some calm, others . . . not so calm.

immediately flipped onto her back for a belly rub. Priorities are priorities, so I obliged. Her name, I was told, was "Bumble," and unfortunately, she often lived up to her appellation. She enjoyed running with her team, but she was not especially adept at it, and frequently collided with the other lead dog during the run. Sometimes, she would even cross over the gangline to see what it was like to lead from the other side for a while. And she would frequently turn around to see if Newton was still on the sled—not that his absence would have prevented her from continuing her present course. I heard that she'd once caused a pileup when she stopped to look at a tree that she found particularly interesting.

Bumble wore a permanent expression of confusion, one that might roughly be translated as "Huh?" But despite being absent-minded, she was an ideal patient, at least during an examination. No amount of probing or prodding could disturb her. She stood upright when you needed her to stand upright, lifted her leg when you needed to examine her paw, and rolled over when her abdomen needed to be inspected. All things considered, Bumble was a sweet, simpleminded dog. She sat patiently all through my examination, apparently finding it so interesting that when I started to look at the dog behind her, she followed. When I examined the next dog, there, too, was Bumble, standing at my side, keeping a careful eye on what I was up to. She kept this up as I made my way down the line. At this point, the dogs were still connected to the central gangline, so she dragged the others along with her. Soon, I had a conga line of huskies following me. When I reached the seventh row, Bumble—her curiosity evidently satisfied—made her way to her bed of straw, oblivious to the tangled mess of dogs in her wake.

As I started my examination of the last dog, I automatically reached for my stethoscope. Not finding it, I whirled around to where I could have dropped it. A stethoscope is a basic piece of equipment, an essential veterinary tool that I can't conduct an exam without. Beginning to panic, I looked up to see Bumble chewing on a long black object. An object that, moments ago, had been dangling from my neck. She must have very gently removed it so as not to disturb me. I ran up to her.

"No! Bumble, I need that!"

She cocked her head to one side, as if to say, "Do you, though?"

"Don't bite it! Don't bite it!"

Just as she began to dig her teeth into my prize, top-of-the-line Cartman Cardiology III Professional stethoscope, along came her musher.

"Drop it," he said calmly. She did so immediately, though probably out of confusion, not obedience. Grinning, he picked it up and handed it back to me.

Newton Marshall, originally from St. Anne, Jamaica, was easily one of the most likable competitors in the field. While many nations and ethnicities are represented in the Iditarod, almost everyone comes from a place not far from the Arctic Circle. It's not all that surprising, then, that Marshall was the only competitor that year—and pretty much any year—from the Caribbean. He'd come to Alaska via Minnesota, and worked as a horseback tour guide at a resort near the White River valley in the Yukon. Newton was a natural at handling dogs, as he was with horses. He began his career in sled dog racing by competing in international events like the 210-mile Percy DeWolfe Memorial Mail Race, a round trip from Dawson City, Yukon Territory, to Eagle, Alaska. He then completed a few endurance sled races, including Alaska's Copper Basin 300 and the Yukon Quest. Anyone who completes the latter qualifies for entry in the Iditarod. He ran his first Iditarod in 2010, but he had to drop out near McGrath, about a third of the way in. This year, he told me, he hoped to make it all the way to Nome, but things weren't looking good. There were about seventy teams in the race and only seven teams behind him. He felt that his dogs were not pulling well, and worried that they might not have the stamina needed to make the treacherous Norton Sound crossing.

Even so, Newton was enjoying the moment. He was something

Newton Marshall is one of the most charismatic mushers I've met.

of a celebrity on the course. He smiled brightly and laughed generously, both traits that made him approachable. Given his charisma and good looks, it was no wonder that people flocked to him at every checkpoint. He was, of course, a media favorite, and he usually had at least one photographer in tow. None of this had gone to his head; he was anything but a dilettante.

I asked him if the Jamaica Dogsled Team was a sort of spin-off of the Jamaican national bobsled team.

"Who?" he asked, furrowing his eyebrows.

"You know, the Jamaican bobsled team, they competed in the Olympics?"

He smiled a smile that let me know that he knew exactly what I was talking about, and that this was far from the first time that he had been asked that inane question. "They are crazy! Zooming down those hills at a hundred miles an hour. Me, I just like taking my time, seeing the sights."

I told him that so far, his huskies looked good. He thanked me and held out his hand for a shake. "See you up the trail!"

With that, he was off. Newton's team gracefully made their way out of the exit zone. At the left-hand turn to go up the incline, they all turned as a unit. All except Bumble, of course, who made a sharp, right-hand turn, pulling against the grain.

❄ ❄ ❄ *FINGER LAKE, AK. 852 miles to Nome. Evening. 10°F. Cloudy.*

BY THE LATE EVENING, nearly all the teams had arrived at the checkpoint, and some were already well on their way to the next checkpoint, Rainy Pass. There were about half a dozen teams who hadn't reached us, but none were expected until the morning, so the veterinary team retired for the night. Huddled in sleeping bags on the hard floor of the tent, the veterinarians drifted off.

Hours later, I was still awake. Giving up on sleep, I exited the tent and stepped into the tundra. As far as I could see, I was the only person up and about. It was a cloudless night, but a cold, brittle wind was tossing snow from the tree limbs around me. The snow glittered like quartz as it fell, squeaking under my boots as I walked. The light from my headlamp caught the flakes, and for a moment, I felt like I was surrounded by stars. Overhead, the Milky Way shone brighter than I'd ever seen it.* Out here, the stars don't twinkle; they're bright, clear points that appear almost as if someone is shining an arc light through a pinprick-sized hole in the sky. Even small stars seem closer in Alaska, glittering with dazzling brilliance, color, and clarity. The sky was so crowded that I had a difficult time making out even the most well-known constellations like Taurus and the Big Dipper. As I watched, a

---

* The air in the northern latitudes is almost uniformly cold, and there's no light pollution, so there's very little temperature inversion.

The open plain.

shooting star brightened above me, then broke into fragments, individual streaks of light that soon faded.

I liked it out here. No board reviews, no hospital inspections, no ringing phones. My job had become far more elemental. I got up in the morning and examined dogs all day long. There were no substantive arguments or conflicts. People took me at my word, and the dogs were better off for it. Eventually, Betsy joined me. She'd seen me watching the sky and, after alerting me that someone had started the coffee machine, stopped to gaze up herself. She pointed out Sirius, the Dog Star, hanging low over the tents. We stood there for a while, just the two of us, watching the heavens. Soon enough, the smell of fresh coffee would lure us inside.

Stu Nelson flew in early in the morning. He'd decided to shepherd the dropped dogs back to Anchorage himself, and he took the opportunity to inspect our work while he was here. Stu had been in charge of the Iditarod veterinary team for over a decade before my first stint. One might expect someone in charge of an operation as big and complex as caring for the dogs of the Iditarod to be a loudmouthed, drill sergeant type; Stu is definitely not that. He's a dedicated, warm-hearted individual who, despite a tendency toward disorganization, manages to keep the dogs in this race as safe as possible year after year. During the Iditarod, Stu is in perpetual motion. He's in constant contact with everyone by fax and by cell, and is more or less aware of every issue raised on the course. He'd already been briefed on which teams remained at Finger Lake, and which problems had yet to be resolved. But Stu doesn't just rely on reports. He likes to see for himself how the race is going, and tries to visit each checkpoint at least once. It's thrilling to see him in action. When he reached the area where the dogs were resting at Finger Lake, he paced up and down the rows, methodically scanning the sleeping pups. I joined him, keen to glean any tidbits of advice he had to offer.

"It's always a good idea to watch the dogs when they are sleeping," he told me. "Sometimes you can see things you missed during your initial exam."

As soon as he said it, something caught his eye. He motioned me over to a lead dog asleep in a pile of straw. Stu stood still a moment, observing.

"Was it you who checked this team?" he asked.

I wasn't sure. I hurried back to the sled to retrieve the log. Flipping through, I found that, sure enough, my initial was next to the entry for the dog in question.

"Yeah, Stu, I looked at him this morning. Normal respiration, normal heart rate. No other concerns," I said as I handed him the log.

Stu didn't say anything. He took the dog's temperature and passed the thermometer to me. 103.7 degrees. The normal temperature for a resting dog should be around 101.5; this dog clearly had a fever. What had he seen that I missed? I crept closer, and as I did, I saw that the dog was breathing at a fast rate, and that breathing was an effort for him. I fished my stethoscope out of my pocket and listened intently to his lungs. There it was: a soft and muffled yet distinctly discernible crackling sound.

Aspiration pneumonia.

I should have spotted it. I had seen it many times before in my own clinic. I was devastated. How could I have missed this? I'd checked everyone on the team carefully, just as I'd checked every other dog I examined. Stu saw the despair on my face.

"I am sure he looked okay when you examined him," he assured me. "This is what aspiration pneumonia does. Sometimes it takes a while to develop."

The team's musher came over. Stu knew all the mushers, and all the mushers knew Stu.

"I'm worried about your lead dog here, Dave. He looks like he might be developing a respiratory problem."

"You think I need to drop him? He has been pulling great all the way here."

"Yeah. We need to keep him here."

If I had been telling the musher this, I'd have worked through a list of reasons before presenting my conclusion. Stu's voice was friendly, but his tone made it clear that there would be no debate. Before he'd even settled the issue with the musher, he'd hailed the dog handlers to retrieve the dog. Dropping a dog this early in the race is a blow to the team and the musher; Stu knew this. He *also* knew that the dog's situation would only worsen as he went farther up the trail. For now, at least, the dog was still in good spirits. He ate heartily when Dave cooked him a meal,* and after he was done, the dog handlers led him to the dropped-dog line. I trudged behind them, Stu alongside me. The dog still wasn't showing many signs of illness, but there were signs, and I should have spotted them. The lesson that morning was simple. You can never assume that a dog you checked previously is still okay; your work isn't done until the team leaves the checkpoint.

---

* We ask the musher to prepare food for a dog before dropping them, since they're more likely to eat when among comrades.

CHAPTER 9

LEARNING THE ROPES

IN ALASKA, STORMS CAN CLOSE IN WITHIN MINUTES. I WATCHED, once, as a clear sky gave way to a cold, enveloping fog. With work winding down at Finger Lake and only a few teams still to arrive, I had been scheduled to fly out with some of the huskies later that day. But we weren't going anywhere. No one could predict when the storm system would clear, and planes would be able to reach us. The Iditarod Air Force had to follow Visual Flight Rules, or VFR, meaning that the pilots can only fly when they can see the ground.

The remaining teams came and went. Taking advantage of the enforced lull in activity, I trekked the snowmobile-hardened paths around the checkpoint. I quickly realized that the reason Carl Dixon built his resort on Finger Lake is because it's located in the kind of wilderness terrain that people pay good money to see and explore. Even though I'd seen the mountains of the Alaska Range every day that I'd been at the camp, I was still mesmerized by the fierce plumes of snow raking across the summits, and the clouds that hung around them. During one of my forays into the foothills, I strayed far from the tracks and spotted a snowy owl sitting on a branch. Stepping toward him, I sunk to my hips in soft, deep snow.

But this was no happy vacation. Word soon reached us that a family of four had gone missing following a plane crash in the mountains. Even in the age of GPS, remote sensors, and emergency beacons, entire planes can still be swallowed by the Alaskan wilderness. Snowmobiles were dispatched. During the day, the incessant whirring of search-and-rescue helicopters filled our ears; when night fell, the helicopters cast great beams of light on the ground in the futile hope of catching a glimmer of metal. As the search radius grew, the searchlights moved farther and farther away. It was a horribly eerie feeling. The family, I later learned, had been traveling down to see the race. It would take a full week before the plane and its occupants were located. All four, it turned out, had died instantly.

As the grayness turned to black and was punctuated by intermittent spits of snow, we began to dismantle the camp. The smaller tents were taken down, first; we needed to sleep somewhere, so we agreed to keep the larger tents up until visibility improved. Now that the teams had come and gone, we were tasked with cleaning up all the straw, dog feces, snow pickets, fencing material, and other detritus on the ice. We started with the parking area, raking the straw and poop into a massive pile before transferring it, via front-end loader, to a pit. We collected trash for burning; what couldn't be burned was packaged for transport back to Anchorage. (The burning of the trash always becomes a spectacle in its own right, one that the guests at the Winterlake Lodge gather to watch.) After the bonfire died down, the ashes were bulldozed into the pit alongside the straw and poop. Everything was made to appear exactly as it had when we arrived, just as Dixon had requested.

❉   ❉   ❉   ❉

DIXON KEPT A KENNEL of sled dogs at the resort for guests so that they, too, could experience the thrill of being pulled by a team of exuberant huskies, of zooming through birch trees. Because the only way into or out of the resort area (short of competing in the Iditarod) is by aircraft, I figured that Dixon's dogs probably don't get too much regular veterinary care. In the afternoon, after everything was cleaned up and the only tents left standing were the ones we'd be sleeping in, I decided to volunteer my services in the hope of fostering goodwill between the race organizers and Dixon. Somewhat to my surprise, Dixon readily accepted my offer. We proceeded to the dog lot, where a chorus of howling huskies waited. I examined each dog and, save for one or two that looked a little thin—likely due to intestinal parasites*—they were in fine shape.

I hadn't been expecting to fall in love with any of Dixon's dogs, but I was totally taken with a black-and-grey husky named Squeaky. (I'm often asked to give school lectures, and the portrait of Squeaky I show is always the most popular slide.) Squeaky was exceptionally cross-eyed and, as her name suggests, had a distinctive, high-pitched howl that stood out even among the yips and yaps of other huskies. Apparently, she enjoyed the sound of her own voice, as she sang frequently and loudly, though not particularly harmoniously. In the rare moments when she was quiet, she fixed me with an expectant look, as if waiting for a positive review. Aside from singing, Squeaky liked to run; she had determined long ago that she would be the lead dog, and Dixon had acquiesced. She wasn't the fastest runner in the kennel, but as he told me, "I couldn't say no to a face like that."

"I am going to take the dogs out for a run," Dixon told me after I finished my exams, "Would you like to go for a ride with us?"

Oh, would I. A sled ride on the Iditarod Trail? Of all the veterinarians I had met in Alaska, I couldn't recall a single one mentioning that they had been offered an opportunity to ride on a sled.

---

* Intestinal parasites—including hookworms, roundworms, tapeworms, and giardia—are fairly common in dogs and rarely life-threatening. A few weeks after I returned from the race, I mailed some deworming tablets to Dixon, and the problem was resolved.

Squeaky seemed to follow our conversation, because at the mention of the "sled," she started dancing and singing loudly. Dixon
selected eight dogs for the evening's run—including Squeaky,
who was adamant that she was already going—and hooked them
up one by one. Those chosen howled with enjoyment; those who
weren't howled with disappointment. The plan was to run down
the trail for a few miles and then turn around. For the first leg
of the run, I would sit in the sled basket, and if all went well—
and if the dogs were open to the idea—then, for the return journey, I would stand on the runners at the back of the sled and
actually mush.

With a firm yet calm "Let's go!" from Dixon, eight huskies
leapt forward, and the sled shot out into the haze of snow and fog.
Slush flew up in my face; to spare my eyes, I lowered my goggles.
The trail twisted and turned, then dropped precipitously downhill. Dixon expertly maneuvered the sled around each bend. The
leads effortlessly relayed Dixon's commands down the line, and
the dogs leapt and bound in perfect unison. Every once in a while,
a dog looked back in my direction as if to say, "Having fun yet?" I
was only a passenger, but the ride was exhilarating. I understood,
now, why Idita-Riders spend a small fortune to do this. The Arctic
wind smacked me in the face, and at times, I had to hide under the
Hudson's Bay point blanket that covered the basket. The dogs ran
with total conviction: I could see the frozen wisps of breath from
their mouths trailing behind them. I had no idea how fast we were
going, but whatever the actual speed, it felt a lot faster, presumably
because I was so close to the ground. This was with eight dogs,
slightly more than half the number in an Iditarod team; I found it
difficult to imagine the power of fourteen elite racers.

I recognized the precipitous embankment where Bill Roth
had positioned himself to take action photos of teams coming to
grief. Dixon avoided the hazard as skillfully as any of the Iditarod
mushers I'd seen. Then we were onto the frozen ice of Finger
Lake itself. Now that there were no other hairpin turns or trees

Squeaky in action.

to worry about, only flat, uninterrupted space, the dogs charged even faster. I could hear the sled runners sizzle across the ice. Upon reaching the far bank of the lake, Dixon slowed the team to a halt. We had lunch and gave some small snacks to the dogs. Then he turned to me and grinned.

"Your turn."

We traded places. Now I stood at the back of the sled, one foot on each of the rear runners. The runners seemed narrow, and I hoped my sometimes-faulty sense of balance wouldn't betray me. Dixon gave me a quick lesson in "Mushing 101," impressing on me the importance of snow anchors. If the sled was unanchored, he said, the huskies might bolt down the trail, with or without me on the runners. When I was ready to go, I had to pick up the anchor; otherwise, it could become entangled or damage a part of the sled. Dixon also encouraged me to think ahead, to anticipate turns on the trail. However good the team, there would always be a delay between the command and action. I recalled a time-honored aviator's motto: "Stay ahead of the airplane."

My training complete, I held firmly to the back of the sled and let out a meek "Go." Nothing happened.

"Louder!" Dixon commanded.

"GO!" I yelled, and off the dogs went. The initial acceleration just about knocked me off the back of the sled, but I regained my balance as the dogs ran back across the frozen lake. The wind blew the hood of my parka down, but I was too excited to care. The ride in the basket had been exciting, but this was something else.

"Right turn coming up!" called Dixon.

"Gee!" I shouted, and the entire team turned right.

The hill that Dixon deftly traversed on the way out now proved a tricky ascent on the return. As the dogs powered uphill, I hopped off the back to push the sled. Mushers are sometimes known to lose control of their teams in this way; I thought of the old sailors' adage that one should always have a hand for yourself, and a hand for the ship. Without my weight on the runners, the dogs rocketed up the hill, and at its crest, I barely made it back onto the sled in time. Later, when I told the veterinarians that I had driven a dogsled team on the Iditarod Trail, I became the envy of the team. Overwhelmed by the joy and thrill of it all, I made a point of repeating the story ad nauseam to anyone who would sit or stand still for more than a few minutes. I'm sure I'll never forget the feeling of the wind and snow buffeting my face as the dogs pulled, or the quiet hiss of the runners, or the sensation of togetherness, the feeling that we were one unit: sled, dog, man.

What I rarely admit when I spin this yarn is that my legs were shaking as I walked back to camp from the resort. I have a mental picture of myself as someone who is in decent physical shape. To be a trail vet in Alaska, to handle hundreds of dogs in freezing weather for weeks at a time, you need to have a certain level of strength and stamina. The ride with Dixon hadn't sapped all my energy, but it didn't leave me with much. The trip was only four miles, and took barely an hour—and I had been in charge of the sled for only half that time. I knew as soon as I stepped off the runners that it would be all but impossible for me to ride on the back of a sled for twelve or more hours for just one day, let alone day after day for more than a thousand miles. We all know that the dogs are capable of extraordinary physical feats, but I left that day with a heightened appreciation for the mushers, too, as endurance athletes.

After several days, the weather finally cleared, and planes were approved to resume flying in and out of Finger Lake. At last, the time had come for me to return to Anchorage; I would be traveling with a colleague and five huskies. My companion took three dogs, and I took the remaining two. My dogs had both been designated "blue," meaning that they were stable. (Any "red" dogs would have been evacuated immediately. Thankfully, nothing had happened at Finger Lake to merit a "red" designation.) I held tight to my charges, knowing that they might try to wrangle free from my grasp to run hopelessly after their teams. A snowmobile pulled us all in a sled across the frozen lake. When we reached the waiting Cessna, we carefully transferred the dogs to the pilot, who clipped their leads onto one of the cables that ran alongside the plane. He had arranged quarters for the dogs in the back of the plane, and everything seemed ready to go, but he kept us waiting on the ice. Every other member of the Iditarod Air Force I'd met had been jumping at the bit to leave. Then, one by one, the dogs began to relieve themselves by the airplane. The pilot grinned at me, and said, "Better out here than up there!" I knew an Iditarod veteran when I saw one.

After all the dogs were done, we loaded them onto the Cessna. I wedged myself in, curling up in the back of the plane with the dogs. One husky, a brown-and-tan girl, remained by the window to enjoy the view. As we flew over the backcountry—gliding over spruce forests, following frozen rivers with pockets of open water—she immersed herself in the vista, looking over her shoulder every once in a while as if to say, "Are you seeing what I'm seeing?" I was. Through the lush canopy of evergreens I could just barely make out the Iditarod Trail. An Alaskan train, with its distinctive canary yellow and deep blue engines, wound its way through the valley, heading to Anchorage. We were low enough to exchange greetings: a waggle of our wings for a tug on the whistle from the train's engineer. Mountains ascended on either side of us as we soared safely through their shadows. Soon, without warning or transition, we were over the ice of the wide Knik arm of Cook Inlet, and there was a city beneath us. The plane descended toward the Millennium Hotel, and then we were on the frozen lake, taxiing over to the spread of tarmac where the dog truck was due to meet us. The propeller stopped and I climbed out, eager to stretch my back. The dogs were still fast asleep. I glanced at the pilot, who sat, unmoved, in his seat. He looked confused.

"Where is the dog truck?" he asked, scanning the tarmac. "I radioed in to let them know that we were landing. They should be here."

I heard stirring. The dogs were waking up and realizing that the flight had ended. We unloaded them carefully, one at a time, and hooked them to the cable on the side of the plane. Ten minutes passed, then twenty. The pilot grew more and more agitated.

"Are you really *that* worried?" I asked. Sure, I could see potential risks, but I wasn't all that worried. That's part of my job, though; it's important to stay calm for the dogs.

"This is how accidents happen," he explained. "We should have someone here so we can just hand the dogs to them." I remember thinking that this was an ominous thing to hear from someone with so much experience on the trail. After checking the leads, the pilot made an irritated phone call.

"They are just now leaving the building," he reported.

It would be another twenty minutes before they arrived. We were exhausted, and it was already evening. I wasn't all that far from my hotel room, and I had no plans except to get there and crash. I reached into my pocket for a pinch of Skoal, and the pilot

A dog waits near a bush plane to be taken back to Anchorage.

stepped away for a cigarette. As his Newport burned to a stub, the dog truck glided into view. Before it had even come to a stop, the driver was on the ice, apologizing profusely. She had two assistants with her. They unclipped each dog in turn, placing them into the cubbyholes of the "kennel" on the truck bed. The driver herself retrieved the last dog, but she stopped just short of the truck to talk to one of her assistants. I have no idea what they were discussing, but she wasn't watching the dog, which began to back out of her collar. I started to jog toward her, my voice failing me.

And then it happened.

The dog gained enough leverage to slip its lead. I stood and watched for a horrified second as she worked herself out of her collar. *Finally*, the driver looked down and saw the husky, who was now nervously backing away. The driver's face turned ashen. She tried to beckon the husky back, but it was no use. The dog bolted. I was tired. Anxious. Furious. All the driver had had to do was put the dog into her assigned cubbyhole on the truck, and then she could have talked all she wanted to. Now, the dog was running free on an active airport. Within seconds, we were all on our phones. The pilot ran hopelessly after the dog. There's still hope, the driver told us; the airfield is fenced in, so the husky is contained. Even if the containment area is a few square miles.

Not once at the checkpoint had anything like this happened, not even during the storms. Now, right at the end, one of the dogs I had been responsible for escaped. We all joined the pilot in chasing after the dog, but it was pointless. The husky was well rested and spooked. More to the point, she was bred to be fast. Even if we could get close to her, how would we catch her? Soon, she was only a dot in the distance. We slowed our pace. To her credit, the driver immediately took full responsibility. She was more upset with herself than anyone was with her. As it turned out, this was her thirteenth Iditarod, and before now, no harm had ever come to one of her charges. For the next few days, she spent every waking moment looking for the lost husky. It took three days, but the dog was eventually found; she had cozied up to a family dog in a neighborhood yard.

My feelings of anger quickly turned to empathy; a brief complacent moment had led to an accident. During the Iditarod, you can never let your guard down, not even if you're "safely back in Anchorage." And this—the journey from Willow to Finger Lake, the first 112 miles of the 1,049-mile Iditarod Trail—is the easy part. From here on out, it only gets harder. For the mushers, for the dogs, and for everyone working to keep them safe.

PART III

THE
HARD PART

CHAPTER 10

DROPPED DOGS GO TO PRISON

WHEN A DOG IS DROPPED FROM THE IDITAROD, IT GOES TO prison.

Since 1974, dogs dropped before the midway point of the race have been collected from Ted Stevens Anchorage International Airport and transferred to the Hiland Mountain Correctional Center for Women in Eagle River, Alaska. A year after the running of the first Iditarod, Dan Reynolds—then, deputy superintendent of the correctional facility—decided to start a program whereby minimum-security prisoners could volunteer to care for dogs dropped from the race. The idea, which was fairly novel at the time, was that the care and compassion the inmates would need to conjure up to help rehabilitate an injured or sick dog would, in turn, help in the women's rehabilitation.

❋ ❋ ❋ *EAGLE RIVER, AK. 998 miles to Nome. 30°F. Fair.*

EACH YEAR, ABOUT SIXTY dogs are dropped before the midway point. At the airport, they receive any urgent medical care they may need. While some stay behind, the others are driven about twenty miles to Hiland Mountain, where they'll be allowed to rest and heal until their owners retrieve them. I've always been intrigued by this aspect of the dogs' care. One year, late in the race, I was loitering in the lobby of the Millennium when I spotted a group of dogs, outside, being readied for transport. I hurried out and asked the staff if they could use some help—knowing, of course, that no one handling huskies would turn down an extra pair of hands. (I was right.) As one of the breathless handlers explained, the dogs were headed to Hiland Mountain.

"The prison?" I asked.

"Yep."

"Can I come?"

It was as simple as that: I was granted a seat in the transport truck. The drive to the correctional facility was pleasant. The sun was just setting, glowing orange in the western sky, its rays muting the greens of the pines. We drove far into the dense woods, first over deeply rutted asphalt, then over deeply rutted dirt and mud. I couldn't make out any buildings at all until we were right there, at the main gate. In the dim light, the prison had an especially melancholic feel. I'd driven by many prisons before, but suddenly, I felt uneasy. This was a particularly grim place; presumably, the people in it had committed particularly grim crimes. Right? There was no "day release" for the inmates here, no activities outside the facility's walls. Would I be allowed to talk to the inmates? Would they be sullen or angry? I should've asked more questions, I thought, before volunteering my services.

The double gates swung open and the guard waved us in. The treatment area rose up to our left, separate from the main cell block. An open-air shelter had been constructed for the dogs. As we approached, I saw generous amounts of fresh straw, water, and food; each animal had its own designated space. Tending to the dogs were maybe a dozen or so inmates, all clad in Day-Glo jump-suits with "D.O.C." emblazoned on the back. I'm not sure what I expected the prisoners to look like. *Hardened*, I suppose. A few fit that profile, but most seemed far too young to be here. The majority were in their late teens or early twenties, and despite their oppressive surroundings, were energetic and cheerful.

Hiland selects about twenty inmate volunteers per year to

participate in the program. The selected inmates work in teams around the clock to log, tag, and treat each arriving dog, paying particular attention to those prescribed medications and other veterinary treatments by trail vets. *So, this is who has been deciphering my handwriting*, I thought to myself. For a few minutes, I watched the inmates, mesmerized by their practiced, efficient movements. The dogs, I realized, couldn't be in better hands; each husky had at least two women stroking its fur, cooing, and kissing it on the snout. The dogs reciprocated this affection fully, frequently licking the women's faces. This, inevitably, drew peals of laughter from the women. It was a joyful scene—but I couldn't entirely forget the fact that I was in a prison. The inmates, I noticed, all carried jackknives. If you need to cut straw bales and bags of food, this is a practical tool to have in your arsenal, but it was still a jolt to see prisoners wielding them. It occurred to me in that moment that the guards must truly trust the volunteers. If they didn't, or if they were wrong, things could get ugly quickly.

Up until this point, I'd shared only cursory glances with the inmates. They were far too busy working with their patients to notice me. Suddenly, there was a commotion; one of the women had noticed the stethoscope hanging around my neck and come running over, followed by five or six other inmates. When the first woman reached me, she didn't bother with introductions. Instead, she pointed to a gray-and-white husky in the corner of the shelter.

"Could you please take a look at Darcy?" she asked. "Her feet look red." The other inmates, just now catching up, murmured and nodded in breathless agreement. The first woman took my hand and led me toward the husky that was, evidently, Darcy. I bent down to examine her feet. Darcy, of course, took this as an invitation to lick my face, much like she took my not bothering to shoo her away as an invitation to *continue* licking my face. I backed away to try again. The same scenario played out. Too many kisses. I mopped my cheeks on the sleeve of my parka and turned to the woman. It was only then that I realized how young she was.

She should've been in a prom dress or a college sweatshirt, not prison overalls.

"Would you mind holding Darcy, so I can take a look?' I asked her. Without another word, she took the dog's head into her arms. As she cradled Darcy, I heard her whisper, ever so softly, "Let the doctor see your foot, then you can kiss him."

She smiled at me, and I took the opportunity to ask her some questions about our patient. Like many teenagers, she was in the habit of inserting far too many "ums" and "y'knows" into her sentences. She squinted into the sun as she spoke. I could see in her some mischief, maybe, but no real malevolence. *What terrible thing could this girl have done to land here, behind a chain link fence with guard towers?*

I pulled out my penlight and examined between each toe and toepad. They all looked perfectly normal to me. Confused, I looked at my companion.

"Where did you see the problem?"

"The front right paw," she answered. "There is a small tear near one of the pads."

I took the paw in my hand and looked it over again, this time using my thumb to probe for a wound. Just as I was about to say that there was nothing there, my thumb passed over a tiny laceration at the base of the main paw pad. Darcy immediately withdrew her foot, so I knew that the tear, despite its small size, was bothering her. I parted the thick husky fur between her toe webbing, and shining my light straight on it, I finally saw it: a four- or five-millimeter cut. I checked for any signs of a splinter or other foreign body but found nothing. The wound appeared to be only skin-deep.

"How the hell did you find that?" Sure, Darcy had winced when I pressed on it, but there was no noticeable limp or change in her stride when she walked.

"Oh, they want us to check each dog very carefully."

I shrugged off her comment. She should be proud of herself. This was a remarkable find. "I'm fairly certain that I wouldn't have been able to pick this up on a routine exam. I don't think I know any vets that could have. Seriously, good work."

At this, her smile broke into a broad grin. Working together, we lightly bandaged the injured foot. I prescribed some routine antibiotics; within a few days, not even my impromptu veterinary assistant would be able to find where the wound had been.

As we finished wrapping, I looked at the young woman and started to ask, "I know it's none of my business—"

"Drugs," she said, not needing to hear the whole question. She told me the story matter-of-factly, without any emotional kow-towing. She and her boyfriend had started using meth, which led into small-time dealing, then escalated into manufacturing in a shed out in the woods. A long-term customer had been picked up by the police, and in exchange for a plea bargain, he'd led author-ities to the makeshift lab.

"Most of the women are in for drugs," she said, gesturing to the other inmates.

I didn't know how to respond in the moment. I just stood and patted her on the shoulder.

"Well, you did a good thing by Darcy here tonight. I am sure she appreciates it," I told her. She nodded and bent down to whis-per in Darcy's ear.

"Do you feel better, honey?"

Darcy responded with a giant, wet kiss. The other inmates, heretofore patiently awaiting their turns, now approached me with problems they wanted me to check. Minor cuts and abra-sions. Slightly elevated temperatures. Sore legs. The women— each and every one of them—were friendly, sociable, and, above all, intensely attuned to the health and well-being of the dogs. The program is mutually beneficial; while the dogs receive excel-lent care and love, the facility reports that the recidivism rate for women who participate in the program is significantly lower than that of the rest of the prison population.

In college, I took a course in criminology. We spent hours

discussing whether prison should be considered punishment or rehabilitation. The Hiland Mountain Correctional Facility maintains that its primary focus is reform. Most of the women, as I've said, are in for minor offenses. None of the inmates I met were violent criminals. To me, they seemed like everyone else. They were, really; they were people you could meet anywhere, people who, like many of us, have made mistakes. Maybe they had family on the outside. Or maybe they were alone in the world. Either way, it can be difficult to truly *see* a person when that person is wearing an orange jumpsuit. But in the simple act of petting a dog and seeing that dog return their affection, I saw the women express something of their identity, the best part of them, the part that wants to love and be loved.

As I rode back to Anchorage, I thought about the girl who had assisted me with Darcy. Someday, I'd love to run into her again, on the other side of the barbed-wire fence. I like to imagine she'd be a veterinarian, too.

CHAPTER 11

RAINY PASS AND THE BURN

N O PART OF THE IDITAROD IS LAID-BACK, BUT SO FAR, IT'S been plain sailing. After Finger Lake, the terrain and weather grow harsher and more unpredictable. The next leg, from Finger Lake to Rainy Pass, is a thirty-mile trek through the Alaska Range. The mountains funnel the warm, wet air from the Gulf of Alaska in the southeast directly into the frigid air from the north. It's a recipe for disastrously high winds and heavy snowfall. The going, as you might imagine, is steep and treacherous. The trail crosses creeks and ridges, so the mushers and lead dogs, especially, have to stay concentrated on the course lest they come across an obstacle.

At an altitude of 3,160 feet, Rainy Pass is the highest point on the Iditarod. From its peak, you can see the wide valley floor, with its thick pine forests and glossy lakes. This is widely acknowledged as the most beautiful view on the Iditarod Trail, if not the whole of Alaska. But to get here, competitors must struggle against gravity, and whatever appreciation they might have for the scenery is likely muted by the knowledge that the next stretch, from Rainy Pass to Rohn, is among the most difficult on the trail. After Rainy Pass, the competitors traverse a charred section of forest aptly nicknamed the "Burn." Fallen timbers, logs, and tree stumps left in the wake of a massive fire in 1978 create a dangerous obstacle course, one that lasts nearly thirty-five miles. Some of the obstructions are the size of houses. Others are hidden, like icebergs waiting for their RMS

Titanic, just beneath the snow. To make matters worse, the whole route is downhill, since the sleds are now heading *out* of the Alaska Range. Mushers must frantically try to regulate their speed; given the dangers, they generally try to complete this stage in daylight.

❋ ❋ ❋ *RAINY PASS, AK. 819 miles to Nome. Morning. 28°F. Clear.*

I've never been stationed at Rainy Pass, and as a veterinarian, I've never witnessed the competitors negotiate the landscape firsthand. But I've been posted to that next checkpoint, Rohn, a few times, and I've seen the aftermath of Rainy Pass and the Burn. I was at Rohn one year when a rookie competitor became disoriented and lost the trail near the Burn. Remember, the mushers aren't given maps; they aren't following a blip or a dotted line on a screen. They're trying to keep to a trail that can easily be obliterated by a blizzard or a particularly strong gust of wind. There are times—on ice plains, during whiteouts, on cloudy days—when the features of the land become all but invisible. The mushers say they lose more than their sense of direction; they lose all sense of movement *itself*. The dogs appear to be running, their legs trotting along like always, but there are no visual cues for forward motion. They could just as easily be on a treadmill.

Dogs, as I've said, will sometimes follow the scent of other dogs, so if the team in front of you heads down one of the hundreds of smaller paths that branch off of the main trail, you'll soon be headed that way, too, unless you're paying close attention. When this happens, and when the musher *realizes* that this has happened, there's no way to know how long ago the wrong turn was taken. The team must turn around and try to retrace their tracks. All competitors carry small GPS devices, but these don't provide them with any information or alerts; they're designed to feed basic location data to the communications team, only. We could only watch, then, as the musher lost in the Burn trudged deeper and deeper into some of the most desolate wilderness on the course. There was no way to contact her, to let her know which way to turn. She wandered throughout the night, crossing and recrossing the trail many times, but never rejoining it.

The psychological toll of the journey on the musher must have been incredible. Even in daylight, Alaskan forests are filled with terrors both real and imagined; in the dark, it must have been horrific. I can only imagine that she felt an initial surge of anxiety when she figured out that she was no longer on the trail. There would have been nothing to allay that feeling. Even if she could make out the shapes and positions of trees, rocks, and other identifying features of the land through the little cone of light protruding from her headlamp, these landmarks would have morphed into a hazy miasma of shapes, and she would have had to make decisions based on those shapes. The sky was overcast that night, so she couldn't use celestial navigation, as many mushers can during late night and early morning runs. Panic and fear may have overcome her; as several staffers noticed, the dot on the monitor that represented her position became increasingly erratic as the night wore on. The rational course of action for a musher in this position would be to stop and camp—to recover your bearings with the sunrise—but who could devise such a plan when gripped by terror?

Bypassing Rohn entirely, the musher eventually found a path that ran roughly parallel to the course, and by chance, regained the trail outside McGrath. When she arrived at the checkpoint, she was a wreck. She was physically drained; I heard from my colleagues that even in the diffuse light of dawn, her face was visibly pale. Her hands shook as she dismounted the sled. She didn't speak, and no one dared ask about her ordeal. After she made her way into the checkpoint building, a volunteer handed her a hot cup of tea. She sat and stared at her drink with the kind of thousand-yard stare that troops who've seen combat sometimes get. No tears, no crying, no movement at all, really. After a while,

Snow and wind can easily obliterate the trail. While we huddle in tents and cabins, the competitors battle the elements.

her husband joined her at the checkpoint. He sat down next to her, and she promptly collapsed in his arms. He stroked her hair, and tears flowed freely now—onto her face, onto his face, and onto many of the volunteers' faces, too. Most thought she'd drop out of the race then and there.

One adage that every musher I've ever met holds dear is that you leave your major decisions until after you've rested. So, the musher slept, safely if not soundly, her husband lying next to her on an army cot, still stroking her hair. Incredibly, after a day's rest, she decided to carry on. Maybe she had to; maybe she didn't want the incident to scar or come to define her. In any case, she finished the race that year, and to this day, it's one of the bravest things I've seen an Iditarod competitor do. I couldn't imagine going back on the trail after enduring a full night lost deep in the Arctic wilderness. The musher's determination to finish emphasized in no uncertain terms that the glory is in participating, not necessarily winning. Finishing the damn thing *is* the victory.

There are no endurance sports in which every competitor at the start line imagines that they are going to win the race. After Rainy Pass, the Iditarod, in a sense, becomes two competitions: one in which a third of the field pushes ahead, seriously believing that they might be the first to cross the finish line in Nome; and one in which the goal is to reach Nome intact. The trail is the same, of course, and no amount of experience or fame can completely shield you from falling foul. I've seen this happen, back in 2014. The race had a few more days to run, but my Iditarod was already over. I'd served as trail vet for nearly two weeks, worked my checkpoints, and was due to fly back to Anchorage. In two days, I'd be on a flight home to Washington, DC. I said my goodbyes at the checkpoint and hitched a ride with a snowmobiler down to the airstrip, where a twin-engine Cessna awaited.

Much to my surprise, I was not the only passenger. The entire back of the airplane was filled with huskies. In the co-pilot's seat was a man in his early twenties. I recognized him instantly as Lev Schvarts, a Ukrainian American musher. Born in Kyiv, Lev had moved with his family to Boston when he was still quite young. After adopting a Siberian Husky named Ollie, Lev became interested in sled dogs and conceived, in his own words, a "pipe dream" to one day run the Iditarod. This was his rookie year, but he'd performed well in the qualifying events, and had been deemed one of the "names to watch." But instead of being out on the trail, here he was, packed into a small bush plane with his entire sixteen-dog team.

Since Lev was already strapped in, I climbed into the back with his dogs. Most of them were curled up, fast asleep. But as often happens, one dog remained alert, absolutely enthralled and fascinated by the flight experience. This time, it was a red-and-brown husky who trampled over her comrades—and me—to get the best view. She watched excitedly as we took off and began our initial ascent, only occasionally turning to her teammates, eyes wide with excitement. I gently stroked her back; whenever I stopped,

A husky peers out the window of a plane.

she placed her muzzle under my hand and pushed it up, reminding me that I was not done yet. I continued petting her as I asked Lev the most obvious of questions:

"What happened?" I watched the musher's cheeks inflate, then quickly deflate as he let out a deep breath. He'd been anticipating this question.

"It was over in seconds," he said. "One moment, I was riding through the Burn at a fast clip. The next, my sled disintegrated from under me."

The snowfall that year had been particularly dismal. Hundreds of exposed roots, deadfall, branches, and rocks that would normally have been covered by one or two feet of snow were exposed. The huskies could nimbly pick their way through the hazardous terrain, but a sled going eight to ten miles per hour downhill—carrying a human passenger and a hundred pounds of supplies—has a great deal of momentum, and anything it hits, it hits with (easily) enough force to crumble a sled with a wooden frame. This isn't the kind of problem that calls for a veterinarian. The dogs were completely unharmed, oblivious, at first, to the fact that there had even been an accident.

"My dogs were all pulling really well," Lev added. "We had weathered through some pretty hairy terrain towards Rainy Pass, so I thought we could make it all the way to Nome. But when we hit that stump through the Burn, I knew it was all over."

There had been some genuine efforts to get Lev back in the race. Once it was clear that the sled was beyond repair, a supporting musher worked to get one of their spare sleds to him, so that he could at least finish. The judges overruled the offer: "outside assistance" is strictly against race regulations.

"I had to concede defeat," he explained, "so we're all heading back to Anchorage."

Lev said this matter-of-factly, but I could tell that he was bummed. Who could blame him? He had logged hundreds of hours training for this event; experienced the exhilaration of finally qualifying; and performed well with a full team of healthy dogs, only to be forced out because of a freak accident. It had to be soul-crushing. I tried to cheer him up with my best "C'mon Rocky, you ain't out of it yet" pep talk, but to no avail. He wasn't in the mood to talk right now. Instead, he looked out the side window, absent-mindedly petting the heads of any huskies that ventured up to the cockpit area.

Only a few determined rookies make it back to an Iditarod after they have scratched. There's a psychological toll associated with scratching, sure, but we can't ignore the monetary toll: Lev had just taken a huge financial hit, and finding or raising the funds to compete again would be the principal factor determining whether or not he'd get another shot at the race. The entry fee alone is well over a thousand dollars, and it costs thousands more to ferry all the dogs and gear up to Alaska. Teams from the lower 48 try to arrive at least a week before the race to rest their dogs and get them acclimated to the harsh Alaskan winter. That's gas money, plus a week's worth of lodging, meals, and food for the dogs, as well as the musher. The mushers also have to pay for the supplies they send ahead to the checkpoint, including shipping costs, as well as medical insurance. Since there aren't too many full-time mushers—as there are full-time race car drivers and full-time Olympic athletes—competitors may have to take time off from work. The costs, in other words, add up quickly, and Lev had been left with very little to show for his investment this year.

We landed at Anchorage shortly before sunset, and in the waning evening light, I helped Lev unload his dogs from the plane and reload them into his truck. His girlfriend appeared from around the front of the truck. Lev—head hung, feet shuffling— ambled toward her. She embraced him, and his face turned pink as he finally, wordlessly began to cry. The time, the expense, the training, the slim chance of being selected to try again—all of it seemed allied to conspire against him. In his mind, at that moment, Lev probably thought it was all over for him and his team. But somehow, when you are young, no obstacle is insurmountable. The following year, Lev raised the $10,000 needed to reenter the race. He went on to finish the Iditarod on his second attempt and continues to compete. By 2021, he had worked his way up to a seventeenth-place finish.

CHAPTER 12

A STUDY IN ROHN

ROHN ONLY EXISTS AS A CHECKPOINT BECAUSE IT'S SOMEWHERE between the Burn and the next challenge—a bleak, marshy area with a flat, icy surface that extends most of the seventy-five miles to Nikolai, the next checkpoint. Rohn sits in the shadow of the Alaska Range, near the Rohn River. It's less than two hundred miles from Anchorage, but it's so remote—cut off by wilderness—that it wasn't until 1898 that a US Geological Survey mapped the area.* In other words, this isn't the kind of place we say Europeans "discovered" though there had been people living here for thousands of years.

Then, in 1908, on Christmas Day, gold was discovered in Otter Creek, kicking off what would become the last great Alaskan gold rush. Many boomtowns sprang up, including one in the Rohn River valley region. The government worked to improve the trail through Rainy Pass (a significant shortcut to the new goldfields) but the route remained hazardous, and a hundred years on, the official population of Rohn is zero. Like many places in Alaska, it's accessible only by plane. Rohn has a single grass-and-dirt runway, which is always covered with snow when the Iditarod rolls around. "Clearing" the airstrip doesn't mean removing the snow, it means using snowmobiles to pack down the snow to make a

---

* The Rohn River was named after a member of the team that surveyed the area, Oscar Rohn.

hard surface. Near the strip, there's a half-buried historical sign noting that the strip was "built" as an Air Navigation Site and incorporated by the Alaska Legislature in 1938 as one of the first federally built landing strips in Alaska. For better or for worse, it's been in use ever since.

So, on my first assignment to Rohn, I found myself, once again, hovering precariously over a narrow airstrip in a small bush plane. Coming into Rohn airspace is, to say the least, challenging. There's no conflicting air traffic, but unlike most airports, there's a mountain looming at the start of the runway. Pilots making the approach have to take a sharp banking turn to get around it. The mountain filled my entire passenger seat window, and even though I knew it was good mile or two away, it definitely *looked* as if we were about to end up on its hillside. The pilot, a retired 747 captain, was calm.

"Yeah, that mountain scares a lot of people out of landing here!" He yelled over the engine. "I never worry so much about coming down, it's the taking off toward it that makes me nervous, especially when there's good crosswind blowing."

With that, the pilot began his descent, occasionally looking back over his shoulder, like a mom parking a minivan, to make sure we had enough clearance between us and the mountain. As we swept in for landing, people flocked out of an old log cabin to greet us. Snowmobiles had already gathered near the airstrip to bring in our gear. I'd stepped out into the snow the moment the plane had come to a halt, but one of the crew had already tossed my pack onto a sled. They were efficient here. Although the temperature was well below zero, the air was dry and still. The sky was completely cloudless, and it had that sapphire-blue tint common to the Arctic regions. Rainbows climbed across the Alaska Range,* and the scent of evergreens and spruce trees filled

* When the sun hits an open ice field, the rays are refracted in such a way that multiple rainbows appear and disappear.

the air. I could hear birdsongs of all kinds, and a creek in the distance, swirling below the embankment. I already wished I could live here. It's astonishing to think that this is generally considered the *second* most picturesque point on the trail.

At the opening of the trail, three mountains jut up from the valley floor. Constant wind sends plumes of snow up and over the summits, making it seem as if they're spewing cotton-white ash. Although the peaks are covered in snow, the granite cliff faces have been wind-blasted clean, revealing the strata in the bare rock, rendered as if painted by an artist—Rothko, maybe—with each striation representing hundreds of millions of years. Scanning the horizon, I could just make out the gully that the sleds take to access the checkpoint. The teams were still several hours away, traveling through a labyrinth of narrow trails and switchbacks between the mountains as they descend from Rainy Pass. The trails converge on a broad plain in the valley. Achieving the valley floor is always a milestone for the competitors, signaling that the perilous trek through the Alaska Range is over. From the

Mounds of ice may become invisible obstacles at night.

base, mushers get their first look at the checkpoint. They still have a few miles to go, though. The camp itself is obscured by dense pine growth; to reach it, teams must traverse a frozen bog and weave a sinuous path among the spruce and pine trees.

The dogs have to be in peak condition for this section. The trail is only a few feet wide at some points, and despite the best efforts of volunteers who spend considerable time and effort cutting back the brush, there are still plenty of arching branches to clip passing teams. As I trudged toward the camp, I made a mental note to be extra careful checking the dogs for any scrapes or lacerations. I noted, too, the unevenness of the terrain. While one of my boots crunched through the ice, the other was supported by the crust. It struck me that I could expect to see dogs with bicep injuries. This kind of injury can occur when a dog's forelegs are "held" by the soft snow, putting undue strain on the shoulder area.

The checkpoint area sits beneath a canopy of evergreens and birches clumped together on a bluff. The trees keep falling snow from reaching the ground, creating a small, green island in a sea of white. The old Rohn River Roadhouse—originally built during the gold rush of the early 1900s, and substantially rebuilt in the 1930s—has now been converted into a checkpoint center. Made of solid cedar, which has excellent waterproofing qualities, the cabin still appears as solid as it did a hundred years ago. Nearby, there's a tree cache in the shape of a miniature log cabin. (The first time I saw it, I mistook it for an ornate treehouse, much to the amusement of my colleagues. I was only later told that it was used to keep meat off the ground, away from scavengers and predators.) Directly in front of the cabin, there's an overhead arch, also made of cedar, bearing a sign that says "Rohn." The upright posts are decorated with antlers and skulls, trophies left by a century's worth of hunters and trappers who'd sheltered here. Leaning against the post is an antique, dilapidated dogsled, its wooden frame bleached grey from sun and rain.

I dumped my bags in my barracks—each team of veterinarians,

communications staff, dog handlers, and so on had their own tent—and headed to the cabin. A pair of large moose antlers graced the doorway. Volunteers had strung Christmas lights between the antlers and among the beams and supports. The inside of the cabin was rustic and warm, thanks to an old-fashioned wood-burning stove. Conversation and laughter filled the building. One of those voices, I realized, was directed at me.

"You look hungry. We have hot moose chili in the cabin," she offered. "I'm Lisa," she added, almost as an afterthought. Lisa stepped forward to embrace me. "We give hugs up here."

Lisa Jager and her husband, Terry, have run the checkpoint for years. They met twenty years ago, at Rohn, as Iditarod volunteers. Each year, they come up weeks before the race and get things in order, cutting back overgrown brush, making repairs on the cabin headquarters, sawing firewood for the winter, and doing pretty much everything else that needs doing. Both Lisa and Terry are natural leaders and doers. As I've learned, they prefer to lead by example; their diligence often prompts other, less active volunteers to help with chores around the camp.

❊ ❊ ❊ *ROHN, AK. 787 miles to Nome. Late afternoon. 25°F. Fair.*

ROHN, FOR WHATEVER REASON, attracts characters. There was a cook there, a man with a sharp wit, who I remember as clear as day. He picked up on a foible of mine: I have trouble recalling names and routinely have to ask new acquaintances for their names, often more than half a dozen times in a single day. The cook, observing this, changed his name every time I asked. He was a great guy, and he made a mean stew, but I never did find out his real name.

Of all the inhabitants of Rohn, the most memorable was probably Tina Scheer. Tina had been a competitor on the first season of *Survivor* and had, at one time, a traveling show featuring an all-woman cast. The Lumberjills, as they were called, performed at county fairs, outdoor festivals, and in local contests, competing in such events as logrolling (Tina's specialty), hatchet-throwing, and wood-chopping. Now, of course, she was volunteering for the Iditarod. I met Tina at Rohn, during a get-to-know-each-other activity led by the Jagers prior to the arrival of the dogs. Lisa and Terry had us all stand in a circle, introduce ourselves, and share what we were doing (or supposed to be doing) at Rohn. When Tina's time came, she dramatically jumped into the middle of the circle, and sang out, "Cheerleader!" I groaned internally. I'm all for keeping the atmosphere fun, but this, I thought, is the last thing we need. Why have someone at the checkpoint with no particular job, and no defined responsibilities? My first impression was totally off the mark. Tina acted as a highly capable catchall; every time I turned around, she was busy doing something for someone. There was no job beneath her. She cleaned up dog poop, fetched drinking water from nearby streams, spread straw, and took care of everything in between.

The first competitors weren't due into Rohn until dusk, and I hoped to make the most of my free time. The creek that ran at the bottom of the nearest slope was mostly covered with ice, but in the shallow areas where the current sped up, water circulated freely to the surface. It seemed like it would be a great place to fish. Back in Anchorage, there had been a simple fishing kit for sale at the hotel gift shop. It consisted of a single block of wood, around which wound a fishing line with a small lure at the end. At the time, I thought it a touristy gimmick, but I wished I had it now, so I could slide down and fish for trout. When I mentioned this to Terry, he chuckled and explained that the streams surrounding the checkpoint area are actually glacial runoffs, barren to most trout. The water is clean, cold, and well-oxygenated—all good conditions for trout—but it contains microscopic traces of silica mineral that can slice a fish's gills like a razor blade. In the deeper pools, Terry told me, I might land a hardier fish, maybe a grayling or two, but forget the trout.

While I contemplated my skills as an angler, the camp began to take shape around me. More tents were set up; wood was chopped and stacked; Christmas lights now adorned the grounds in even-greater numbers. The smell of fresh moose chili beckoned from the cabin, and for the first time that day I realized I was starving. During the Iditarod, it's important to eat when you can, as it can be difficult to find time to break away for a refuel or bathroom break. Equally important, if not more, is staying hydrated. A lot of body fluids are lost through perspiration, and dehydration only amplifies the effects of the cold. After a quick bowl of chili, I scoped out the dog lot. Already, it was difficult to navigate; the cabin is deep in the woods, where no moonlight touches. The lot had been fenced off with fluorescent tape to help the teams find their parking spots. It dawned on me that I'd be performing my veterinary exams in the dark, with just a headlamp to guide me.

The first team in was led by Dallas Seavey. No surprise there. For many years, the Seavey family dominated the event. Dallas won in 2012 and 2021, and for three years straight between 2014 and 2016. What happened in 2013 and 2017 to break his winning streak, you ask? His dad, Mitch Seavey, won in both years; he also won in 2004. Not to mention, the legendary Dan Seavey—Mitch's father and Dallas's grandfather—competed in the first two modern Iditarods, in 1973 and 1974. You don't win the Iditarod without a superb team of dogs, and Dallas Seavey's huskies were more than just well rested. They were all smiling as they approached the check-in station. Even as the sled glided to a halt, several of them continued to pull, and Dallas had to throw down his snow anchor to keep the team from sliding forward. Still, the dogs leapt up and down, ready to put another twenty miles or so under their paws. Usually, the arriving huskies can't wait to burrow into their straw nests after a hard run, but these pups seemed energized by their trek down the mountains. Terry Jager's booming voice rose over the noise of the crowd, directing the dog handlers to a resting spot among the trees. The huskies paced back and forth, a few looking quizzically at Dallas as if to say, "Why are we stopping so early?"

After Dallas's team located its "parking spot," I examined the dogs with Ronald Hallstrom, a veterinarian from Virginia who worked just as hard, if slightly slower, than I did. We began at the head of the line with the lead dogs. Crouching down, I inspected my patient's forelegs, then his hindlegs. Everything looked and felt fine. Moving down the line, I examined each of the dogs' paw pads, expecting to find some lacerations or tears from the rock-strewn trail near the gully. As they avoid obstacles, rapidly shifting their body weight from one side to another, dogs may get minor abrasions (especially on a rough course), but this whole team had nice, healthy feet. The skin between the toes was dry and unscathed, and despite the warmer than usual weather, the dogs seemed no more tired than I would expect them to be on a typical day. A few minutes after running seventy miles, their heart rates had returned

A quizzical look from one of Dallas's dogs.

to below average, as if they had been resting all day. It was incredible. There were no problems at all with Dallas's team.

Rohn is not like Finger Lake, where everyone seems to arrive at once. The mushers arrive in roughly ten-minute intervals. When there are no complications, ten minutes is almost exactly the time needed for a pair of vets to fully examine a team, write up their notes, and sign off on the team's logbook. But this essentially meant that we had a conveyor belt of dogs to examine. A conveyor belt of sleeping dogs, at that. It was now around midnight, and nearly every dog—utterly weary, yet with the contented heart that follows from a hard day's work—had circled once or twice in the dog lot, and, finding that perfect position, fallen asleep within minutes. It's always harder to work on a sleeping dog; they no more like being rustled awake from a deep slumber than we do. Try as I might to examine these Sleeping Beauties *before* they got comfortable, I couldn't overcome the trend.

In rare moments of inactivity, I scurried into the cabin for caffeine. Opening its door was like suddenly entering summer. A wood-burning stove fired at full force, and with various mushers, support personnel, techs, and vets filling the domicile, the temperature inside had to be at least eighty degrees warmer than it was outside. At each break, I let the warm embrace of the cabin envelop me; I took off my frozen parka and mitts, allowing the air to touch my bare skin. It was a wonderful feeling, hot meeting cold. The coffee, too, was delicious. It didn't matter that it was a bottom-shelf brew, whatever brand was on sale that week. It was warm and fresh. Sitting down for five or six minutes, holding my steaming mug of coffee, may be as close to Nirvana as I'll ever come.

Nothing would have given me more satisfaction than to stay there, in the cabin, napping in the comforting glow of the stove, but I had to get back to work. While vets are actively encouraged to take breaks, we try not to take breaks that are too long or too frequent, lest we become known as a "shirker." Having finished

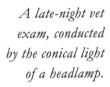

A late-night vet exam, conducted by the conical light of a headlamp.

one coffee, I poured another to go, and put my parka back on; it was now twice as heavy, thanks to the melted snow. As I stepped outside, a particularly icy gust of wind refroze my lips and nostrils. The frigid night air felt all the colder because I'd spent a few moments out of it. I buried my chin in my parka and walked quickly in the direction of the veterinarians' station. Suddenly, I was blinded by a flash of light. The beam of a musher's headlamp cut through the dark a mere few feet away. I leapt backward, just in time to prevent a pileup (though not in time to miss a verbal barrage from Terry Jager). The incoming musher was one of a few Norwegian competitors that year. Even as he sped by, I noticed that one of his lead dogs was resting in the basket at the front of the sled, which is never a good sign. After apologizing profusely to Terry, I leapt from the snow and chased after him. As I approached, the husky in the basket perked up, scratching and yawning. I felt a wave of relief; at least she wasn't severely ill.

"She not like pull," the heavily accented Norwegian declared. "Wants to ride and petted." He attended to his other dogs first, taking out frozen fish fillets and distributing them down the line. The huskies didn't crowd him; instead, they waited patiently in place for their treats. As he worked his way down the gangline, he gave each dog a pat on the head. Finally, he came back to the dog in question.

"When I put her on the line, she not pull, so I put her back in sled and pet her all the way here. I would like to drop her here. She wants to stay here and rest," he explained.

The husky refused to budge from the basket, and eventually had to be lifted out of the sled. The Norwegian gently undid the fastener that connected her to the gangline, then paraded her up and down the line so I could observe her gait. In the basket, all had seemed fine; the husky was clearly bright and alert. But as soon as she began to walk, I could see that she was limping. While the musher stood next to her, I stooped to examine her right fore-leg, introducing myself by patting her head. Carefully, I took the injured leg in my hand. She winced as I flexed her shoulder joint. Uh-oh. While mild soft tissue tightness might resolve itself during the course of the race, shoulder injuries, you may recall, are much more concerning.

I advised the musher to drop her, and he agreed. I was due to fly back to Anchorage the next day, and I suspected she would be sharing a plane with me. Before I led the husky away to begin treatment, the musher bent down and gave her a tender kiss on the snout.

"Rest now," he said. "We see you back in Anchorage. You did good."

I carried her to the dropped-dog line, where she made short work of the food Tina Scheer gave her: a bowl of kibble made into a stew with warm water. I went to fetch some medication for the inflammation. By the time I returned, the husky was fast asleep, and Tina was gently massaging her injured shoulder. I can't think of a better therapy for this kind of injury. Muscles that are strained or damaged accumulate lactic acid at a faster rate than normal tissue. Massaging the legs doesn't just *feel* good, it allows the lactic acid to dissipate. Our patient was clearly enjoying the treatment. She lay with her eyes closed, and even in her sleep, groaned softly with relief.

While I was caring for the injured husky, another team arrived. By the time I found their designated resting spot, nestled in the woods, the dogs had already been fed and watered. A young lady sat with a husky cradled in her lap. Thinking something was wrong, I rushed up to her and introduced myself as a veterinarian. She smiled, shook my hand, and introduced herself as Anna Berington. (And no, the dog was fine, she had just been cuddling with it.) I'll admit that I was somewhat starstruck: Anna and her twin sister, Kristy, are iconic Iditarod competitors. Neither musher has won, and though they're usually in the middle of the pack, they're impossible to miss. Everyone recognizes them because they're about as identical as identical twins can be. (Both women wear their long, blonde hair in braided pigtails during the race, which makes it even harder to tell them apart.) They run together as Seeing Double Sled Dog Racing, and they've been racing since they were kids. Their first sled dog team consisted of the family's pet dogs—a border collie and a Great Pyrenees—which they harnessed to a milk crate and some skis. Kristy was the first to take up the sport seriously; she began practicing with a few dogs of her own in Wisconsin. Eventually, Kristy and her family, including Anna, moved from Wisconsin to Alaska to learn more about competitive sled dog racing. Since then, Kristy has run the Iditarod, the Yukon Quest, the Kusko 300, the Copper Basin 300, and many other races. Anna ran her first Iditarod in 2012, during my rookie year as a trail veterinarian.*

---

* That year, in 2012, the Berington sisters became the first twins to complete the Iditarod.

Kristy Berington's husky rolled over for a belly rub as soon as she approached.

I had just finished signing off on Anna's team when Kristy's team appeared. While Kristy parked the sled, I noted that one of the team dogs was heavily favoring his left forepaw. Before I could approach the team, a reporter and his cameraman stepped in front of me to ask Kristy for an interview. Removing her goggles, she politely told them that she'd be happy to give an interview, but she needed to tend to her dogs first. I smiled. *That's a good musher*, I thought. I shook Kristy's hand and told her about the lame dog I had spotted.

"He just started doing that over there," she said, pointing to an abstract point near the gates. "He had been running fine until then."

We both knelt down in the snow. The husky in question was trying to pull off his racing bootie. I leaned in to help, undoing the Velcro strap. From the top, the paw looked fine. But in turning it over, I revealed a small ulceration on one of the paw pads. While it wasn't bleeding, it *was* raw, and it was right where the dog would be placing most of his weight. I looked in between the toes and at the skin between each digit. There were no other injuries.

"Is it bad?" Kristy asked.

I shrugged. "No, not really, but it will probably get worse if he keeps running. I would recommend you drop him here with us. I promise you, in a couple of days, he'll be completely healed."

Kristy immediately agreed, and I called for one of the volunteers to escort the husky to the dropped-dog line. I continued with my exams. Most of the competing dogs are friendly, but hers were exceptionally so. It was obvious that she loved them, and they loved her right back. When I needed to examine a dog's belly, Kristy sat down next to them, and they'd plop into her lap for a belly rub. It didn't take long to examine her team; for the most part, the dogs were in excellent condition.

While I finished with the canine athletes, the human athlete excused herself to speak to the reporter. He asked questions that I'm sure Kristy and Anna have endured countless times before: What made you get into sled dog racing? What do you do during the off-season? What's it like to race against your sister? Sitting on a bale of straw, with a couple of huskies at her feet, Kristy answered each question with poise and grace. She was eating a cup of soup, animating her answers with pointed movements of the spoon. She smiled a lot—a genuine smile, not a painted-on grin. The reporter, safe to say, was putty in her hands. After they wrapped, Kristy appeared at my side again, as if she'd never left. I told her that the rest of her dogs looked good, and that we would take care of her husky.

"You're impressive with the interviews," I added. "I imagine you and your sister get that a lot."

She nodded and thanked me. We talked for a while longer, me with my cold cup of coffee, her with a hot mug of tea. I tried to impress her by rehashing the tale of the fire at Finger Lake, explaining that it was the reason for the lack of rest areas for mushers that year. (Much to my dismay, Kristy said she didn't remember any problems that year.) Soon enough, Anna joined her, and the sisters went off, arm-in-arm, to fetch water and straw for their teams. I watched as they disappeared into the woods.

❧ ❧ ❧ *ROHN, AK. 787 miles to Nome. Dawn. 34°F. Fair.*

DURING THE SUMMER, when the undergrowth develops, the woods become impossibly dense. But in March, the ground is still soft, covered only by moss and light snow. In certain parts of the woods, walking on the moss feels like walking on a sponge or a down comforter. Just before dawn, I found a bare patch overlooking a river, complete with a fallen tree for a seat, and sat there, sipping coffee. I read a little, then wrote a little; mostly, though, I just took it all in. In the distance, the sun began to crest. It felt like I'd been at Rohn for a week. Today, the checkpoint would be torn down. Some of us would be heading up the trail; others would be heading home. After Rohn, I'd be flying north to Cripple, and I was due to leave in just a few hours. I would barely have time to tear down my gear and stow it, much less get some shut-eye. Still I sat, watching the sun rise over the mountains.

Back at the camp, the volunteers loaded Kristy's dog into the bush plane. As the propeller wound up, the pilot threw my (hastily packed) bags into the cargo bay. Both Linda and Terry came to say goodbye. As she had done when I first arrived, Linda gave me a great, big hug, and together, they handed me a plaque carved from virgin cedar by Terry himself.

CHAPTER 13

THE GREAT HUSKY AIRLIFT

AFTER HALF A DOZEN CHECKPOINTS THAT CONSIST OF NO MORE than a handful of tents, maybe a log cabin or two if you're lucky, being in McGrath, a town of 341 people, actually feels like city living. The town sits on the south bank of the Kuskokwim river, and is the hub for the Iditarod Area School District. (Appropriately enough, the district's mascot is the husky.) McGrath has exactly one café, a hardware store, a radio station, two bars, and a large, concrete runway with space for cargo planes and other large aircraft to land and take off, making McGrath a critical hub during the race. The bush planes that flit along the trail can't fly directly from Anchorage to the various checkpoints on the second half of the course and back. McGrath offers a place for pilots to land, refuel, and drop off volunteers. Dogs dropped from the northern checkpoints also congregate at McGrath, where they're cared for while they wait for transport back to Anchorage.

The first time I traveled to McGrath, it was on a Sunday afternoon, via an Alaska Airlines flight—a world apart from the single-engine Iditarod Air Force planes I'd become accustomed to. The three hundred miles from Anchorage to McGrath takes the Iditarod front-runners three to four days; Alaska Airlines can make the same trip in about an hour. I arrived just as day turned to evening, and the sun cast pink and blue shadows across the

Sun glares off the snow.

snowfields. The McGrath Café, located conveniently by the airport, is the de facto headquarters for race volunteers. The break
room there serves as the flight operations center, a makeshift
affair run by a woman named Rebecca. Upstairs, there's a dorm
for us to lay out our sleeping bags. A lucky few get cots to sleep
on. The ceiling up there is low, and a wooden beam running
through the center of the room makes it even more hazardous.
The beam is low enough that if, say, a 6′1″ veterinarian got up
in the middle of the night, it would smack him squarely in the
forehead.

The plan was to stay there for a night before continuing on, the
next morning, to the checkpoint in the town of Iditarod, about a
hundred and fifty miles away. As often happens, things didn't go
as planned. Early on Monday, a barometric low settled over the
town, bringing with it fog that enshrouded the entire basin, all of
McGrath, in a dense blanket of gray, the kind that makes the coldest of days seem somehow colder. It would be days, maybe even a
week, before conditions changed. Each morning, I would walk to

Flight Ops, and each afternoon, I would walk back to my bunk, dejected, because all outgoing flights had been canceled. In fact, *all* flights to and from the area had been grounded. To pass the time, I read—I never travel anywhere without at least two books—and, when not ensconced in the warm café, explored the town. One afternoon, I followed a picket fence decorated with moose antlers to a building with a gold-lettered sign. The McGrath Museum consists of just a few rooms, each showcasing a different aspect of the region's history. There were ancient canoes, mastodon bones, and Stone Age weapons, as well as photographs of European pioneers. As I spoke with a kindly, bespectacled docent, I wondered how many visitors the museum had ever had; McGrath is not a large town, even by Alaskan standards. But here was its museum, lovingly kept open by a small group of locals.

While McGrath boasts many luxuries that other stops lack—indoor plumbing, for one, and hot showers, too—competitive mushers often bypass the checkpoint and push the additional eighteen miles to Takotna, the next checkpoint. This year, there was just one competitor staying at McGrath, a musher by the name of Ellen. I'd met her, not even three days ago, back at Finger Lake. There, Ellen had been positively ebullient, eyes alight with the excitement of her first Iditarod. She'd told me of her journey while I examined her dogs. (All were in excellent condition.) The stretch from Willow to Finger Lake is a sizable part of the course; Ellen said she was proud to "have made it this far." I remembered her laughter as she joked with the other mushers. I was thrilled to see her in the McGrath Café; I sidled up next to her and offered a cheerful, "Hi, Ellen! How ya doin'?"

"Oh, hey," she replied. Ellen barely lifted her eyes. I recognized something solemn in her voice.

"How is it going out there?"

Ellen shrugged her shoulders. She played at her food with a plastic fork, head down, shoulders slumped. She seemed to have

The Alaskan wilderness can be densely wooded or completely bare. Sometimes, it feels like there's no end in sight.

aged twenty years since I last spoke to her. I could see that she was bruised and battered. While I'd spent a leisurely hour on a commercial airplane en route to McGrath, she'd experienced a three-day ordeal, a trek through some of the roughest terrain on the course, and she looked very much worse for the wear.

"How are your dogs? They doing okay?" I asked. She responded with a slight nod of her head. It was hard to believe that this was the person I'd met three days ago. "How about you? Are you okay?" I offered, leaning in a little.

Finally, Ellen looked up. Her eyes were red, maybe bloodshot, and quickly filling with tears. She shook her head. "I don't think I can do this anymore," she said. "It's too hard, too rough. I shouldn't have even started."

We sat in silence for a moment. She sunk lower, down toward her half-eaten plate of mashed potatoes.

"Ellen," I said softly, trying to sound soothing, "You're almost halfway there."

As soon as the words left my mouth, I knew I'd said the wrong thing. If I were in Ellen's shoes, the absolute last thing I'd want to hear is that my ordeal is not over and, in fact, the worst is yet to come. Unsurprisingly, Ellen now responded with audible sobs. I felt terrible. She must be exhausted. Out there, on the trail, every ounce of her concentration had to have been on staying the course—on avoiding every low-hanging branch, patch of ice, and rock that threatened to unseat her. If a musher is hurt on the course, or if she falls off her sled, or if a dog is injured, she's alone. There are twenty- and eighty-mile stretches without assistance; sometimes, a distressed musher's best chance of finding help is another musher, someone coming up the trail behind her. But in most circumstances, all that musher can do is relay a message to the next checkpoint. Then what? It could be hours or even a day before help arrives via snowmobile or helicopter. Those hours may very well be the loneliest and most excruciating hours of her life. So, yes, Ellen seemed shaken. But who wouldn't, with all that weighing on them?

Ellen fanned her hand in front of her face and sniffed. "I'm sorry," she apologized, "I'm just tired."

I bit my tongue. I had wanted to say, "Of course you're tired!" At best, Ellen would have only taken catnaps on the trail. Maybe she'd slept an hour, maybe two.

"No, no. *I'm* sorry," I stressed.

It was clear that she needed to be alone to contemplate her next move. I wondered if she would choose to drop out here. The next section of the race, after McGrath, is relatively plain sailing—at least until the Bering Sea, the Iditarod's toughest challenge. But that was still several days and hundreds of miles away. Besides, every competitor, whether a rookie or veteran, identifies with Ellen at some point during the race: tired, stressed, beaten up, hungry, and aware that there is so, *so* much farther to go. It must be tempting to say to yourself, "Well, I made it this far. Maybe next year?" The walls of McGrath Café are lined with posters made by local schoolchildren, each with an inspiring message, like "You are just about to the halfway point!" or "Only 600 miles to go!" Some had been personalized; a neon pink sign read "Go, DeeDee, go!"* I wondered if these enthusiastic banners helped or hurt mushers like Ellen. Had I been in her position, I might've stayed there, at McGrath, where there was hot food and a warm, soft bed only a few hundred feet away. What resilience, what unmitigated fortitude it would take to pull on your mukluks and parka and return to the trail. In the end, that's exactly what Ellen did. The last time I saw her, she was headed out the door to her team. From across the room, I yelled, "Good luck!" She didn't turn around, only waved her hand wearily.

❋ ❋ ❋ *McGRATH, AK. 664 miles to Nome. Dawn. −2°F. Fog clearing.*

Several days passed before the weather began to improve. My last morning in McGrath, ironically enough, began without wind or cloud cover: excellent flying weather. I had been inside all night, sheltering from the then-raging wind, and desperately needed fresh air. I left the checkpoint with the intention of snapping yet more photographs of the dogs. (Who can resist?) But once outside, I found that what most captivated me was an older woman standing on a knoll overlooking the frozen Yentna River. Her parka was well worn, and she had wrapped herself in a red woolen blanket. Although the glare from the snow was blinding, she wore no sunglasses, only a fur-lined, beaver-skin Alaskan aviator's hat.

Every once in a while, she removed her arm from the blanket and shielded her eyes with a great, furred mitten. I had seen her

---

* DeeDee Jonrowe is one of the most popular Iditarod mushers. Her signature color is pink, signifying that she's a breast cancer survivor.

several times before—in fact, I'd seen her almost every day that I'd been stationed at McGrath. Her self-appointed task of many years is to direct teams out of the checkpoint, toward Takotna, about fifteen miles away. I learned from my colleagues that no one had ever asked her to perform this activity; she had simply decided that someone should assist the dogs. Each morning, she situated herself atop the knoll, like a sentry at her post, and left only when she no longer felt needed. I had wanted to speak with her for a while, but I hadn't found an appropriate time or, more to the point, worked up the nerve to address her. This, I realized, was my last chance. Composing myself, I climbed the riverbank to her lookout station. From below, she seemed to be of average height, maybe taller, but I now saw that she barely rose to my chest.

The woman appeared to be in her seventies or eighties; she emanated the kind of calm contentment that comes with age and wisdom. Her tanned face was etched with wrinkles. Smile and laugh lines crawled from her cheekbones to her forehead, traversing small, deeply set eyes and a broad, flat nose. Despite her age, she had only sparse streaks of gray running through her coal-black hair. I thought she was beautiful, but when I asked to take her picture for my lecture audiences—this being the excuse that I used to approach her—she broke into a cheeky grin, revealing a few yellowed teeth.

"Why would anyone in Washington, DC, want to see a picture of me?" she said, giggling.

"I think they would be very interested in seeing a picture of you!" I countered. The trickles of laughter became a hearty guffaw.

"Why do you come out here all day, anyway?" I asked.

She shrugged her shoulders as if she didn't really know, and hadn't wasted time asking herself. "I like to see the dogs," she offered.

This proved to be the structure of our conversation: I'd ask a question, and she'd reply with never more than one-sentence answers. In the course of our exchange, I learned that she was an elder from the local Athabascan Tribe, and that she had lived here, in McGrath, her whole life. She'd never been out of the state, nor saw any reason to leave.

"Everything I love is here," she explained. While we spoke, she scanned the course for sled dog teams. Not once did her gaze leave the riverbed. After a while, she pulled a piece of whale blubber from her pocket and offered me a small chunk, taking a larger chunk for herself. Whale blubber is a special delicacy, with the consistency of chewing gum, if chewing gum were fish-flavored.

"Good," she said. Whether it was a question or a statement of affirmation, I couldn't tell. Ready to take my leave, I moved to shake her hand, but she seemed uncomfortable with this gesture and instead gave a slight bow. I snapped a photograph as I descended the crest.

Germans have a term, *Fernweh*, that signifies "yearning for a distant place." Having grown up in small-town Ohio, almost literally in the middle of a cornfield, I've always had a particularly strong sense of *Fernweh*. When I went to college, I took every opportunity to travel, working in Hawaii with dolphins, attending a semester abroad in England, and even backpacking through Greece. There have been countless vacations and trips. The world is a vast and infinitely interesting place, and in truth, I've always looked down on people who chose not to wander, not to see and experience different cultures. Maybe there was something deeply ironic in the fact that this chance encounter with an elderly Athabascan woman pushed me to reconsider my stance. She was content, serene. Could I say the same? Not really. She didn't need to tell stories about wild sled rides to make her friends jealous; she didn't need to supplement her life with cheap souvenirs from tourist traps. She only needed the now of the weather, the dogs, and the mushers. I wondered if all the adventures in the world could ever bring me such peace.

❄   ❄   ❄   ❄

BY MID-MORNING, ALL THE mushers had passed through the checkpoint, and the woman had returned to village life. But we still had nearly a hundred dropped dogs to care for. With flights to and from McGrath grounded, there had been no way to transport the dogs to Anchorage. Fortunately, they were all in stable condition; most had been dropped for relatively minor aches and pains, such as pulled muscles, strains, and what we call "general soreness." Many of the dogs had already recovered, and were fit to run again. While only a few huskies required medication and observation, all of the dogs had to be monitored, fed, and watered. With nothing else to do, I volunteered to pitch in. The huskies yipped and howled when they spotted me. One of the black-and-white huskies that I'd examined earlier that week threw back her head and crooned a deep, mournful song. One by one, the others joined in, creating a kind of sad, wilderness chorus.

Our upcoming task was, in principle, simple. We would load the huskies into a single cargo plane via the cargo door, whereupon they would be airlifted to Anchorage. The whole operation had to be organized down to each movement. We couldn't have any escapees. After the episode in Anchorage, I was all too aware of the fact that even the slightest amount of slack in a lead can allow a husky to wriggle free. It had taken several days to find *that* dog, and that had been in a city, with a large populace to help search. A dog who freed himself here would surely dart for the dense birch forest, where he would be all but impossible to find, unless he returned on his own. We decided on a kind of bucket brigade, with the first person unhooking the dropped dog and passing him or her to a handler, who then walked the dog from the runway to the cargo door. At the plane, a third person would lift the dog up to yet another person—me—waiting on crates by the door, who would then hand the dog to one of the technicians aboard the plane. Finally, the technician would secure the dog to a tugline strung across the aircraft floor. Simple enough, right? From our perspective, maybe. The plane, on the other hand, was late, and as it taxied toward the wrong end of the runway, one of my colleagues had to leap onto a snowmobile to chase it down. This particular air freight company had never transported dogs before, but felt its crew was up to the challenge. When the cargo door flew open, several cardboard boxes fell to the ground.

"Once all the huskies are loaded, we'll use these boxes as barriers," the pilot shouted.

"Why will we need it, when the dogs are going to be secured to a tugline?" I asked.

"What's a tugline?"

"It's the cable that we secure the dogs to during flight."

"Oh no, no need for that." I could hear the confidence in the pilot's voice. "We will just load all the dogs into the cargo bay, then block the exits with these here cardboard boxes."

A dropped dog waits to be transported back to Anchorage.

Not pictured: the cardboard boxes.

"Huskies can chew their way out of a wooden crate," I said, trying to keep my voice calm. "Cardboard boxes won't stop them."

"They will the way I stack them," he said with a wink.

I took a deep breath. *This is absurd*, I thought. A single loose husky is a problem. What kind of hellacious bedlam might be caused by a hundred dogs, free to roam the underbelly of a large aircraft? There would be scruffs, fights, and enough bite wounds to keep veterinarians back in Anchorage busy for more than a few days, not to mention mating attempts.

In their "expertise," it turned out that the pilot and his singular crewman had not even *brought* a tie-down cable, so there was nothing to secure the dogs to. There was no time to grab one, either. We all knew that the blue skies above could turn gray in a matter of minutes. None of us wanted to keep the dogs in McGrath for a moment more than we had to; already, they had been restricted to the compound for several days. They were tired, bored, and irritable. With every passing hour, the risk of an escape, or a fight, increased—and the volunteers here urgently needed a break from caring for the dogs around the clock. Weighing the risks, we ultimately decided that the dogs should still leave today, on this plane, despite its, well, novelties. There was nothing to do but get to it.

One by one, we loaded the dogs into the plane. As anyone but our pilot could have predicted, the cardboard barriers were next to useless. The huskies were everywhere, wiggling under and over the cardboard, sometimes chewing it right through the middle. Some had found their way into the cockpit; others had roamed into the tail section and were now squeezed between boxes of cargo. Dogs began fighting, and John, one of the volunteers inside the plane, did his best to separate them. I watched in what felt like slow motion as one of the huskies, a red-and-brown male, saw the open cargo door and sprinted toward it. I barely caught hold of his harness as he leapt over my head. Another husky tried to follow, this time by running between my legs. I now had my hands full with two wiggling huskies. If a third tried to make a break for it, there would be little I could do to prevent his escape. I yelled for help. Susan, the veterinary technician who had heretofore been handing dogs to me, nabbed another would-be escapee. There were close to thirty dogs on the plane before the two crewmembers agreed that a solution other than flimsy pieces of cardboard was needed.

Ronald Hallstrom, my partner vet, watched the whole ordeal unfold. He spoke to the pilot, who then sheepishly ambled over to suggest that we remove all of the dogs. In the meantime, he would run into town to get a tie-down cable to secure the huskies.

"That's a great idea," I mumbled.

It takes significant physical effort to lift a single squirming dog, let alone a hundred of them. This change in strategy meant that my colleagues and I had to expend the energy to maneuver sixty dogs to and from the aircraft—for nothing. We'd be right back where we began, with all the dogs chained to the perimeter fence of the airport. As the pilot steered his valiant steed (a snowmobile) toward the city, we began the long, arduous process of offloading the dogs. It would be hours before the pilot returned with the golden cable, but when he and it finally appeared on the horizon, there was a collective sigh of relief. We secured the cable to the bulkheads and began the whole process again. Except now, of course, the dogs that had already been inside the airplane didn't want to return; they had to be carried all the way from the fence, up through the cargo door, and into the aircraft. The rest of the huskies went voluntarily, but still had to be lifted through the door before being secured to the cable.

By the time we loaded and secured the last husky, my back was in searing pain. I rubbed my aching arms as I watched the plane taxi down the runway, grateful that the dogs, at least, were safely on board, and on their way back to Anchorage.

Chapter 14

HONEY, THERE ARE NEVER EXTRA PIES

MUSHERS ARE REQUIRED TO MAKE AT LEAST ONE TWENTY-four-hour layover, and many elect to skip McGrath, instead taking their mandatory rest in the tiny community of Takotna. What the hamlet lacks in infrastructure, it more than makes up for in pies. Yes, pies. It is a truth universally acknowledged—by locals, volunteers, and mushers alike—that in Takotna, pies await. Never mind the roomy, spacious bunks, or the exceptionally friendly volunteers. The main draw are the mounds of apple, peach, chocolate mousse, banana cream, coconut, lemon meringue, and berry pies. The residents of this small mining town, all fifty of them, start baking days ahead of the race. During my stay, I asked one of the local women what they do with the extra pies once the checkpoint shuts down.

"Honey," she said, "There are never any extra pies."

Takotna is a small village that, like many Alaskan communities, boomed when the mines flourished. In the early twentieth century, Takotna was the last stop on the route for steamships carrying supplies before the southernmost port of Bethel. In the early 1900s, gold was discovered in the nearby Innoko Region. The town expanded, and by the mid-1920s, boasted several commercial companies, roadhouses, a post office, and about fifty residential houses, as well as an airfield. At its height, Takotna had its own radio station and printed a daily newspaper. Long after the gold rush died down in the rest of Alaska, the community became an operations area during the Cold War.

The White Alice Communications System (WACS) was deployed in Takotna during the Cold War, officially to extend telephone service to remote areas of Alaska, but locally widely understood to allow the US Air Force to eavesdrop on the Russians. The system provided early warning of Russian military activities, including missile launches. In the 1990s the gold veins began to dry up, and the Iron Curtain fell. Fate finally caught up with Takotna, and like so many Alaskan settlements before it, it became something of a ghost town. One of the few remaining buildings from that era is a library that houses thousands of books, a number totally out of proportion to the current population of fifty-three.

I traveled to Takotna with three colleagues, including Gretchen Love and Gayle Tate, who were by now old friends. Our plane dropped us off at dusk, then promptly turned around and left. The airport was deserted, the fading light casting a gloomy atmosphere over the runway. The city of Takotna was still a good mile or two away, so we couldn't see any buildings aside from the small shack that had been designated as a "terminal." We hunted for any sign of our ride to town. Supposedly, a snow machine had been sent to pick us up, but there was no one in sight, and we couldn't agree which direction the town was. Night was falling, so we huddled together, resting on our backpacks to keep from sitting directly on the snow. Finally, we heard a snowmobile in the distance. As it glided down the road, we collected our belongings and made our way to the gate in the chain-link fence. The snowmobile started to slow, then rounded a bend in the road and continued on.

"Was that our ride?" Gretchen asked. The rest of us could only shrug.

"Maybe they forgot about us?" someone suggested. Again, we all shrugged. Gayle removed his Arctic cap and scratched his head.

"It's going to get dark soon," he said. He paused, then

added, "We should start down the road. Maybe we'll meet them halfway."

None of us relished the idea of walking a mile or more down a dark, snow-covered road with all our gear, but it seemed to be a better option than remaining at the airport, in the cold, waiting for a ride that may never show. We hunched into our backpacks and grabbed our duffels. Even with layers of cold-weather gear, it was a frigid journey. Thankfully, there was only a light breeze. We soon crested a small rise, from which we could see the distant, flickering lights of the Takotna Community Center. By the time we reached the building, it had gone dark. We were tired and hungry; we had only just entered the building when someone informed us that we would be bunking not there, but in the library. I braced myself for another trudge through snow and ice, but I was reassured that it was, literally, next door, a mere twenty feet away.

Teams had begun to reach the checkpoint, but the veterinarians already on-site had agreed to handle the night shift so we could turn in for the night. As I laid out my sleeping bag, Gretchen brushed her teeth; Gayle was already snoring. Finding myself more awake, I retrieved my headlamp from my duffel and scanned the shelves for books, eventually pulling a copy of Jon Krakauer's *Into Thin Air*. In the back of the book, there was a paper card for a borrower to initial and date. Evidently, this book had been checked out a dozen times or more in the last few years; apparently, there were bibliophiles in Takotna. As I began to read, my thoughts raced, pirouetting between the rocks and crags of Everest and the snow-covered mountains outside. The wind sung between the trees, just as it did for the protagonists in the book. I lay comfortably in the dark, warm room, closed my eyes, and when I opened them again, the sun was rising. I rubbed the back of my head where it had been resting on the shelf, and made my way carefully around the slumbering volunteers strewn throughout the library, back to the Takotna Community Center.

The veterinarians on duty were surprised to see me so early (much to my quiet delight). I acquired some coffee, then joined them in the small room we had designated as a "clinic." There was a dog resting in the corner. To the untrained eye, she might've looked like a black Lab, but I immediately recognized her as an Alaskan husky. When she saw me, she yawned, stretched, and gently thumped her tail on the floor. There was a catheter in her arm, and a bag of Lactated Ringer's solution* steadily dripping fluids into her vein. One of the veterinarians came over to brief me.

"This is Midnight," the volunteer explained. "She came in on a team last night after you guys hit the sack. She was running a fever, so we decided to bring her in and give her some fluids. We were going to get you guys up if it got any worse, but she did well overnight. Her fever is down now, and she is responding well."

I looked at Midnight, who returned my gaze with big, brown doleful eyes. She began thumping her tail harder, as if in agreement.

"You guys need to be fresh," the volunteer warned. Another veterinarian spoke up.

"There are a lot of parked teams out back," he clarified, pointing out a window in the back of the room.

There were, indeed, sleds and dogs in every available parking space. Huskies were curled up, end-to-end, in beds of straw. Many of the mushers were still fast asleep in the sleds, preferring to sleep with their dogs to a heated cabin. (I asked about this once. The musher explained that he prefers not to "get used to" these comforts between stops.) Slowly but surely, the vets I'd come to Takotna with began to filter in. Midnight perked up with the arrival of these new faces. She was especially smitten with Gayle; picking him over all of us, she settled by his side as he sat, cross-legged, in the cordoned-off clinic that had become her private hospital. Someone had volunteered to get her some food, and

---

* Lactated Ringer's solution, or LR, is an intravenous fluid used to replace water and electrolyte loss in dogs with low blood volume or low blood pressure.

Huskies resting
in nests.

she was now enjoying a meal—a clear sign that she was improving. Gayle stroked her head. When he tried to rise to stretch his legs, Midnight pressed her head down, onto his lap.

"Hold on, I'll be right back," he told her, gently, as he left for a bathroom break.

Midnight's gaze never left the door. Only when Gayle resumed his position did she relax; again, she gratefully rested her head in his lap. While we waited for race updates, we began to devise a game plan, eventually settling on six-hour shifts. Takotna is almost exactly halfway through the course, and the teams, by now, are spread out. Having just one team of two veterinarians on duty *should* be adequate, providing nothing went awry. There was, of course, an understanding that if those two vets became swamped by new arrivals or encountered complex medical issues, they shouldn't hesitate to fetch an off-duty veterinarian to assist. It was agreed that someone would need to stay with Midnight, at least until she was off intravenous fluids, and—obviously—that someone would be Gayle Tate.

The route from McGrath to Takotna is only eighteen miles, some of it running along the frozen Takotna River. About a mile from the town, the sleds must climb a steep bank, then take a dirt road, buried deep in layers of snow, to the checkpoint area. The Iditarod Committee had kindly arranged for a spotter to watch for approaching teams. With the checkpoint right outside, the volunteers would have plenty of time to take one last bite of pie, or gulp of coffee, before heading out to greet the musher. As our meeting came to a close, the spotter's cry rang out, right on cue: "Teams on the ice!"

❋ ❋ ❋ *TAKOTNA, AK. 646 miles to Nome. Afternoon.*
8°F. Light wind.

I PAIRED WITH GRETCHEN, who was already fully dressed and organized. As I struggled to put on my mukluks and parka, I noticed another young woman doing the same.

"Looks like we better get a move on," I smiled to her.

She smiled back, a little blankly. I repeated myself, but received the same look. Another young woman approached and said something to her in a foreign language. Finally, I spotted the Norwegian flags sewn on their coats. As she exited, the woman I'd spoken to smiled and waved. I quickly finished zipping my parka and, grabbing my stethoscope, followed her outside. The sun shone from a crystal-blue sky; squinting into it, I saw that the young women were now flanked by two or three other people, all milling about a television camera. Intrigued and—as ever—willing to do just about anything to appear on TV, I went over and introduced myself. (Fortunately for me, a few of the crewmembers did speak English.) I learned that they were journalists from the Norwegian Broadcasting Corporation, *Norsk rikskringkasting AS* (NRK), there to film a documentary about their countryman, Joar Ulsom, and his Iditarod bid. Somehow, they knew that he was the musher who was about to arrive, though no name had been called.

While many of the mushers stop to rest at Takotna, by no

means all of them do. Usually, if a team makes a long stop at McGrath, they blow through Takotna. A few teams will make a mini-stop, gathering water for the dogs, maybe gulping down a sandwich or two, restocking whatever essentials they may need, and then going on their way, all inside of fifteen minutes. We knew from the timing data that Joar Ulsom had rested his dogs at McGrath, but the rumor was that he would make a mini-stop here to load up on essentials, and to give a quick interview to NRK. Joar was a rookie that year, but he had an impressive résumé. He had finished the Yukon Quest, as well as the *Finnmarksløpet* and *Femundløpet* races in Norway. He set a record at the Russian Nadezhda Hope Race, becoming the first non-Russian to win there in twenty years. At twenty-four, he was one of the younger competitors on the Iditarod course that year. As the television crew scurried around, making ready, Gretchen and I watched for Joar's team to crest the hill before the official checkpoint line. Several dog handlers preemptively went to fetch straw bales for Joar to take with him. It dawned on me, then, that Gretchen and I would have just a few minutes to perform our examinations.

Soon enough, the sound of yipping huskies carried over the wind, and not long after, the dogs appeared above the hillock. Joar tried to slow them down by yelling "Whoooaaa!" but the dogs pressed on at the same pace. As his instructions became more forceful, the dogs reluctantly slowed to a trot, but they never came to a full stop. Instead, they jogged by the checkpoint area and all the staffers there, prompting two members of the support staff to chase after them. While the sled continued to glide, Joar, unphased, requested two bags of food from the depot area. He leapt theatrically from his sled as the TV crew approached. Taking advantage of the momentary lapse in activity, Gretchen and I began to visually inspect the dogs. I smiled. The dogs appeared to be in excellent shape, but clearly, a storm was brewing. One of the leads—a trim, black-and-white husky—was straining against his harness. He had just rested at McGrath; it was a beautiful, cold day; and he had only run eighteen miles so far. His excitement spread down the gangline.

As Joar spoke to the TV crew, the sled began to inch forward. Several volunteers tried to hold the huskies back, but an entanglement was quickly becoming inevitable. Someone shouted to Joar for help. Joar whipped around, and now seeing the commotion, broke off the interview mid-sentence. A dramatic exit followed a dramatic entrance: the musher raced up to his sled and jumped on the back, instantly restoring order, but the dogs took this as the signal that their human was finally ready to go. His pleas to stop fell on deaf ears. The huskies were beyond listening; they were on their way, regardless. Joar frantically reeled in the snow anchor, which was bouncing along the ice behind him. The volunteer with the bag of dog food was just barely able to toss it into the open bay of the sled. One of the cooks came sprinting out with a plate of hot food and—somehow—caught up to Joar in time to hand it off like a baton in a relay race. Joar turned and waved.

"Well, I guess we are going now," he announced. Within seconds, the team had turned the bend and disappeared, once again, into the wilderness. There was a moment of silence. Then, slowly, we all began to laugh.

"The huskies were too impatient to wait for an interview," one of the Norwegian women remarked.

It wasn't long before another team arrived. Unlike Joar, this musher had not rested his dogs at McGrath. He decided to stay here for a longer rest. Most of the competitors who hoped to win or place had passed through hours ago. Those coming in now were in the middle of the pack, and while they might hope to overtake a handful of rivals to place higher, their main goal was to finish. As far as I could tell, the dogs were still taking things in stride, but the strain was now beginning to show on the mushers' faces. From a practical or strategic point of view, with over half the field now focusing on finishing, rather than speed, it meant that from here on out, we

could expect most of the teams to be making longer stops, quite leisurely ones compared with what we'd seen so far. The competitors
would not be taking any undue risks; instead, they'd be looking to
preserve themselves and their huskies. From a vet's-eye view, this
meant we'd have ample opportunity to examine their dogs.

When the team pulled up to the checkpoint line, Gretchen noted
that one of the wheel dogs, the pair right behind the lead dogs, had
a slight limp. As the volunteers parked the team, we both gravitated
toward the limping dog. The lameness was by no means obvious, but
it was definitely there. But where exactly? Believe it or not, it can be
difficult, sometimes, to determine which leg a dog has injured just by
watching their gait. Gretchen and I knelt in unison. The dog stood
still without prompting. *A veteran*, I thought. She could be tricky, like
Andy, Hank DeBruin's dog of long ago. By way of introduction, I
patted her on the head. She leaned into me affectionately. I breathed
a sigh of relief; she'd be cooperative, after all. After a short examination, Gretchen and I agreed that there was tension in her right carpus, or wrist. The tension could be from overexertion, or it could be
from an actual injury, such as a strain or sprain.

Carpal injuries are a common problem in racing dogs. It's not
at all unusual to see them at this stage in the race. Dogs with *more*
pre-race conditioning actually tend to sustain carpal injuries at a
higher rate than dogs who did not train as hard; it signifies that
the joint has been overused. Interestingly enough, though, as a
dog's age and experience increase, the likelihood of orthopedic
injuries decreases. I know from my work in Washington, DC, that
canine athletes over four years old are less prone to injury. Sled
dogs generally begin conditioning and training around the age of
seven to nine months, and are considered experienced veterans
at about three to four years. Over time, dogs learn to adjust to
difficult obstacles and trail conditions, and such skill acquisition
and increase in expertise with experience could be why we see
decreased injury for more practiced, older dogs.

Who doesn't love a good massage?

Carpal injuries tend to be easier to pinpoint and manage than shoulder injuries. With minor carpal overexertion, many dogs will simply rest out of them. If the injured dog's team is taking a longer break, they may not even have to be dropped from the race, though, as always, we err on the side of caution. Sometimes just a short nap is all it takes for the dog to become sound. Invariably, mushers will massage the sore area with a substance affectionately known as "Pink Goo" (or "Pink Goop"). There must be an official name for the stuff, but in truth, everyone, including the veterinarians, refers to it as Pink Goo. It's a concoction comprising all kinds of oils and salves, from Thuja-Zinc Oxide to mineral oil, that—you guessed it!—takes its name from the hot-pink color of the medicine. Mushers swear by it, and a trail veterinarian would be deemed an "irredeemable quack" if they didn't have a tube or three on their person at all times.

Mushers will often spend *hours* hunched over their patients, rubbing this malodorous, sticky glob on sprains, strains, and muscle aches. Whether it's the actual pharmacologic properties of the goo or the constant massaging that does the most good, the injuries do seem to respond to the treatment. Sometimes, a thick bandage will be placed over a generous application of goo to act as a "sweat bandage," similar to those used in equestrian sports.

Both Gretchen and I thought the wheel dog's injury would resolve itself given time, so we continued down the gangline, checking the other dogs on the team. Without exception, the rest of the huskies were in good condition and, evidently, looking forward to a hot meal and some shut-eye. They curled up into balls as soon as we finished our exams.

We were just wrapping up when the musher returned with the dogs' meals. We informed him that the only problem we'd seen was the one case of mild lameness. He told us that he'd be taking one of his two mandatory rest stops here, so we agreed to reexamine the dog later, knowing that we'd have plenty of time—up to eight hours—to evaluate her progress. Meanwhile, another team had arrived, and was ready for inspection. Just as we turned to leave, the musher asked, "You wouldn't happen to have some Pink Goo on you, would you?"

The last time I saw our patient, she wore a blissful smile. The musher was gently massaging her paw with Pink Goo. Her dinner had just been delivered, and the sun shone warmly on her black-and-white fur coat. As far as she was concerned, she was fine.

AT THREE YEARS OLD, the dog Gretchen and I treated at Takotna was a veteran. "Puppies" is a term used for sled dogs that are between one and two years old. The dogs are technically adults—which is to say, they've stopped growing—but it's none-theless a good descriptor for a team of novice racers. Iditarod puppies, like all puppies, are disorganized, undisciplined, and chiefly concerned with having fun. But experienced mushers will often include a few puppies on their teams so that they can learn from the more experienced dogs. This, as I've mentioned, also substantially reduces the risk of injury. One (particularly popular) strategy that mushers employ involves running younger dogs for only part of the race, then dropping them at a predetermined checkpoint.

At Takotna, the veterinarians were given advance notice that one of the arriving teams consisted almost *entirely* of puppies. It was comical to see the "Puppy Team," as it came to be called. Most dogs will cross the checkpoint line and wait while their driver signs in. They'll stay in their assigned position, sometimes standing, sometimes sitting. When the Puppy Team stopped in Takotna, the lead dogs ran to the middle of the team, yipping, rolling, and wrestling each other, until not even the musher was sure who was who. Evidently, for the puppies, every stop—for food or water breaks, or even crossing a small stream—was an opportunity to meet in the middle and play, which inevitably created a knot of dogs, leads, and tuglines. It was a giant, fuzzy puzzle, one that the musher was having great difficulty untangling. The lead dogs were eventually separated and placed at their position at the front. This left the unsupervised sled dogs mingling with the other dogs, creating yet another tangle. It looked more like a recess for a bunch of kindergarteners than the midway point of a grueling endurance event.

Forget everything I ever said about sled dogs being relatively easy to examine. This batch was squirmy and all but impossible to hold still. Kneeling down to examine one dog meant another four dogs trying to climb on you to see what's going on. One of the puppies found that the sleeve of my parka made a great tug toy, and that I wasn't a natural at standing on snow and ice. She made a game out of periodically grabbing my cuff and pulling me over. Another puppy had fun jumping between me and the dog I was checking, muzzle in my face, blocking my view. The noise they made by themselves more than compensated for the endless quiet of a calm day in the Alaskan wilds. Finally, defeated and exhausted by this one team, I laid down, spread-eagle on my back, on the ice. This was way too much fun to resist: the puppies made the most of my resignation by gleefully leaping over me, licking my face, and I imagine, laughing all the time.

Boisterous and unseasoned as they were, the Puppy Team was totally fine. Happily, I left them to their own devices, and later watched as they galloped away, into the sunset.

CHAPTER 15

CRIPPLE

B Y THE TIME THE RACE REACHES TAKOTNA, IT'S RUNNING IN territory with hardly any human settlement. The next checkpoint, Ophir, is twenty-three miles to the northwest. Ophir is another ghost town that had thrived during the gold rush; in fact, its name is derived from the Old Testament, where "Ophir" was the mysterious source of King Solomon's gold. Today, Ophir, Alaska, is an unincorporated area, with an official population of zero.

The Iditarod takes slightly different courses on alternate years. After Ophir, there's a fork: a northern route to Nome through Cripple, Ruby, Galena, and Nulato; and a southern route via Iditarod, Shageluk, Anvik, Grayling, and Eagle Island. This was decided for seemingly contradictory reasons. Representatives from several villages not on the original course—this being the northern route through Cripple, Ruby, Galena, and Nulato—expressed a desire to be included in the race. Yet hosting the race places such a concentrated strain on resources that smaller settlements simply can't bear the burden of hosting the race each year. The Iditarod Committee thus conceived of a plan to alternate the routes on different years. Race organizers, however, do occasionally switch routes due to trail conditions, usually because not enough snow has fallen on the southern route.

This may become increasingly common as the climate continues to change. Since records have been kept, there have been warmer and cooler years in Alaska, and always some variation in annual snowfall totals and the thickness of ice in Norton Sound. Since 1980, though, there's been a distinct trend towards warmer weather, and that's accelerated even since I first volunteered. Spring in Alaska now falls two weeks earlier, and is a few degrees warmer relative to average temperatures in the 1990s. In March, when the Iditarod is run, there can be heavy rainfall that turns ice fields into slush or even floodplains. The real problem, though, is that winters in Alaska are much warmer than they once were— seven degrees Fahrenheit over averages in the '90s. Things don't freeze as solidly, and less snow falls. This means that when winter ends, the trail isn't as hard-packed or solid as it needs to be for racing. Conditions along the trail have become more unpredictable. Certain rivers are no longer frozen; vegetation and debris from summer wildfires have created new obstacles. Areas that were permafrost are now mud. Race organizers have responded by rerouting the race—and even shipping in snow for the Ceremonial Start.

The Iditarod may soon be in trouble. In July 2019, temperatures in Anchorage reached ninety degrees Fahrenheit. If and when that becomes a normal summer in Alaska, there will be profound changes to almost every aspect of life in the state. For now, the race can still be run. Volunteers can monitor the trail and set up diversions where there are patchy hazards like wet or exposed ground. In time, the northern route will likely become the only route. Until then, the two routes will coexist, converging at Kaltag, forty-two miles from Nulato, sixty miles from Eagle Island.

I've almost always been posted to checkpoints on the northern route. On this route, the checkpoint after Ophir, Cripple, is located in a wide valley, a bleak, barren plain where snow is swept into frozen waves by near-constant wind from the mountains. It's not the most visually dramatic location on the course, but it's not entirely flat and featureless. The area is surrounded by hillocks and spruce forests; a mossy arctic tundra grass grows in small, scattered patches. Like islands in an ocean, the grass, with its brownish-purple hue, stands out in the sea of white. During the summer, the entire area transforms into a swampy wetland that, while pristine and beautiful in the way that bogs are, also prohibits travel. The ground here is still permafrost, so even on the warmest summer days—which rarely exceed sixty-five degrees—frozen ground lingers a few feet below the mud. When the marsh freezes again in winter, a plate-glass ice sheet forms, extending for miles and miles.

Cripple barely registers on the maps. If you look closely, you might see a kink in the road near Caribou Creek. That kink represents Cripple. It's even more lonely in person. After being dropped off by the Iditarod Air Force, I trudged up the trail to the veterinarians' cabin. The snow was deep and covered with crust, making it punchy and treacherous. With each step, I sunk up to my calves in soft, wet snow. Walking quickly became tedious; in the distance, I spotted the Cripple checkpoint line, marked only by an arch consisting of two gray, weathered timbers connected by an equally beaten crossbeam. Appropriately enough, the arch was set several yards from the buildings behind it, making the gateway appear all the more forlorn. There are a handful of permanent structures, all set around the former Innoko River Lodge. This is owned by Ed Gurtler, who runs a guide service for anglers and hunters. The Cripple checkpoint came about through the efforts of Ed, plus the husband-and-wife duo of Leslie and Jules Mead. Until Jules's passing in 2017, the Meads operated a small general store in nearby Wasilla, Alaska. Years ago, they offered their cabin and surrounding property in Cripple to the Iditarod Committee for use during the race. The race organizers readily accepted their offer and eventually bought the cabin. Built at the turn of the twentieth century, the lodge comprises two rooms, each heated by a single wood-burning stove. At one point in time, the checkpoint consisted of only this, but the area has now grown to include three additional log-hewn cabins, adding not-insignificant creature comforts to the spot.

I'd be staying in "the Bungalow," a cabin which was, essentially, an empty dorm. There was a nice heater in one of the corners, and bunks lined the wall, but otherwise, nothing. Still, I'd spent the last week in an unheated tent, so this was a significant upgrade. I found a nice place to settle in—an upper bunk with a small lookout facing south—and placed my pack items, including my book, on a plank conveniently laid across the ceiling beams. That year, I was deep into Hampton Sides's excellent *In the Kingdom of Ice*, a history of the polar voyage of the USS *Jeannette*. It felt like an appropriate choice; already, I was looking forward to climbing into my sleeping bag to read it by the light of my headlamp. Before I could settle down, though, I wanted to explore more of Cripple. I wandered toward the cabin where the meals would be prepared. The smell of coffee permeated, and people chatted across split-cedar tables. The walls, I noticed, were adorned with taxidermy, fish and game that looked like they'd hung there since before I was born. There were signed photographs of Iditarod heroes and their dogs, too. Between the cabins there's a dilapidated outhouse. Someone, at some point, had pinned a full-size cardboard hula dancer on the inside of the latrine door—to make it more festive, I suppose. I snapped a few photos for the road, resolving that, maybe, there wasn't too much to explore here, after all.

❋ ❋ ❋ *CRIPPLE, AK. 550 miles to Nome. Morning. –10°F. Mostly cloudy.*

THE NEXT DAY I awoke to a blinding sun that shimmered all over the plain. It had snowed while I slept, and a glaze of white powder still clung to the branches of the birch trees. I threw on my clothes and hurried to the mess cabin to grab some coffee. Sitting there, on the porch, was a haggard-looking fellow, a little older than myself, and judging from all the patches on his parka, a veterinarian. At least, that was my first impression of Dr. George

Stroberg. In short order, he would become one of my closest friends on the trail. The first time I met him, George had a full head of white hair and wore a small beard; he had a weathered, good-natured face, and warmly stood up to introduce himself. He explained that he had just flown into Anchorage from his previous posting when he was dispatched to Cripple, with no time to change his clothes, let alone shower. As we made our way inside, George told me that he had worked at Cripple several times in the past. In fact, this being his twenty-somethingth Iditarod, he had worked just about every checkpoint.

The other veterinarians filtered in, and we began to divvy up assignments. George was enthusiastically appointed our leader. It was apparent that he had become accustomed to being "Chief Vet," and so would be here as well. But George isn't cantankerous or overly commandeering. He's exactly the kind of person you want to take charge. When participation in an event is voluntary, decisions are made on a communal basis. This can quickly become a problem; since we hardly know each other, we all go out of our way to be diplomatic, even deferential. In general, I've found that teams work best when they appoint one person as the "boss," provided that the boss is a strong leader who can cut through clutter to make *and* articulate clear and concise decisions. George can do this as well as anyone. Back in his home state of Colorado, he oversees a multi-doctor practice. He's been a trail vet on dozens of courses, including the Yukon Quest, which can be as taxing on the volunteers as it is on the competitors, given that much of race is through the Alaskan wilderness. Critically, then, George had not only the knowledge but the experience to lead.

George instructed us to park the teams atop a nearby bluff. The dropped-dog line would be strung there as well; if the bluff became overfull, we were told to take the other teams down the hill to a small plain. We decided that with five vets we could split into two teams, working four-hour shifts. For me, this was ideal: I can usually do about four hours of intense labor before I need a breather. There would be no time for eight-hour rests, but there would be no eight-hour shifts, either. We were at a point in the race—perhaps the last point—when the vast majority of the teams arrive within a day. We agreed to work these shifts until the bulk of the field passed through, at which point we would convert to longer shifts (with more downtime built in) as the rearguard trickled in. It was universally agreed that we would all catch up on sleep at Anchorage. As if.

We split up, with George and two other vets, Richard and Mark, taking the first shift, from 6 to 10 p.m. I paired with Ronald Hallstrom, the vet I'd worked with at Rohn and McGrath. Our shift would be from 10 p.m. to 2 a.m. Since the first competitors weren't expected to arrive for several hours, and I wasn't on the first shift, I elected to take a hike on the snowy plain. I walked toward the only defining feature that I could see, which was what appeared to be a pile of wood. As I approached, the pile began to take shape, and finally, I realized what I was looking at. Back at the lodge, I'd read a brochure by the Iditarod Historic Trail Alliance that contained a reprint of a 1912 article describing how Colonel Walter Goodwin, head of the Alaska Road Commission Expedition, created simple structures to mark treeless sections of the trail in a way that couldn't be buried or toppled. These structures consisted of three planks of dark timber: two eight-foot-long boards, propped in a V-shape, and a third, eleven-foot-long board lashed to the other two, creating a kind of tripod.

Colonel Goodwin called these "tri-posts." These structures—possibly even some of the original tri-posts—are still in use today. Through the valiant efforts of public land managers and volunteer groups, they're repaired and refitted each year. So important are they to the history and legend of the Iditarod Trail that a silhouette of a tri-post graces the official badge of the Iditarod Historic Trail Association.

Tri-posts have saved countless lives. Even on large swaths of

Simple structures consisting of three planks of timber, tri-posts have saved countless lives in the tundra.

tundra, they can be seen for distances of ten or more miles; they're even visible to bush pilots at 1,200 feet. Because of their shape and size, they're almost never fully buried, even in the worst of whiteout conditions. Just the sight of a tri-post can be an enormous boon, offering reassurance that you're on the right path, that you haven't hopelessly wandered into the wilderness. Many of the older mushers that I've met have told me of the extreme relief they felt when, after losing the trail, they regained sight of a tri-post. One modern musher, who was lost on the snow plains of Cripple in a blizzard, told me that she'd only found her way when her lead dog sniffed out such a marker to pee on it.

❄ ❄ ❄ ❄

I WASN'T THERE WHEN the race leader arrived; in fact, I was fast asleep in my bunk. Dallas Seavey had told me about some sleep apps he used to rest "in the noisiest of places." I'd downloaded a few of these myself in the hope of drowning out the

Examining dogs often involves long hours crouching in snow.

sound of other people sleeping. (Nobody, I've learned, snores louder than veterinarians.) By the end of the first shift, there were perhaps a dozen teams in the parking area. All the dogs had been fed, inspected by the vets, and bedded down. A couple dogs with lameness issues had been dropped, but otherwise, all was well. Work had been steady but not overwhelming.

Naturally, the situation changed as soon as I was on duty. Even before Ronald and I had finished setting up, teams began to arrive in quick succession, one after the other. No sooner had one set of dogs been parked than another arrived at the entry point. All day, the sun had been shining on the powder-fresh snow, melting it into a deep, sloppy, Slurpee-like mixture. Now, it was night, and the temperature was falling, the bottom layer of slush hardening into ice, with new, wet snow accumulating on top of it. The wet snow clung to everything it touched; every time my boot lifted from the ground, it carried in tow a few extra pounds of snow. It was a slow, treacherous slog from one team to another. The decision to string the dropped-dog line on top of the bluff proved to be a mistake. Transporting dogs up and down the embankment became more and more grueling as the snow grew deeper and icier. Soon, my legs were sore and burning from the strain.

The mushers, even the dogs, became a blur. I usually enjoy playing with the dogs a little before I give them an exam. (This helps calm them down.) But now, my whole world existed in just the spotlight of my headlamp. Every physical was muscle memory and rote action. Eyes, paws, heart and lungs, gum color. Next dog. Fish out the Vet Book. Scribble my notes. Trudge over to the next team. As the teams started piling in, more and more dogs had to be dropped. Two mushers came in with dogs in the sled basket; luckily, these were both non-life-threatening injuries. I looked to my partner, Ron, remembering from Rohn that he tended to operate slower than I do. *If I was struggling*, I thought, *he must be underwater.* I was right. Try as he might, Ron couldn't catch up. It wasn't his fault. Each time Ron carried a husky to the dropped-dog line—a Herculean task by night's end—he was pulled aside on the descent by a musher who thought he was free. More than once during our shift, I whipped around to look for him. Each time, I'd find him standing by the bluff, swamped by mushers mobbing him with pertinent and trivial questions alike: Where's the food drop? How's the trail ahead? Can you check my dog's sore? One time, I watched as Ron was stopped while literally holding a dog, plodding up the hill.

When Ron finally caught up with me, he looked pale and out of breath. He started to apologize for leaving me with the lion's share of the checkups, but I stopped him.

"You've been a star, Ron," I told him. His eyes softened. "The exams will get done. The dropped dogs will be taken care of." I didn't know if I was speaking to Ron or to myself.

By the grace of God, we didn't have any true emergencies that night, but there were plenty of first-aid issues: dogs with scraped or torn paw pads; dogs with bits of ice forming on their fur that needed to be knocked off; two or three minor lacerations. Ron and I conferred in hushed whispers about waking one of the other veterinarians, but ultimately decided against it. There was an unspoken credo among the volunteers that you do your work and do it without complaining. Back in a warm lecture room in Anchorage, we had been warned that this event would be physically challenging, that it would push us to and beyond our limits. Experience is the ultimate teacher, and nights like this simply had to be endured. There had been patches at earlier checkpoints where I'd been rushed off my feet, or two or three things had happened at once, but this was the first time that I'd felt truly overwhelmed by the task at hand. Ron and I found ourselves admitting this to each other. Still, we agreed that we could handle it—that this, too, was manageable. The night may not have unfolded as we hoped, but things were getting done. Most importantly, every dog was getting a thorough physical exam, and every dropped dog was getting the primary medical treatment he or she needed.

The minutes crept ever so slowly toward the 2 a.m. mark. In the distance, Ron and I began to see the glowing lamps of incoming mushers. A whole new cluster of teams would be arriving soon. As soon as this thought crossed my mind, though, I looked up to see George leading his troops, Richard and Mike, toward us, coming to our rescue a full ten minutes early. The mere sight of them brought a sense of relief. I must have looked how I felt, because the first thing George said to me was, "Get some sleep." Not yet ready to relinquish our duties, Ronald and I gave a quick report on the status of the dropped dogs. A few yards away, Richard and Mike had begun work on the new arrivals. George waited for us to finish, then nodded, patted me on the shoulder, and said, "See you in four."

PART IV

ALMOST THERE

CHAPTER 16

ZIRKLE AND KING

B Y THE TIME THE RACE REACHES RUBY, ON THE NORTHERN
route, the teams are spread out, and there's no need for more
than a couple of vets at each checkpoint. Most years, once
the teams clear Cripple—112 miles south of Ruby—and the checkpoint is dismantled, that's the end of the Iditarod for me. After
Cripple, I hopscotch my way back to Anchorage, first on bush
planes, then a commercial airliner from McGrath, and finally a taxi
back to the Millennium Hotel. My flight back to Washington, DC,
is always the day after I arrive in Anchorage. With my responsibilities for the race finished, I usually relax by the fireplace, catching
up on my reading and reflecting on the past couple of weeks.

2016 was different.

Early on the morning of Sunday, March 13, 2016, I wandered
down to the communications room at the Millennium, juggling
a hot coffee and book in one hand while balancing my notes in
the other. The staff are always there, sitting around computer
monitors, providing race updates, and printing items of interest (pinning them, it seems, to every visible surface). I like to
browse the news and human-interest stories. By then, I'd met
most of the mushers, and I'd become invested in their progress.
Most of what I read were notes about position changes, or lists
denoting who had already taken their twenty-four-hour layover,
but there were also interviews with volunteers, pieces by local
journalists, often with color photos that I like to scan—or, more

appropriately, squint at—for familiar faces. Today, however, one posting caught my eye. It was a terse fax, taped to the wall, and apparently, it'd caught the eye of several other volunteers, too. The room was crowded with people staring at the fax. The headline read:

MUSHERS HIT BY SNOW MACHINE; ONE DOG KILLED, SEVERAL OTHERS HURT

There was an article pinned underneath. It reported that a snowmachiner* had hit both Aliy Zirkle and Jeff King. Shockingly, according to both mushers, it hadn't been an accident, but a determined attack. The driver had aimed his machine at them, repeatedly crashed into their sleds and teams, then turned around for renewed attacks. This was extremely confusing—not to mention upsetting—news. With nothing to go on but that report, we had so many questions. The article said that the driver had targeted the dogs. Who would want to hurt the dogs? Could this be a response to being bitten? It seemed unlikely, as the huskies are trained and used to being among people. Their temperaments are those of well-trained support dogs. Was it someone who was opposed to the Iditarod? It's common knowledge that some animal rights activists oppose the race, and have had run-ins with the organizers, but there was no way that they'd try to make their case by killing dogs. That made no sense. Might it have been a local who objected to the race? Maybe, though the Iditarod is the biggest sporting event in Alaska, and the communities along the route all benefit from increased revenue during the race due to tourism. Were the competitors targeted personally? Both "Zirkle" and "King" were big names in the world of sledding. Aliy Zirkle had been the first woman to win the Yukon Quest; Jeff, meanwhile, had won the Iditarod four times between 1993 and 2006.

---

* This is local vernacular for a snowmobile.

Slowly, specifics of the event percolated into the room. An unknown attacker had smashed his snowmobile into the side of Aliy's sled about five miles from Koyukuk on the Yukon River. As reported, he had then turned around and charged her, not once, but several times. After the initial attack, the snow machine vanished. Aliy righted her sled, checked on her dogs, and set off again, shaken, but still able to tell herself that it hadn't been, couldn't possibly be, deliberate. Fifteen minutes later, the snow machine returned and renewed its assault. After several passes and collisions, the machine turned toward Aliy for what she thought would be the final blow. After revving the machine for several minutes, the attacker wheeled it around and finally disappeared for good. Incredibly, Aliy was uninjured. Only one of her dogs had sustained an injury, and a minor one at that. That there were no fatalities is a small miracle; at top speed, a snowmobile on open ice can move about as fast as a car on a paved road.

Aliy reached Nulato in tears, clearly in shock. She told volunteers waiting to receive her that she had never been so scared in her life. This, may I remind you, is someone who has faced the hazards of a dozen Iditarods and countless wilderness endurance races; she's braver than just about any of us.

"Someone tried to kill me with a snow machine," she breathlessly told race judge Karen Ramstead. There was no better person for this moment than Karen. A former Iditarod competitor, Karen had herself had several life-threatening encounters, although nothing as personal as Aliy's. At about five-and-a-half-feet tall, and with a grandmotherly appearance, Karen is one of the most universally beloved figures on the trail, in no small part because she's stood where the competitors stand, and understands innately what they're going through. Once, Karen told me the story of how she and her team had survived a moose attack.

If you've never seen a moose in the flesh, the idea of a "moose attack" may sound preposterous, even comical. Make no mistake, though, moose are huge beasts. A full-grown bull has an average shoulder height of about six feet, and at 1,400 pounds is heavier than a buffalo or bison. They're capable of charging at about thirty-five miles per hour, and have the endurance to swim in a freezing river for at least a few hours. Resources are scarce in the snowfields, and moose are aggressively protective of patches of vegetation and sources of drinking water. Being charged by a moose is like being rammed by a small car—or snowmobile. They represent a serious threat during the Iditarod, and mushers sometimes carry guns specifically to protect against moose.

When Karen rounded a bend on the Iditarod Trail and saw a moose standing in her path, she did exactly what you're supposed to do. She stopped her sled to signal to the bull that her sixteen dogs were not there to start a fight. The moose decided to attack anyway, charging straight for the dogs. Karen brought a double-barreled shotgun to bear on the moose and fired a shot over its head. When the animal kept charging, she was forced to shoot to kill. As she later explained, she didn't want to kill the moose at all, but if it came down to a choice between her dogs and the moose, she'd protect her team, always.

"I am sure they would do the same for me," she added.

Karen knew all the competitors by name. She greeted them all and inquired about trail conditions and their huskies—and, most importantly, asked the mushers how they themselves were doing. When news reached us at the Millennium that Karen was with Aliy, there was a collective sigh of relief. Karen would be able to talk to her, to calm her down. She was someone that Aliy could trust in a moment when she really, *really* needed someone to trust.

Jeff King's team was not as fortunate. He was attacked close to where Aliy's second attack had occurred, out on the Yukon. In his telling, a snowmobile traveling at about eighty miles an hour sideswiped his sled, hard enough to tear off a piece of the machine's fender. The impact instantly killed one of the team's two lead dogs, Nash, and severely injured two other dogs. One of the dogs, Crosby, had clearly sustained serious injuries. At first, Jeff thought the other dog, Banjo, had been killed in the impact; the dog remained unconscious until after Jeff arrived in Nulato. Unlike Aliy's encounter, the attacker did not return for a second assault. Still, Jeff had no doubt that the incident was intentional. He told a reporter that the snowmobile driver had to have seen him. He had all his lights on, and both the sled and the dogs were outfitted with reflectors. The trail at that point was forty feet wide, well-marked, and following the Yukon at a point where it's a mile wide. He had loaded Nash's body and the other two injured dogs into the sled. As he'd checked the rest of his team, he found the piece of the snow machine's fender and brought it with him to the Nulato checkpoint. It was the evidence that would ultimately connect the perpetrator to the crime.

The next morning, twenty-six-year-old Arnold Demoski, a Nulato resident and natural resource coordinator for the Nulato Tribal Council, turned himself into the police. An officer from the Alaska State Troopers was flown in from Galena to take him into custody. The police immediately incarcerated Demoski, charging him with second-degree assault and reckless endangerment, as well as half a dozen other offences. On April 29, 2016, the *Anchorage Daily News* reported that Demoski admitted to drinking heavily that night, though he claimed he didn't remember anything. He stated that he had heard the news like everyone else in his village. Wondering who could do such a thing, Demoski had opened his garage door, and saw his damaged snowmobile. Allegedly, it was only after he saw the missing section on his own machine that he put two and two together, then turned himself in. His explanation failed to satisfy almost anyone involved with the race.

Questions swirled. The biggest, of course, was "Why?" Why did he repeatedly ram Aliy's team? Aliy Zirkle is one of the most well-known, well-loved Iditarod competitors. Fame hasn't tainted her personality in the slightest. She's invariably kind, and known to be friendly with anyone. After Demoski charged Aliy, why did he go after Jeff King's team? In his confession, Demoski said that Jeff was one of his favorite mushers. The only explanation that he could offer was that he had blacked out. Modifying his initial statement, Demoski suggested that the adrenaline of the collisions had jolted him out of his stupor. After the assault on Jeff's team, he claimed to have stopped and turned around to make sure everyone was fine, but didn't stay for fear of being pegged for drinking and driving. Initially, Demoski was cooperative with authorities, but he quickly ceased to speak on the attack, only pleading with his community to forgive him.

After the incident, Nulato residents gathered in the village gymnasium to hold a fundraiser for the mushers and their injured dogs. Residents brought piles of food: giant bowls of pasta, sandwiches, a huge pot of moose stew. Desserts like brownies, pies, and muffins were crammed onto collapsible tables. Both Jeff and Aliy made an appearance. People lined up to share their condolences. Many were in tears. Jeff was extraordinarily gracious, more than I imagine I'd be in his situation. The snowmobile could have easily killed him. When he told newspaper reporters, "Six inches over and I would be dead," he wasn't exaggerating. One of the dogs who was hit, Banjo, was a wheel dog—in other words, one of the pair closest to the sled, and to Jeff. He made it clear that he didn't hold the village accountable for the errant actions of one of its citizens, but said that he felt sorry for the town "and for the person involved, because it obviously sheds light on social problems, not shared by the whole village, but unfortunately the weight is carried by the whole village."

Back at the Millennium Hotel, hundreds of miles away, the whole ordeal sounded unreal. I hadn't attended to a seriously injured dog at any point, in any Iditarod, and now there was one dead, and two others needing immediate transport to a tertiary facility in Anchorage. Dr. Kim McCreedy was responsible for receiving the injured dogs. A dropped-dog vet, she was extremely experienced with critical-care medicine—the right person, in other words, to have when the injured animals arrived. I asked her if I could help, and she agreed to let me accompany her to collect the dogs. She was calm, focused. She probably didn't need my help. But I needed to help.

Later that afternoon, a chartered plane would arrive in Anchorage with Jeff's injured dogs. It had already been determined that Crosby had a probable broken radius and ulna. The veterinary staff had placed him in a splint, but it was clear that orthopedic surgery would be needed. We arranged with a local veterinary orthopedic surgery specialist to have Crosby brought straight from the airport to his clinic, where he would take over his care. Banjo, the dog who'd been knocked unconscious, also needed critical care. I joined Kim as she went to meet the plane. We were accompanied by her vet tech, Caylee, who had been working with Kim at the Hiland Mountain Correctional Center.

As soon as the plane touched down, Caylee extracted Banjo and placed him in the van. All things considered, Banjo looked alright. He had only superficial scrapes and bruises, and he seemed to be walking normally, with no neurological impairment. As with any human patient who's been knocked out in an accident, though, we'd need to conduct all sorts of scans to rule out a brain injury. He would need to be monitored for a long time, but Banjo would recover. Crosby was a different story. When Caylee emerged from the plane cradling Crosby, my eyes began to burn. The husky had a thick splint on his right forearm, extending from his foot to his elbow.* Crosby was clearly uncomfortable, though the vets had given him morphine. His head hung low, resting on Caylee, who was trying not to cry. We decided against placing him in a transport cage. It would be too difficult, we thought, to try to maneuver him into one with his split. Instead, I just held on to him in the back of the transport van. Crosby curled up and placed his snout

---

* With a fracture, it's important to immobilize a joint above and below the break to keep it from shifting and causing yet more damage.

on my leg. He didn't try to make eye contact. Both Caylee and I were crying now.

Kim gripped the wheel, wearing a grim expression. We hit every red light, fell behind every snowplow. With each pothole I winced, terrified that the jolt would further injure Crosby. When we finally arrived at the emergency clinic, the staff met us at the door. We took Crosby back to the exam room. Radiographs were made of his arm, and treatment began. Eventually, a plate would be surgically placed to internally stabilize the fracture and allow the bone to knit together. Crosby would live, but he would never race again. He seemed to understand that. As I packed up my things, I turned to see him staring blankly at the wall, wondering, I'm sure, why anyone would wish him so much harm.

CHAPTER 17

UNALAKLEET

A FTER RUBY, GALENA, AND NULATO, THE NORTHERN AND southern routes converge at Kaltag. From Kaltag, the trail leaves the Yukon River behind and continues overland across a mountain and mountain pass called "Old Woman" and "Old Woman Pass." There's a cabin there, not an official checkpoint, but one where many mushers elect to rest. Old Woman Pass marks the point on the course where the terrain transitions from a relatively sheltered, inland section of frozen marsh dotted with ghost towns—like Ophir and Iditarod—to the exposed coastline of the Norton Sound. Teams travel through rolling hillocks that get smaller and smaller until they reach Norton Sound, a 150-mile-long inlet where the Yukon River empties. The checkpoint is in Unalakleet, a town on the coast of the Sound with a population of less than 700. The final third of the race, after Unalakleet, runs along and over the Norton Sound. This is the most difficult sustained section of the race. It's not quite in the Arctic Circle, but it's much farther north than Anchorage, and a markedly different climate. The temperatures are always bitterly cold, and the wind is constant. Storms and blizzards can crop up with little to no warning.

To mark this new phase of the race, the first musher to reach Unalakleet is awarded a trophy and a "bag of gold" worth about $2,000. (The amount was upped, in 2023, to $3,000 worth of gold nuggets.) Rumor has it that some racers "go for the gold"—that

Two teams rest at Old Woman Pass.

is, they put in just enough effort to win the bag, then drop back and take it easy for the rest of the way. Winning the gold certainly comes with bragging rights, and it's true that the person who wins the gold isn't always the person who wins the race. But it doesn't make much sense from an economic standpoint to *just* go for the gold. The prize purse for the Iditarod is divided based on position, with the fastest teams—everyone in the first half of the field, which typically includes the team that reaches Unalakleet first—receiving something. Each place dropped in the top ten can cost a musher about $10,000.

Unalakleet is one of the older settlements in the region. The name comes from the Inupiat word *ungalaklik*, meaning "the southern side"—specifically, the southern side of the Norton Sound. The town is on a small peninsula close to the conjunction of the Unalakleet River and the Kouwegok Slough. It was at Unalakleet that the Athabascan Tribe, which historically inhabited the interior, first met the Inupiat, who lived along the coast.

It was established as a place of trade between the groups at least two thousand years ago, and shortly thereafter attracted Yupik-speaking peoples from the more southerly coasts of Alaska. When the Russian-American Company was chartered by Tsar Paul I in 1799, it built a permanent trading post at Unalakleet. During the early and mid-nineteenth century, fur traders from Russia used the port. As well as copper cooking ware and tea, the Russians also brought sickness. A smallpox epidemic that raged throughout the late 1830s killed at least a quarter of the Alaskan population, including almost everyone in Unalakleet.

Before the building of the airport in the late 1940s, citizens of Unalakleet relied on the annual visit of the cargo ship *North Star* for provisions. The ship, which originated in Seattle, dropped provisions off at several villages up and down the Alaskan coast. It typically made a stopover in Unalakleet sometime between June and September, then continued up to Point Barrow, where it turned around before the winter ice could freeze it in place. Now, the airport is the primary source of provisions for the populace, though supply ships still visit occasionally. Today, most of the inhabitants of Unalakleet are Inupiat, with a smaller mix of Yupik and Athabascans. Commercial fishing for herring is a major component of the local economy, as is king crab harvest. Many locals support themselves by subsistence fishing and hunting, with caribou, moose, and bearded seal being the favorite game.

Despite its long history, Unalakleet remains remote. There are no roads that go to or from the town, but a few airlines operate cargo flights and passenger service. When I first arrived, I was struck by how close together the homes are. The houses themselves, like those of many other towns in the wilder places of Alaska, are compact, mostly prefabricated frames with a main living room and kitchen, plus two or three bedrooms. They're heated by propane stoves, which carry with them serious risk of carbon monoxide poisoning. While I've always flown in via a commercial flight, one of the other veterinarians once snow-mobiled from Eagle Island to Unalakleet. Snowmobiles are about as fast on fresh snow as motorbikes are on tarmac, and this is a straight-line distance of forty-five miles; still, his trip took a full four hours. When he finally arrived, he told me that he felt like a desert traveler stumbling upon an oasis. Maybe that's the best description for the towns of the North. They're little pockets of heat, comfort, and other people.

❊ ❊ ❊ *UNALAKLEET, AK. 261 miles to Nome. Evening. 18°F. Light wind.*

I WAS FIRST ASSIGNED to Unalakleet during the 2017 race. I looked at the map, saw just how far north I would be heading, and assumed the worst, but by checkpoint standards, Unalakleet is about as good as it gets. Along with Anchorage and McGrath, the town is one of three major hubs for the Iditarod. There were permanent, heated structures to live in, so I didn't have to spend a whole day helping set up tents. The berths in the bunkhouse where we'd be staying were warm, and the rooms we'd be sleeping in were dark. There would be well-cooked food, hot showers, and indoor toilets.

I had just entered the checkpoint building when a volunteer announced that the first teams were on the isthmus, five miles away. They would be here, in other words, in less than an hour. By this point, several days into the race, the field is spread out to the point that teams would be passing through the checkpoint all week, arriving at any time of day or night. We'd be given an hour's advance notice of each arrival, so the veterinary staff agreed to adopt a "whoever's available" approach, rather than a shift sys-tem. Since I was freshly rested, I gathered my medical equipment and hurried down to the checkpoint finish line to take the first shift. The checkpoint building sits on a gentle, slippery slope

Watching the television crews set up on the best sledding hill in Unalakleet.

leading down to the frozen bog where the dogs would be arriving. I was navigating successfully down this slope when I hit a particularly smooth section of bare ice and, devoid of any pedal friction, landed butt-first on a snowbank. This amused the children of the village very much. I looked to my left and right. Flanking the slope were two large hills. I realized that by far the most efficient way to get from the checkpoint building to the actual checkpoint would be to "butt-slide" down. The children were way ahead of me; they had been tirelessly climbing, "sledding," and working their way back up the hills for hours. The best run, it seemed, was from the top of the hill to my right, down a steep gradient and then out onto smooth ice. Unfortunately for us, this was precisely where the television crews had set up their aerials and dishes. The technicians harangued the children for getting too close to their equipment, telling them how valuable it was and that they should find some other place to play. (In my mind, if you set up your broadcast antennae on the best sledding hill in town, you deserve whatever fate comes to you.) I shared the kids' fascination when one of the TV crews broke out a drone to capture aerial views of the race. We watched the drone lift off and flit out of sight, then hurried to the nearest monitors to see the live overhead images of the competitors.

The first team to arrive at Unalakleet in 2017 was Dallas Seavey's. In reaching Unalakleet first, Dallas earned his trophy, gold nuggets, and bragging rights. Remembering my experience with Dallas at Rohn, I hurriedly asked to examine his team before he was mobbed by reporters. His dogs had looked good coming into the chute, and as I worked my way down the gangline, my suspicions were confirmed: the Seavey dogs were in great shape. As before, they were happy, friendly huskies, and apparently well-accustomed to the hoopla surrounding their musher. This would be a memorable year for Dallas, though surely not in the way that he'd hoped. His team ultimately finished in second. His father, Mitch, beat him by a matter of hours. After the race, though, a few of Seavey's dogs tested positive for trace amounts of tramadol, a pain relief medication.

Human endurance sports—from baseball to bodybuilding, and from track and field to cycling—have had enormous problems with performance-enhancing drugs. I suppose it's natural, then, that when I tell people I'm an Iditarod vet, one of the most common questions involves doping in the world of sled dog racing. Certainly, there are substances that you can give to a dog to improve its performance. The Iditarod bans about twenty different substances. Anti-inflammatories and pain medications are both on the list because they can cover up the pain of an injury. That Dallas's dogs had tested positive for a pain-relief medication was a shock. After the news broke, I talked to many veterinarians. This was the first time that anyone could remember anything serious being found following a pee test. Most human sports that have problems with performance-enhancing drugs involve an arms race of sorts. Many professional athletes have justified their own use of steroids and other drugs because they know their rivals are doing the same. It was an open secret, a part of the culture in which even trainers and team medics were complicit. The Iditarod just isn't like that. Still, as a precaution, it has a "pee team," a group of technicians who take random urine samples from the dogs—and all the winners—to make absolutely sure that there's nothing in their system that shouldn't be there.

The mushers, as I've emphasized, would never want to mask any pain that their dogs have. The *last* thing they want is to run an injured dog that might give out on them between checkpoints. While sled dog teams have star performers, no musher is ever completely reliant on one dog. If a dog—any dog—is injured, the musher drops the animal from the race at the next checkpoint and carries on. Naturally, after Dallas's dogs tested positive, there was an investigation. Dallas vehemently defended his name. Even accounting for metabolic degradation, he argued, the samples taken from the dogs were of such low concentrations of the banned substance that there was no way it'd have any physiologic effect on the dogs, which was absolutely true. Besides, Dallas knew enough about sled dog racing to know that he'd gain no advantage using tramadol. The most compelling argument in favor of his innocence was that he was a veteran of the race, someone who had previously won and knew that all the top finishers have their dogs' pee tested after the race. Not once had any of his dogs "peed hot" before.

It's worth asking what any competitor stands to gain by using performance-enhancing drugs in the Iditarod. At heart, even for "big name" racers like Dallas Seavy, the Iditarod is a personal challenge, a matter of honor. There's a reason that it's called "The Last Great Race on Earth." Where's the honor in winning by cheating, especially if cheating harms your dogs? If there was a *real* financial incentive, that would be the obvious answer. The reality, though, is that endurance dogsledding is never going to be a spectator sport with lucrative TV rights—the kind of sport, like cycling or running, that millions of people do as a hobby. The top competitors get a few meager sponsorship deals, but nothing on the level of Carlsberg sponsoring Liverpool FC, or Gatorade sponsoring the NFL.*

The most important question, of course, is that of the character of the musher himself. As someone who had met Dallas many times before, I found it inconceivable that he would deliberately use a banned substance. To me, it seemed that someone either inadvertently gave Dallas a small dose of tramadol, or it was accidentally ingested by the dogs. I believed Dallas when he told the press that he didn't drug his dogs. There is a small possibility that his dogs had been sabotaged, that someone else had doped them. If he named names, he only ever did so in private, and I never heard of action being taken against anyone—and in December 2018, Dallas was absolved of all blame by the Iditarod Committee.

* Despite its fame and popularity, the Iditarod itself has only a few brand-name sponsors, including GCI, Ryan Air, and Alaskan Brewing Co., among others. It relies primarily on merchandise sales, contributions, and small business advertising for funding.

CHAPTER 18

LUCY'S CRIME

EVERY TIME THAT I'VE BEEN POSTED TO UNALAKLEET, THERE have been long gaps between the arriving teams. Unalakleet is a small town, and I took advantage of the opportunity to explore. The building I find most interesting is an old wooden schoolhouse that was once part of the Bureau of Indian Affairs Unalakleet School, a historic school complex. Originally constructed in 1933 as part of a major federal program to improve the education of Alaska's Native population, it served the community for forty-five years, until a new school was built just east of the airport. Unlike the other structures in town, this one is not hemmed in by other buildings. Built in the Georgian Revival fashion, it stands two and a half stories high, and has balloon framing and a gable roof with octagonal cupola. The boards are weathered; the front steps have been worn by years of student traffic; and the paint is peeling off the sides. It is forlornly beautiful.

Unalakleet has precisely one pizza joint, Peace on Earth, and it's a legendary, must-visit spot for Iditarod veterans. Peace on Earth has become the social center of the town, attracting more visitors than the official community center up the road. Here, people sit and chat with locals, and card games carry on all day. Only occasionally does someone order a pizza. Prices start at $36 for a plain cheese pie, but the food tastes so fresh that you forget every ingredient has to be flown in from elsewhere. An impressive glass case full of local artwork caught my eye. The prices, like those of the

218   ❄   Four Thousand Paws

pizzas, are high, but easily justified. The craftsmanship is exquisite. There are carvings in walrus ivory, whale bone, wood, and—because this is a prime area for finding fossils—mastodon teeth. The materials were collected following traditional practices, so it's legal to sell them. Many families, I came to learn, depended on the extra income. I purchased a few seal sculptures, hoping to decorate my clinic with them.

By the time I returned to the checkpoint, it was past midnight, but there were groups of children skating along the frozen sea ice. Up on the hill directly across from me was a group of kids learning to cross-country ski. The Iditarod, as it turned out, coincided with spring break, and the children were relishing the chance to stay up late.

"Hi! My name's Johnnie." The voice came out of nowhere. I was totally startled; I thought I had been alone, or at least at a safe distance from the schoolchildren. Johnnie extended his right arm for a handshake. Beneath the crux of his left shoulder was a clipboard. Twelve-year-old Johnnie Katchatag was, as he would soon tell me, the "Official Checker" for this overnight shift. A combination of youth and caffeine kept him sharp, even in the middle of the night. Johnnie clearly had everything under control. Throughout the night, I watched as he confidently marched up to volunteers and asked how many dogs were on the approaching team. When told "eleven," he'd jot the number down in its proper column, then order his crew to bring hot water and food for eleven huskies. Directly, without question or reply, a handful of eight-to-ten-year-olds would race up the icy slope to carry out his order. Johnnie and his team carried water and fresh straw down to the dogs, brought the mushers hot food, and did all the miscellaneous tasks that a large operation demands. Johnnie was proud to have been chosen as an Official Checker, and he was determined that all the things he could control went off without a hitch. If he saw a member of his crew goofing off or disturbing a sleeping dog, Johnnie promptly addressed the offending party and sent them back to work. When one of the kids wanted an autograph, it was Johnnie who would politely address the musher and ask if it was okay for the autograph-seeker to approach him or her. He was, unfailingly, well-mannered.

In the wee hours of the morning, when the next team wasn't due for a few hours, we all retired to the bunkhouse. Some of the parents were there, and the kids excitedly recounted their work with the dogs. Hugs were given all around. There was hot cocoa galore. The sugar high and excitement of the day wore off quickly, though, and within an hour of coming inside, all the children were asleep. All of them except Johnnie. He had forms to fill out. As I drifted off to sleep on the sofa, I saw him bent over, scribbling his notes by the light of a gooseneck table lamp.

✳ ✳ ✳ *UNALAKLEET, AK. 261 miles to Nome. Dawn. −2°F. Partly cloudy.*

The first exams of the morning.

The dawn in Unalakleet was cold and brilliant. As I made my way toward the veterinarian's station, I sipped my still-hot coffee, happily taking in my surroundings. By now, dense mountains have given way to coastal plain. Ensconced by land and water, the competitors rest at the true edge of Alaska.

The first team of huskies greeted me in unison as I kneeled to examine them. As often happens, I was the recipient of many wet dog kisses; long, pink tongues warmed my cheek. I'd met the musher before, and she honored me by remembering my name. After the initial cordialities—How was the trail? How were the dogs pulling? Was she keeping herself properly fed and hydrated? and so on—we got down to the matter at hand.

"Most of the team is pulling well," she said, "but I have one girl who seems a little lame. I think I'd like to drop her here."

I examined the team. She was right. Everyone was fine, all except one, cinnamon-colored Alaskan husky with alert, soul-searching blue eyes. I sat down next to her. Her fur was smooth and glossy. She was happy, and she expressed her pleasure by tilting her head toward me in that cute, heart-melting puppy way.

"She started limping right before we reached the checkpoint," the musher explained. Sure enough, her left carpus was tender. While not a serious injury, the prudent thing to do would be to drop the dog. Keeping her in the race might exacerbate the injury. The musher filled out the necessary form and handed her leash to me.

"Lucy," as I'll call her (to protect the name of the truly guilty), was now under my care. Unlike so many of the huskies I'd seen and treated, she didn't seem particularly upset by the prospect of being left behind. She trotted happily up the embankment with me. I secured her to the dropped-dog line, giving her extra room to roam since all the other dogs had already been taken to Anchorage. As far as I could tell, there didn't seem to be any opportunities for mischief. I was wrong—and Lucy's crime was of the most odious nature. At Unalakleet, as at every other checkpoint, mushers have at least one dedicated bag of food. The bags, as I've said, are labeled, flown in days in advance, and carefully stored. Finding Lucy's cache was easy; I opened the bag, went inside to fetch hot water, and mixed the water with the food, making her a nice, warm soup for dinner. She must have appreciated my culinary skills because the entire bowl was finished almost immediately. Content, she curled up and fell asleep on her fresh bed of straw. I went inside to retrieve some more coffee.

After an hour, I went out to check on my only remaining charge. I fully expected to find that she'd been fast asleep the whole time. What I saw instead puzzled me at first. Lucy was standing upright, her muzzle under the chain link fence. In the dim moonlight, all I could make out was that she was intent on reaching something outside of the designated dropped-dog zone. Still, she seemed fine. I returned to the bunkhouse to read for another half hour. Only when I returned did I notice the morsels of dry food scattered in the snow. The greatest concentration was at her feet.

"Lucy!" I yelped, realizing what had happened. When I hooked her up to the dropped-dog line, I had carefully checked to make sure the bags of dog food were well beyond her reach. But I'd underestimated her. Somehow, Lucy had reached under a gap in the fence and dragged another musher's bag of food toward her. She had then torn the bag open—no small feat, considering the bags are made of a braided nylon material—and spilled the contents into her enclosure, where she'd enjoyed a late-night snack. I rushed toward her and pulled the bag out of her reach. There was still some food left on the ground, and I tried my best to clean up the leftovers. It wasn't easy to work out how much she had ingested. If she had gulped down a lot of food quickly— which, based on the food remaining in the bag, I assumed she had—she could make herself sick. In dogs, as in people, eating too much too quickly can lead to gastrointestinal issues: vomiting, diarrhea, gas pains. More worrisome was the prospect of pancreatitis. During races, mushers feed their dogs high-energy food mixtures. Some foods are commercial; some are concocted by the mushers themselves. All of them are high in protein and fat. Racing dogs quickly burn the calories, and as such, are at low risk of pancreatitis. Needless to say, a dog sitting in the dropped-dog area who has gorged the better part of a whole team's rations isn't going to burn those calories.

Lucy hadn't vomited yet. Dogs developing any form of severe gastrointestinal distress will often feel intense pain in the belly, but during her physical exam, she didn't show any signs of distress when I palpated her belly. I examined her again and again. Physically, she seemed fine, almost contented. Most dog breeds would hang their head, but Lucy, as a husky, smiled that goofy husky smile, the kind they have when they've done something naughty, know that they've done something naughty, and are telling you that they don't care that they've done something naughty. I swear, Lucy knew that she had bested me, and she was proud. Satisfied—and no doubt experiencing postprandial drowsiness—she curled up again and fell asleep. I inspected the damage. The entire side of the bag had been ripped open. Each bag has the checkpoint and musher's name on it; in black felt-tip marker, the musher had written "UNK," standing for Unalakleet. I rotated the bag to see who it belonged to. Statistically, given the fact that most of the teams had already passed through the checkpoint, the odds were in my favor that this would be a bag of food left behind by someone, one that wouldn't be missed. My heart sank. Not only did the bag of food belong to one of the mushers yet to arrive, but he was due to arrive at dawn, when the sun would be up, and the crime scene would be obvious to all.

Lucy might not have eaten enough to make herself sick, but I was nauseous. I looked at Lucy, asleep on the straw. She rolled onto her back, comfortable and oh-so-content. I watched over her until daybreak came, bringing with it a fresh batch of well-rested volunteers. I went in to get my morning coffee, secure in the knowledge that Lucy would not pull any more shenanigans. By the time I came back, three or four people were hovering over the ripped open food bag. There were murmurs of who might be responsible for this crime. One theory held that the bag had ripped during transport. No, another countered, this was certainly the work of an animal, perhaps one of the village dogs. Many people owned dogs here, and sometimes they stayed outside. There were also some strays that survived by going through people's garbage and pilfering other dogs' food from their bowls. I had seen one of these very dogs myself, a mixed breed that had growled at me. No one put forth the theory that an absent-minded veterinarian placed a dropped dog too close to the food depot.

Meanwhile, the musher—*the* musher—arrived. I went down the sledding hill again for the hundredth time, and started my exam of his team. The dogs were in good condition. I didn't find anything on inspection that would warrant the musher having to drop any of the dogs. After my work was complete, I approached him to report my findings and countersign his Vet Book. On the edge of my toes, I asked him how his race was going. He appeared sleepy, much more so than the dogs.

"Yeah, a good race so far, except apparently a stray dog got into my food bags last night," he said. I nodded in support.

"Do you have enough to feed everyone?" I asked, a genuine concern.

"The stray dog only got into one bag," he said, adding, "We should be fine. Still, I wish they would keep better care of my stuff."

Again, I nodded, more piously this time. I stood for a moment, my conscience screaming, trying to confess. But I had important things to do, such as go back down the hill and pick up a piece of plastic that I'd seen blowing across the yard, so I silently sauntered away. The musher opened one of the other bags of food and began feeding his team. There were no further inquiries, which was good, because I'm sure Lucy would have dimed me out in a second.

❄   ❄   ❄   ❄

MOST OF THE RACERS who'd come into Unalakleet had already stopped, rested, and left, but a few were still trickling in. Out of the original six-person veterinarian team, only a veterinarian named Jennifer and I remained at the checkpoint; the rest had moved up the trail. Still feeling guilty, I volunteered to work the night shift. Jennifer, a rookie, went off to get some sleep, with promises that she'd be readily available in the event of an emergency. While Jennifer slept, I sat at one of the cafeteria tables, a fresh cup of coffee in hand. One of the villagers was still awake. We chatted to pass the time. He told me stories of his childhood in the Unalakleet area, fantastic tales about seal hunts with his grandfather when hunters still used a spear. Seals, he explained, are considered one of the most important animals for hunting. During the spring and fall, the seals migrate past Norton Sound, often surfacing near an ice fissure to bask in the sun, where they could be hunted. I'd seen several seals sunbathing during my stay in Unalakleet, though no one was hunting them.

With the winter months comes caribou hunting, which—as the villager told me—is considered a more "manly" sport. He was planning to leave for a three- or four-week caribou hunting trip in a few days. He still had the high-powered hunting rifle he'd been given for his tenth birthday, and planned to use it then. The ability to find and kill game is considered an important early life lesson in a region where subsistence living is still practiced. Extra money can be had by selling the furs. He was fifty or sixty now, but just as excited to get out in the field for a few weeks as he had been as a boy. We spoke late into the night. Secretly, I hoped I'd never have to leave. Eventually, though, duty called.

❋ ❋ ❋ ❋

THE MORNING SUNLIGHT REFRACTED and reflected off the snow with such a dazzling intensity that the volunteers had to wear sunglasses. Moderate gusts lifted a few loose snowflakes. Eighty miles southeast, though, a storm had just passed through, obliterating the southern trail between the checkpoints at Eagle Island and Kaltag. Most racers had reached Kaltag before the blizzard, but the back two had been caught in it.

The screen at the comms center showed two GPS position flags, numbers 59 and 44, the bib numbers of Steve Watkins and Tara Cicatello. They were near Eagle Island, far, far behind the pack. The only other person who hadn't reached Unalakleet—forty-five miles north of Eagle Island—was Marcelle Fressineau, the French musher, who was maybe five or six hours away from us. Magnus Kaltenborn had been here for many hours and was still puttering around. Everyone else had come and gone.

For hours, Steve and Tara remained fixed in place. We spent an anxious day trying to guess what, exactly, had happened. Had one

The trail between Unalakleet and Kaltag is dense with trees. At night, it's easy to make a wrong turn.

of them been injured? Had their sleds crashed into each other? *Had something happened to their dogs?* I wondered. They hadn't activated their emergency beacons. Maybe they were feverish—two veterinarians had come down with severe flu, and had been forced to leave the trail.

This was Tara's first year on the Iditarod, but she was an experienced musher. Steve, too, was an experienced musher, and an Iditarod veteran, not to mention all-around formidable athlete and survivalist. He'd first competed in the Iditarod in 2015. That same year, he attempted to climb Mount Everest. During his summit bid, a 7.8 magnitude earthquake struck Nepal, killing over 8,500 people across the country. Twenty-two people died on Everest in the ensuing avalanches, making it the deadliest day in that mountain's history. Ten members from Steve's own team perished. He was 19,200 feet up when the earthquake hit—and somehow still made it safely back to base camp.

While I was concerned about the two mushers, I knew there was next to nothing that I could do to help, and I was beginning to get cabin fever. For the first time in an Iditarod, I truly had nothing to do. Presumably, Kaltenborn would be leaving soon, and he didn't need my services. The last of the dropped dogs had been dispatched south to Anchorage. Of our four-person vet team, two had already traveled up the trail. I surveyed the site, watching as a gust of wind carried snow across the plain. It hit me, then: there would have to be at least one veterinarian on duty when Steve and Tara showed up. Jennifer, though a brilliant veterinarian, was still a rookie. I needed to stay.

There were, of course, broader logistical issues. The two stragglers were already at least a day away, and falling farther behind all the time. Was it fair to the volunteers to ask them to keep this and subsequent checkpoints up and running for only two competitors? Most of the volunteers have jobs, families, and other responsibilities away from the race. It costs money to house and feed the volunteers. Despite its fame and popularity, the Iditarod has only a few big-name sponsors, primarily relying on merchandise sales, contributions, and small business advertising for funding. Allowing the race to run for three or four more days than planned would burn through the Iditarod Trail Committee's shoestring budget, sinking this year's event deep in the red. At some point, the organizers would have to call it a day and start shutting down checkpoints.

It was the end of the day before a message was received from Steve. The blizzard, he reported, had obliterated the course, submerging most of the wooden trail markers. He and Tara had decided to stay put rather than chance it out in the open. All things considered, it was probably a wise decision. He requested trailbreakers—snowmobilers with special equipment—to pat down the trail. Throughout the camp, there was a collective sigh of relief. At least they were safe. It would be a few hours before Marcelle Fressineau arrived, so I decided to catch some shut-eye. When I woke up it was near dawn, and Marcelle's headlamps had been spotted. More astonishingly, Steve and Tara were now well on their way. With the path clear, they'd made up a lot of time, breezing through Kaltag, and were now on schedule to arrive early tomorrow morning, if not very late today.

Marcelle arrived just as Kaltenborn was leaving. Her dogs caught sight of his and tried to chase them. Magnus tried to get his team to leave the checkpoint, but the huskies stayed put. Finally, Marcelle threw out her snow anchor, and Magnus was able to set off. I worked alone examining Marcelle's dogs. There was no need to wake Jennifer this early for just one team. Besides, the new arrivals were in outstanding shape. They were playful and barking raucously. Much to my sleeping comrade's delight, I'm sure.

As I signed Marcelle's Vet Book, I noticed the race marshal talking animatedly with a few other volunteers—too animated for this early hour. Something was brewing. As it turned out, marching orders had come down from on high. The race committee had unanimously agreed that it wasn't feasible to allow Steve and

Tara to continue. Unalakleet would be their final stop. There was no way to communicate this to them out on the course; the race judge would inform them on arrival. Out of courtesy to the competitors, we were sworn to secrecy. But rumors spread quickly in a small town, so much so that by the time I got back to our building, it seemed that everyone had heard. Conspiratorial whispers and quiet debates about the wisdom of the decision abounded.

Steve and Tara kept a respectable seven miles per hour speed on the approach to Unalakleet. Their dogs were no doubt well rested and delighted to be on the move again after their unscheduled forty-eight-hour break. It was after 6 p.m. when they arrived. Theirs was a courageous effort. They had made up much more time than anyone expected, but it wouldn't be enough. As they pulled into the checkpoint, the race judge motioned them over. Steve took the news solemnly. Tears welled in Tara's eyes.

Jennifer and I gave the dogs a short veterinary exam. One and all, they were in fine condition, despite the weather and trail conditions. But that didn't matter now. They and their mushers would be flying back to Anchorage on the next flight out. As the camp packed up around us, Tara thanked me. Steve sat by himself on a bench, his head in his hands, his Iditarod over.

CHAPTER 19

2020

THE WHOLE WORLD WAS AFFECTED BY THE COVID-19 PANDEMIC, and the Iditarod was no exception. In late February, the virus was just beginning to emerge in the United States. The week before I left Washington, DC, for Alaska, there was general confusion. At Ronald Reagan Washington National Airport, there were still no travel restrictions, border-crossing closures, or mandatory mask requirements. All that would change in just a matter of days.

I made it to Unalakleet by the narrowest of margins. The Friday before everything shut down, I checked the departure sheet at the Millennium Hotel for my name. I was not on the list, nor did I expect to be, but I checked in with the Iditarod Air Force to be sure.

"No, Lee, not today," the master of transportation told me. "But you're all set for tomorrow morning."

I was on my way back to my room when I decided to grab another cup of coffee. As soon as I reentered the lobby, a woman with a clipboard gripped my arm, relieved.

"One of our veterinarians overslept. Can you be ready in fifteen?" she asked.

This, at least, was familiar territory. I stuffed everything I could into my duffel bag and raced to the waiting airport shuttle. The plane's propellers were already spinning by the time I arrived; within fifteen minutes, we were in the air. *That*, as it turned out, was the last flight out of Anchorage. That night, Governor Mike Dunleavy announced that no new people would be allowed on the trail. I had been hoping to travel farther north this year, but by the time I arrived in Unalakleet, it had become clear that this was as far as I'd be going. Personal hopes and dreams aside, we had a much more significant problem. With these travel restrictions in place, no additional personnel would be able to join us, and as a consequence, there would be far fewer veterinarians and other support staff on the trail.

It was around this time that the elders of several villages on the trail voted to close their towns to the Iditarod. No one involved with the race, including the competitors, would be permitted within the confines of their towns. This included Shaktoolik, the next checkpoint after Unalakleet. Glibly, you might joke that the Iditarod represents the ultimate form of social distancing—sleds miles apart from each other, mushers often wearing masks—but, of course, those mushers have come from around the world. Not to mention, there are hundreds of volunteers up and down the course, many of them, like me, who'd just passed through international airports and sat on large commercial flights. People from the outside bring in viruses that they themselves may be immune to, but the residents of the isolated local communities most definitely are not. The history of contact between outsiders and Alaska villagers is a list of epidemics. These were the early days of the COVID pandemic, and there were plenty of unknowns. Different branches of the US government were making different predictions, ranging from cases falling to zero in the next few weeks, right through to the possibility of millions of deaths.

Contingency plans were quickly adopted. The Indigenous community, especially, was sympathetic to the plight of the mushers and their dogs. At Shaktoolik, a compromise solution was put in place. It was decided that no one from outside the town would be allowed within the limits of the settlement, but they could skirt the edges of the town. All night, volunteers from the community hauled straw, food, tents, communication devices, and any other necessary supplies to an area about a mile away from the town. Within a day, community members had successfully transported tons of material to the makeshift checkpoint. Still, it was an unmanned checkpoint. The teams would have to find their own supplies, bed their own teams down, and secure shelter for themselves. The restrictions also meant that veterinary care would not be available until the next checkpoint, in Koyuk, some ninety miles from their last checkup in Unalakleet. To make matters worse, Koyuk is on the other side of the Norton Sound crossing, one of the biggest hurdles in the race. There were clear, and unnerving implications for the safety of the dogs. But we had no choice but to press on: they were already out there, on the ice.

❄   ❄   ❄   ❄

ALIY ZIRKLE'S TEAM WAS the first to arrive. The dogs were quite a sight, festooned as they were with azure-blue LED lights. Aliy explained that she had done this to help her lead dogs see better at night. The strings of bulbs strung along the dogs' harnesses *did* give them a magnificent glow, one that I'm sure could be seen for miles in the dark. I recognized a few of her huskies: Decaf, Perky, Violet, and Bruno, all smiling big husky smiles, pink tongues lolling out the sides of their mouths. The pride they had in their musher was evident. It had been four years since the attack on Aliy's team. She'd competed every year since, and remains one of the most popular mushers in the field. Whenever Aliy arrives at a checkpoint, people flock around her. Even in the most difficult circumstances, Aliy carries herself with grace, and her dogs are no less agreeable. While most of the dogs I meet on the course are friendly, Aliy's team—her "Iditarod Superstars," as she calls them—are a level above. Not only are they consistently

among the sweetest dogs on the course, but they'll stand in perfect form for an examination; only when I've finished do they
curl up to sleep.

Aliy had heard Richie Diehl had chosen to leave three of his
dogs behind after hearing one of them cough. She noted that
Decaf, a four-year-old male running in his second Iditarod, had
coughed twice in the final stretch before Unalakleet. He was
still pulling hard and eating well, and she hadn't observed any
additional episodes of coughing or breathing irregularities. Still,
after Diehl's team, any respiratory concern for the musher was a
concern for the veterinary staff. I bent down to examine Decaf
and he dutifully held out his forepaw for me to look at. I had
wanted to listen to his lungs, first, but clearly Decaf knew that
this wasn't normal procedure, and he needed things to be done
in the correct sequence. So, I examined his paw. After I finished,
he lifted his other forepaw. He then laid down and turned onto
his back, all without command, so I could examine his abdomen. Only after I finished these assessments did he stand to let
me listen to his lungs. I couldn't detect any wheezes or other
harsh sounds. The thought of an incipient lung infection nagged
at me. If something contagious was starting, it could overtake
the entire team before they made it to Koyuk. I looked up and
down at the team. Every dog was resting comfortably, breathing
normally, not coughing. At the moment. The notion that drove
me crazy was the inability to predict the future. Would everyone
still be all right in an hour? Tomorrow? And what if they started
to cough on the way to the next checkpoint? No one would be
able to reach Aliy and her team for at least a day. I pondered the
question—maybe too much. Aliy and I discussed the pros and
cons as Decaf slept peacefully on his straw bed. The idea struck
me that perhaps warm vapor on the trail might have caused
some wheezing. Pockets of warm air can cause localized vapor
to form. If the ambient temperature is cold and a dog breathes in

Huskies snuggle at a checkpoint.

this warm air, then the lungs can spasm, causing a dramatic but largely clinically benign cough.

Whatever the cause of Decaf's previous episode, it was gone now. We agreed that as long as Decaf didn't start coughing here, while she rested, and that no one else on the team started coughing, Aliy would proceed. I asked her to please let me know when she successfully crossed the Norton Sound. I'm not sure, in retrospect, how I imagined she would accomplish this, since I had no cell phone reception, but the gesture made both of us feel better. As it turned out, neither Decaf nor any other member of the team developed any problems, respiratory or otherwise. Aliy's team made it all the way to Nome. After the race, Aliy sent me a letter, alongside Decaf's race tag, signed with a big, furry pawprint.

❊ ❊ ❊ *UNALAKLEET, AK. 3,663 miles to Washington,
DC. 29°F. Light snow.*

Being without cell service is usually a blessing for me.
The downside is that when something truly important, like a
global pandemic, is occurring, it's hard to stay informed. I was
more or less in the dark about what was going on in the world
around me. Myths, truths, and half-truths all swirled together in a
maelstrom of rumor. I remained broadly optimistic. That changed
when I caught up with a national news crew hauling their gear to
Peace on Earth.

"It's pretty bad. They are closing all the Canadian borders
tomorrow," one of the camera operators told me. "There is also
talk that they might close the airports. The governor is supposed
to make a statement this afternoon."

I was stunned. Obviously, any talk of getting to a new checkpoint this year had long been out of the question, but it hadn't
even occurred to me that I might have problems getting home.
The worst-case scenario, I'd thought, was that the airports closed,
so I'd have to hire a car. But if the Canadian border closed, I
wouldn't be able to drive. If I didn't have a family, if I didn't have
a clinic in Washington, DC, maybe things wouldn't have been
so awful. But I had both. There was no way that my clinic would
survive financially if it was forced to close for any length of time.
The teams trickled into Unalakleet throughout the day, and I did
my best to focus on the work at hand. Still, nagging thoughts of
what I would do if I couldn't leave encroached. I felt that if I left, I
would be leaving Stu Nelson and the Iditarod Trail Committee in
the dust. Stu was already down on staff. He was here, in Unalakleet. I hovered over him as he strategized about filling personnel
gaps. He had asked one of the other vets to stay longer, but she
declined. She, too, had a family and clinic at home.

By now, volunteers from some of the earlier checkpoints had started to filter into town. They had been asked by the various municipalities to pick up their evacuation of the checkpoints once the last of the dog teams were through. Unexpectedly, this new influx of people contained several veterinarians. This was my chance. There was one flight out in the afternoon, with exactly one seat left. Gathering up all my nerve, I approached Stu with my request. Could I leave early?

He stared at me for a second.

"Is it that important, Lee?" Stu asked.

I said that it was. He had more than enough people now, most of them Alaskan residents, to boot. I was still unsure, as was everyone else, when the international airports would close. He nodded solemnly. I thanked him and ran to stuff my belongings in my duffel. I raced by Kim Henneman, who wished me well; I thanked her, too. I made my way to Anchorage, then to Seattle-Tacoma International. Both reminded me of the ghost towns on the trail. All the shops were closed. There were barely a dozen people on the overnight flight back to Washington, DC. Before I'd even landed, I was convinced that I had made the right decision. I arrived home just as Reagan National closed down for incoming flights.

The mushers had less luck. Thomas Wærner went on to win the 2020 race—I'm sure my pals at NRK were thrilled—but he had to live with friends in Alaska for three months before he could return home, to Norway, to celebrate with his countrymen.

PART V

TO
NOME

CHAPTER 20

THE BELLOWS

EVERY MAN HAS HIS LIMITS—AND FOR ME, THAT LIMIT'S NAME
is Shaktoolik. After Unalakleet, the trail runs over a road
constructed on top of a levee toward the town of Shaktoolik. We're now 750 miles into the 1,049-mile course. Shaktoolik
is where many mushers will make one of their mandatory eight-
hour stops, because the next segment of the race is considered the
most dangerous. From here, teams must cross the frozen sea ice
of Norton Sound—a fifty-mile dash over the frozen Bering Sea.
The wind roars down from the north with nothing to impede it.
Scientists in Knud Rasmussen's epic 1902–04 exploration in this
part of Alaska derisively referred to their camp near Shaktoolik as
"The Bellows," on account of the ever-present wind. With it can
come sudden blizzards, sheer whiteouts, and if a team is caught
out in one the results can be tragic. The veteran mushers tell of
heroic crossings, sometimes at night, sometimes in full gale winds
with absolutely no sense of direction.

Sled dog racing is always physically demanding. There have
been earlier stretches of the race that have required intense concentration, and even the clearest, cleanest parts of the trail might
hide a fallen tree or sinkhole. The Bering Sea is a whole new type
of psychologically imposing ordeal. Mushers need to navigate in
a barren white, featureless ice field for at least six hours. Guide-
posts are set up along the route and snow machines have packed

down the route days prior to the event, but wind gusts frequently blow down the signs and the trail is easy to lose in a constant, unchanging canvas of white on white. Karen Ramstead once told me she was caught in the middle of one of these frequent storms just as she crossed the halfway mark over the Sound. Conditions deteriorated so rapidly and severely that she had no hope of backtracking the way she came. The dogs refused to go forward because they could not see the trail. Another team approached, and both mushers got out in front of the dog teams and led them miles across the ice to the safety of Koyuk. It's no wonder, then, why competitors need a few hours to rest and gather their courage. They do this in Shaktoolik, a small community that sits on a spit of land with the Norton Sound on one side and vast wetlands on the other. There are 250 year-round residents who make their living chiefly from fishing. It's a colorful place. Literally: the houses there are painted in bright colors, as if to ward off the blandness of the all-encompassing white. A sunset orange house sits next to a deep purple one, which is next to one painted in crimson. It would drive a Homeowners Association bureaucrat insane (something I applaud enthusiastically). I was there in the winter, when most people had their boats pulled into their backyard, stored securely away from the crushing ice of the bay. Fishing nets and gear were stored in nearby sheds. Fences divided one yard from the next, but the snow drifts were so high, only the tops of the posts were visible. The airstrip there is behind a stretch of rampart that keeps the town's only road high and dry above the swamp. There are about thirty or forty of those colorful houses, a hardware store right in the middle of the town, and a brand-new elementary school.

The checkpoint was an old National Guard station built in the early 1980s, a prefabricated Quonset hut, with the major sections made in Anchorage and then shipped up to Shaktoolik for reassembly. It was just a wood-framed structure with corrugated metal exterior the size and shape of a double-wide mobile home. There was one large single room, with a bathroom set off to one side at the front. All the cooking, eating, sleeping, and talking happened in that one big room. A small sleeping area was created by lining up old grey metal lockers side by side, but these did nothing to abate the constant noise and fluorescent lights that blazed all day and all night. Sleep was difficult for anyone, and almost impossible for me. The National Guard hut was way too small for all these people. There were mushers, volunteers, cooks, tribal members, spectators all clambering around. In the "Sleeping Area" each one of us staked out a small sliver of space to wedge our sleeping bags into. Gear was kept at your feet to maximize sleeping space.

The bathroom contained the notorious "Red Beast," a giant, ill-tempered red composting toilet that would often and inconveniently stop working. Needless to say, people ate and slept as far away as possible from the Red Beast, but in the tight quarters of the Shaktoolik checkpoint, it was never far enough. As the days went on, it would be a brave or desperate soul that entered the confines of the Beast. Aside from the bathroom, the only enclosed space was a small office at the front of the building, which the comms staff had annexed for their computers and satellite phones.

❋ ❋ ❋ *SHAKTOOLIK, AK. 221 miles to Nome. Morning. −12°F. Windy.*

CROSSING THE FROZEN SEA *after* Shaktoolik is rough, but getting to the town is its own ordeal. It's forty miles up the trail from Unalakleet, so a relatively short run. The first section winds down from the mountains onto the plains of the sea. Most of the mushers I have talked to say that this part is relatively easy. The trail is

A frosty muzzle.

wide and smooth, the hills and forest help protect you from the elements, and the route is generally downhill. That changes as soon as the teams leave the hills and emerge onto the flood plain. The wind hits with all its might, enough that it has been known to flip entire sleds over. Every year, one or two mushers show up to the Shaktoolik checkpoint sporting a sprained ankle, or black eye, or a wrenched wrist.

During my time there, I saw only one musher go through the checkpoint without resting. The distance from Unalakleet wasn't overly long, it took the average musher six or seven hours, but battling the wind and cold drained a person. The mushers arrived in Shaktoolik haggard and shattered. The dogs' muzzles, and any musher beards, were covered in sheaths of ice. Some racers had developed frostbite on their fingertips, despite wearing thick, seal-fur gauntlet-style mitts. After feeding and bedding down their dogs, the mushers staggered into the close confines of the checkpoint station. They crashed into bed, dozed on a chair. The ones who stayed awake usually just sat and stared. Ironically, and thankfully, the dogs seem to thrive in the conditions. They're at home in the cold, running on hardpack.

At most of the checkpoints, parking the teams is an issue as more and more teams arrive, and such was the case in Shaktoolik. At this point in the race, the competitors were spaced apart by many hours, but balancing that out, no one seemed in a hurry to leave, and new teams kept coming in. There was a small shelf of land directly behind the old National Guard quarters, but this quickly filled. The headquarters area, too, became overrun. Once the backlot was filled to capacity, room was made down by the beach area. We did not place teams on the sea ice, as fissures could unexpectedly open up in a matter of moments.

Stairs had been carved into the snowbank to get down the bluff to the beach area, but after a while this became too much wear and tear on my knees. I started to just plop down on my butt and slide down. As in Unalakleet, this tactic was an effortless way to get down to where I was going—and to bring out the local children in peals of laughter.

❄   ❄   ❄   ❄

WE PARKED SCOTT JANSSEN's team down by the beach. Like Dallas Seavey and the Berington twins, Scott is something of an Iditarod celebrity. He owns a small chain of funeral homes in Anchorage, and so calls himself "The Mushing Mortician." Everyone has a story about Scott. He'd earned a reputation as a big talker and liked to entertain listeners with wild tales of past adventures, some of which were even true. Scott is a man with a great sense of humor, a man who appreciates a good self-deprecating joke—someone, in other words, in a serious position who didn't take himself too seriously. Two years before I met him, he'd received national press, even appearing on *Today*, when he claimed to have brought his lead dog back to life.

The way he told the story, his team was only a few miles out from a checkpoint when his lead dog collapsed in the harness. He jumped from the sled, and immediately ascertained that the dog had had a heart attack. He began giving her CPR, and breathing down her snout as a form of artificial respiration. He cried out "Not today, you don't!" and the dog was miraculously revived, whereby he placed her in the sled and transported her to the waiting veterinarians at the next stop. While the story was swallowed wholesale by the press, most veterinarians who've heard it are somewhat skeptical. Even in an ER, with endotracheal tubes, pure oxygen, and various lifesaving drugs close at hand, the survival rate for resuscitating a dog in cardiac arrest is less than 2 percent. I wonder if the dog maybe collapsed from a different issue, and was breathing all along, unbeknownst to the musher. The dog could have had a respiratory arrest, where the chances of survival are somewhat higher. It could be true, though; Scott had a tendency to exaggerate, but he never outright lied, and in any case, he was an engaging person to be around. I, like everyone else, sat in rapt attention while he wove his tales.

Now, Scott wanted me to check one of his dogs, coincidentally named Morgan. She had a plastic sweat wrap around her wrist joint to reduce inflammation. Morgan wagged her tail as I approached, offering up the offending paw for inspection. I have always been amazed how often these dogs seemed to know to present their injured area for exam. I had found many a frostbitten prepuce when a dog would roll over to be rubbed on their belly. Maybe it wasn't that they wanted their belly rubbed at all, maybe they were saying, "Hey Doc, look here, it hurts right there." Giving Morgan a pat on the head, I settled down next to her, and gingerly unwrapped the plastic. The "Turtle Sweat," a malodorous concoction favored by horse trainers and mushers alike, was still present. It was an oily brown goo that truly reeked. As with many folk medicines, the worse it smelled, the better it was perceived to work. The carpus was not swollen at all, and the joint moved freely. Morgan was wearing a bootie, which I didn't remove. I replaced the wrap and called out to Scott.

"It looks good to me," I said, "The wrap seems to have done the trick."

Scott nodded in agreement. I looked back at Morgan, who still had a doleful expression on her face, like I'd missed something. I went back to the National Guard hut and shed my parka. As I was grabbing another cup of coffee, Scott came rushing in the front door.

"I need to drop a dog. Morgan's paw pad is falling off!"

I was mortified. I hadn't checked her pads because she was still wearing her booties, and I had not wanted to remove them. Still, it should have been done. Feeling chagrined, I put my wet parka back on, and hurried to meet Scott at the bottom of the hill. Morgan still sat with her injured paw held high and that doleful expression on her face. I knelt down beside her. Sure enough, the paw pad was cracked and inflamed. While not quite "falling off," it was a painful injury. There was no doubt we would have to drop her here. I could sense Scott's dissatisfaction with me, and I didn't blame him. I secured a lead around Morgan's collar, and carried her up to the dropped-dog station. She settled down into a fresh nest of straw. The paw pad was detached in some places from the skin, and the pink subcutaneous tissue peeked through. I had seen many cases similar to this back at my clinic in Washington, DC. People often play with their dogs on tennis courts. Unfortunately, the abrasive surface tears up the paw pads, resulting in an ulcerative erosion. The wound tends to heal quickly, but it's on the bottom of the pad, where a dog places most of its weight.

Morgan stretched out, and then laid down with her tail curled elegantly over her snout. I continued to work on her wound as she drifted off to sleep. I gently applied an antibiotic cream to the exposed sore, then placed a vet wrap bandage loosely over the wound so it could breathe. Feeling lousy, I sat down next to her with my back up against the building. We were comfortably away from the wind. You often miss the most obvious thing, I thought, because you're looking in the wrong place.

Years later, I had the chance to check Scott's team when I was stationed at the Unalakleet checkpoint. Before starting with the exam, I introduced myself and asked permission to examine his dogs, following the appropriate etiquette. All his dogs were strong and healthy. As I was signing off on his Vet Book, I mentioned the incident that had occurred in Shaktoolik. He looked at me quizzically and pondered the comment, trying to fathom his memory.

"Oh yes, Morgan!" he said. "Didn't she have a problem with her paw or something?"

Clearly, the event hadn't had the negative impact on his psyche as it had on mine. He gestured to the same dog I'd seen two years ago.

"That's her."

I made doubly sure to check her paw pads.

❊   ❊   ❊   ❊

BECAUSE RACE CONDITIONS HAD changed with the new terrain, teams would often arrive later than expected to Shaktoolik. We had GPS to give us an estimated time, but it was anyone's guess as to when a particular team would show up at the checkpoint. Delays happen. All it takes is one dog to pull up lame, or a lead line to get tangled, or a runner on the sled to smack into a rock, and the entire team grinds to a hobble. It is up to the musher to stop, fix the problem as best he or she can, and then continue. On a bad run, delays appear to occur almost continuously.

We took turns standing sentinel outside on the porch. It seemed appropriate that someone had eyes on the horizon. No timetable dictated when one person would stand watch, and another would relieve them. I usually sat with Archie, the village elder. We rested on a straw bale with our backs against the wall, him with a lit cigarette, the glowing ember made all the brighter against the inky blackness of an Alaska night. When I got tired, I would go in and someone else came out. I never saw Archie take a break.

In a small town such as Shaktoolik, village elders are not elected officials, they've earned respect and admiration over the years, becoming the people to seek out when there's a problem to solve. If you had bad luck hunting or fishing, you'd go to an elder. There were no magical solutions here (although I sensed a great respect for the spiritual world), it's that any man or women who had survived for a long time in a hostile wilderness was the repository of hard-gained knowledge. Elders would also help settle small disputes, an especially important task in tiny communities where tiny grudges could quickly morph into large feuds. I felt honored to be sitting next to Archie, even just for professional reasons. His knowledge of dogs had taken a lifetime to accumulate. I might know the science of it all, but he knew huskies on a far deeper level than I ever would.

The wind had picked up sharply, and Archie and I sat, not saying much. The gentle snowfall of the early evening had started to give way to blizzard conditions. Wind whipped the snow across the road, obscuring its path. Somewhere out there, beyond the steadily decreasing light of the streetlamps, the teams were all alone with their dogs.

CHAPTER 21

THE MACKEY BROTHERS

THE BAYING HUSKIES COULD BE HEARD EVEN OVER THE HOWL-ing wind. I stood up to shake out the stupor from my body and walked over to greet the musher as he came into view. Reams of ice adhered to his full-length beard, completely obscuring his face. The only indication that he was even human was when he removed his hood, and a pile of brown tangled mane cascaded down to his shoulders. This was Lance Mackey of the Mackey brothers, Iditarod icons and epitomes of what it is to be a full-born son of Alaska.

In Alaska, Lance—who passed away in 2022—was a true sports hero. Not that this would be apparent from first glimpse—even in a country of hardtack people, where actions mean everything and respect has to be earned, there are people who supersede even this high threshold of toughness and ethics. If you see the head-shots of the Mackey brothers that accompany their biographies in the Iditarod Race Guide, you'll know why neither of them ended up on a Wheaties box. Lance's photo shows a man with a long, thin, grizzled face. Jason's photo shows a man quite similar in appearance, wearing an Alaska aviator's cap. They both have the same wide-gapped grin.

Lance and Jason Mackey were born in the Mat-Su Valley area. Both were mushing as soon as they were big enough to hold onto a sled. Their father, Dick Mackey, won the Iditarod in 1978 and taught the boys at an early age how to handle racing dogs. The

Mackey brothers became extremely capable and experienced Alaskan outdoorsmen; together, they competed in hundreds of sled dog races. From 2007 to 2010, Lance won the Iditarod four years in a row.

There's tough, and then there's capital-T Tough. In 2001 Lance was preparing for his first Iditarod when doctors diagnosed him with throat cancer. Lance deferred his entry until 2002, when he set off on the world's harshest sled dog event with a feeding tube surgically attached to him. When he stopped to feed and rest his dogs, he would take a meal of liquefied protein drink and pour it directly into his stomach through the tube. Unfortunately, he was not able to complete the race, but just the attempt tells you a great deal about him. In 2005, he won his first Yukon Quest, and he went on to win it the next four years. In 2007 he also won the Iditarod, making him the first person to win both events in the same year.

By the time the brothers arrived in Shaktoolik, they were haggard and gaunt. Granted, this is how they usually looked, but even allowing for that, I could see the stress wrinkles in the face, the dehydration of the body, and the slumped-over position that signals total exhaustion. Lance appeared to have aged ten years in the days since I'd seen him at Finger Lake. His face was drawn out and weather-beaten. He had lost more weight off his already rail-thin frame. He'd used duct tape to repair tears in his parka, as well as a deep cut on his hand. Lance Mackey tended to his dogs, then headed into the National Guard shed, where he sat in a fold-out metal chair, trying to doze among the noise and bright lights. Just as his chin dropped to his chest, in burst a hailstorm of children from the local elementary school. They crowded into the building, shepherded by their teacher. As soon as they caught sight of Lance, they froze and stared at him like he was a lion at a zoo.

Then Lance bounced out of his chair.

"Hey guys!" Gone in an instant was the tired, weary man. The children looked upon him admiringly.

"So, you kids have some things you would like me to sign?" He rubbed his hands together eagerly as he spoke. Almost immediately he was joined by his brother, Jason.

All the children pressed forward, chattering excitedly and waving programs, school paper, pennants, and any other odds and ends they thought befitted an autograph from one of the true heroes of the North. Lance and Jason happily started to sign their name to everything that was offered. Jason asked who among the group hoped to become dog mushers when they got older. A sea of hands rose, outstretched with the eagerness only an elementary school child can show. Jason laughed, and told them that it would be better if they found "real jobs." I doubt they were persuaded. It was hard to tell who was having a better time, the brothers Mackey or the schoolchildren.

I've seen this phenomenon many times during my time at the Iditarod, and it applies to all the mushers, not just the star names. Every year, a group of people who have day jobs get to be the hero. Most of the race spectators out on the course, who live surrounded by the wilderness, understand the realities of competing in the Iditarod better than we ever could. The mushers act with according aplomb, enjoying and relishing the attention from the fans. The fans, of all ages, were thrilled to talk with their heroes. I didn't get the impression this is something the mushers thought they "had" to do, although I am sure they are instructed to treat the volunteers and fans with politeness.

❈   ❈   ❈   ❈

It doesn't matter if this is your first Iditarod or your twentieth: disaster can strike at any time. Earlier in that year's race, the Mackey brothers tackled an emergency situation. They had stopped at one of the emergency shelters scattered along the route to rest and snack their dogs. The shelters are not staffed by support personnel, there's very little equipment left in them, but they're landmarks on the course, and offer some respite.

As the Mackeys were thawing some food for their dogs, another team arrived. The musher was carrying a dog in the sled basket. The musher had spotted blood in the snow, stopped the sled and found one of her younger dogs with blood bubbling from its nose. She'd wrapped him in a blanket, but had been unable to stanch the bleeding. She couldn't see a wound. She'd remembered passing this emergency shelter, so she turned back. The rest of her dogs were spooked by the smell of blood, but had sensed the urgency, and moved faster than they'd gone all race. When the brothers first saw the dog, they feared she had died, but were relieved when the dog sneezed, sending a shower of blood that covered Lance's face. At least she was still alive.

It could've been nothing—a small cut just inside the nostril. It could have been an abscessed tooth that had ruptured into the nasal cavity. Messy, and the dog would have to be dropped, but no big deal if treated quickly. It also could have been an exercise-induced pulmonary hemorrhage, a condition that race-horses sometimes get while competing. That would make it a very serious problem. Out on the trail, there was no way for a musher to send a message. In fact, that year, 2015, a competitor would have been disqualified for carrying a walkie-talkie (need-less to say, very little of the trail between checkpoints is in range of a cellphone tower). Mushers do carry a GPS tracker, and that tracker has an emergency response button. The problem, how-ever, is that the unit only sends out a signal that a musher needs assistance. There is no capacity for the sender to describe what the emergency is, or how bad. You forfeit the race if you use it. She triggered it anyway.

Without a way to communicate the dire situation to the race veterinarians, with no way to even confirm the message had been received, the Mackeys decided that the best chance the dog had was for one of them to backtrack along the trail to the previous checkpoint. If the message had been received and a relief team dispatched, then they would likely meet up en route. Jason volunteered to go, and with the help of his brother bundled the still-bleeding husky into his sled. Jason kept his dogs up at a considerable clip, trying to buy precious time for his injured cargo. After about ten miles, he glimpsed a mobile dog kennel being pulled by a snow machine, clambering along at a leisurely pace, answering the emergency signal.

The driver of the snow machine casually climbed off his seat, but upon seeing the injured dog and its bloody dressing, immediately went into overdrive. Luckily, one of the veterinarians had come along for the ride. The dog was still bleeding, but the gushing had slowed to a trickle. The dog was bright and alert, appeared normal, save for the blood that drenched his fur. The vet sprayed epinephrine into the husky's nostrils, which stanched the blood flow. Once the husky was safely in the hands of the rescue personnel, Jason turned his sled around, and made his way back to the cabin. Rather than put the dog into one of the carriers in the snowmobile's trailer, the crew elected to hold the dog throughout the ride back to the checkpoint and the awaiting veterinarians. This was a risky move since a husky, sensing it is unbound, will try to run free. Give a husky a fenced four thousand acres to roam, and it will make a beeline to the fence to look for a gap. By the time the dog made it back to the checkpoint, the bleeding had all but stopped, and by the next morning it was feeling fine. There was never any clear diagnosis on the cause of the nosebleed. In any event, the dog recovered well, thanks to the efforts of the Mackey brothers and its own musher.

That's how I remember the Mackey brothers. But there was another side to Lance. After winning the Iditarod in 2010, Lance displayed an alarming drop in form. In five attempts, he failed to finish in the top ten; in 2020, he failed a drug test and was retroactively disqualified from the race and banned from the next.

Lance Mackey (1970–2022) was a four-time winner of the Iditarod.

Lance promptly entered rehab, and it became clear that he had struggled with drugs and alcohol for some time. A few months later, his longtime partner, Jenne Smith, passed away in an ATV accident, and the throat cancer he had battled in his early thirties returned. Lance Mackey died on September 7, 2022, at the age of fifty-two.

❄ ❄ ❄ ❄

AFTER TWO FULL DAYS at Shaktoolik, with barely two hours' sleep, I had become irritable. I was ugly to the volunteers around me, short to snap at unintended slights. I was becoming a perfectly miserable S.O.B. So much so that I would spend most of my remaining time at Shaktoolik apologizing to the many people I had growled at. Sleep deprivation also has a way of feeding on itself. As the body wears down due to lack of reparative REM sleep, the body secretes adrenaline and stress hormones to help keep it functioning. These enzymes also act as stimulants, so the act of sleep becomes harder. More importantly than my

At this point, we're all a little sleepy.

irritability, lack of sleep was starting to allow me to make mental errors. It was crucial at this stage of the race that I remained focused. The dogs would soon be headed out to the most difficult section of the trail, they needed to be good to go, and I needed to be fully alert and emotionally competent in my physical exam checks. Right then I was a wreck.

The same problem, of course, affects the mushers. They stop for sleep where they can, and there are sections of the trail which are long enough, and smooth enough that they can catnap as the dogs pull them along, but in my experience mushers are far more attentive to their dogs' need for rest than their own. Even though the wind was still blowing around thirty knots, and the temperature was dropping below zero, I decided to see if I could sleep outside. One of the other veterinarians had brought along a small tent and slept in it a couple of nights. I didn't have a tent, but I did have an Alpine bivy sack like the ones mountaineers carry. In addition, my down sleeping bag was rated to −20 degrees.

Logically, the most windless place, I thought, would be on the lee side of a hill. We had been parking dogs down at the beach area, which was protected by a small berm. I made my way out there, and just as I approached the crest of the small hill, a particularly strong gust ripped my air mattress and sleeping bag from my arms. I stood there in disbelief as my gear went tumbling over near the Bering Sea ice. I tried to make my way out to retrieve my things, but the snow got deeper and deeper, and of course I had forgotten to wear my snowshoes. Each time I fell, I cursed as I got back up, and my stuff slid farther out toward the sea, and I felt a profound sense of being defeated, building and building. It couldn't get much worse than this, I thought. I'd come out here because I'd sensed I was on the edge of a complete meltdown. Now I felt it arriving. The Iditarod had finally got to me. It had beaten me. Or so I thought.

Now, I have my own religious beliefs, and I do think that God intervenes in people's lives every once in a while. There are miraculous recoveries and spectacles, sure, but more often than not, He meets us one-on-one in the form of the kind act of a stranger. God's stranger for me that day in Shaktoolik was an eight-year-old boy by the name of Devon. As I stood there, utterly beaten—watching whatever chance I had of getting some sleep blow steadily toward the frozen sea—I heard his small voice.

"Need some help?" The voice emanated from the hood of a parka jacket hood. Devon was in elementary school, and a tribal member. His class had come down to see the dogs earlier and we had chatted a bit then. I took a moment to respond. I wondered, at first, whether it would be dishonorable to ask a child to help out. These thoughts were soon dispelled. I was too far gone, too defeated, tired, and upset.

"Yes," I replied wearily.

With that, Devon scurried out onto the snow-covered beach. In only a few moments he had retrieved my way-gone gear. He smiled a bright, toothy smile as he handed it back to its owner. His curiosity now piqued, he wanted answers. As with children everywhere, I was submitted to a barrage of queries that ran into a string of questions, one right after the other: What was I doing out here? Why was I carrying my sleeping stuff? Was I really going to bed at only six o'clock in the evening? Every answer I gave generated five more questions, but as tired and grumpy as I was, there was something in Devon's demeanor that brought back my good humor.

Now I was in a better mood, I started to think my strategy through more clearly. Of course the bottom of a beach barrier would be windier than anywhere else: the wind accelerates downhill against the contour of the hill. What I really needed to find was a solid structure, one that would block out all the wind. Buildings are good for this. But because of the basin-shaped layout of our checkpoint, wind buffeted by the building was just curling around the edges and regrouping on the lee side to blow back against the structure.

We had put the dropped dogs up against the back of the National Guard post, and then piled straw bales on top of one another to create a little windproof fence. Certainly, if that was good enough for the huskies, it was good enough for me. Devon and I grabbed several extra straw bales and started stacking them together. After a while we had a cozy fort, with the bales as one side and the building as the other. We laid down a bed of straw. Next, I placed a heat-reflective tent pad on top of the straw. I adjusted my air mattress so it fit tightly into the makeshift camp. Fully clothed, I wormed my way into my sleeping bag and Devon zipped me into my bivy sack. Devon scurried up to the top of the bales. As he got to the top one, he unleashed an avalanche of snow that hit me square in the face. He started giggling, then burst into outright laughter. I laughed too.

As Devon kept a watchful eye on me, I felt the warmth of the sleeping bag creep through my sore muscles. The sun was still out, but low in the sky. The only sound was the white noise of the wind. I fell asleep almost instantly. A delicious, deep, unfettered sleep, the kind you have when you have worked hard all day. I awoke four hours later. By then the stars were out and shining brightly against the cold arctic night. Devon had long ago abandoned his perch. I felt rejuvenated. I lay on my back for a long time, just looking up at the sky. I thought of my wife, Kris, and my son, Spencer. They were probably just now getting up. Soon, Kris would be dropping Spencer off at school before heading to our clinic in Georgetown to open. Kris, who had supported me in all my far-flung adventures and misadventures, who loved me as deeply as I loved her. It was because of her that I could be in places like this. I felt the appreciation that many mushers do for their loved ones at the Ceremonial Start.

At breakfast, Devon was seated with Archie, the village elder, and broke into a wide grin when he saw me.

"I watched you sleeping outside last night!" he exclaimed.

"I know you did, Devon," I said. "Thank you very much for that."

Then, inspiration struck. I leapt from the table and ransacked my backpack. I showed what I had found to the boy: a Swiss Army knife my brother Scott gave me when we were teenagers. I've carried it with me on every single fishing and camping trip I have been on since. I opened the main blade.

"It needs some cleaning, and the blades need sharpening," I said. I demonstrated all the little gadgets: the file, fishhook remover, corkscrew, scissors. Devon watched carefully, not entirely sure where this was going.

"Devon, I treasure this because my brother gave it to me. I would like to give it to you now," I said. With that, I gently slid it over to him. Devon's eyes grew wide. He picked it up and carefully unfolded each utensil. For the rest of the day, Devon sat with his newfound gift, cleaning it, sharpening the blades with a whetstone, folding and unfolding the tools.

Archie caught up with me later that afternoon. We walked out amongst the teams, with all the huskies curled up, fast asleep.

"That was a kind thing you did," he said.

"It was a kind thing for Devon to help me last night," I replied.

Archie looked out over the frozen Bering Sea thoughtfully, and lit a cigarette. "Devon is a good kid. Very eager to help. He will have many challenges growing up here. There are a lot of negative influences. Perhaps your gift was spiritual, perhaps it will be a good talisman for him."

When I returned home that year, I phoned my brother Scott. There was a small part of me that felt guilty for giving away his gift to me. Scott listened to the whole story. When I was done, all he said was, "You mean the knife I gave you is now in the hands of a boy who lives by the Bering Sea? That's the coolest thing ever."

❊ ❊ ❊ *KOYUK, AK. 171 miles to Nome. −5°F. Windy.*

After Shaktoolik, the teams must cross the frozen sound. On the opposite shore, fifty miles over the ice, is Koyuk, a village of 347 people. After Koyuk, there are only about 171 miles to go.

Me and Devon.

As I strolled back to the checkpoint, I noted a lady with her small child admiring a flock sitting on a telephone wire.

"Look at all the pretty birds," she cooed to her daughter. "You know what that means, right?" Her daughter nodded excitedly.

"Spring is coming!" she said. Indeed, it was. Not only here, but at home in Washington, DC, too. By now, the Tidal Basin near the Jefferson Memorial would be ringed in fragrant, soft-pink cherry blossoms. Bunches of yellow daffodils would be blooming. In a few days, I'd be on a flight home, and it would be a full year before I returned to the Arctic wonderland of Alaska. I buckled up for one last adventure: to Nome.

CHAPTER 22

THE SERUM RUN

FROM SHAKTOOLIK, THE COURSE RUNS ACROSS THE SEA ICE OF the Norton Sound to Koyuk, then hugs the coastline and turns inland westerly until it hits Elim, an Inupiat village with a population of 339. The trail then stays inland and cuts across a small peninsula to the town of Golovin, another Inupiat village—so named for Captain Vasili Golovin of the Russian Navy, who surveyed the area in 1818—with a population of 148. The race heads onto the frozen Golovin Lagoon for ten miles and traverses the delta of Fish River until it reaches White Mountain. Mushers make a mandatory eight-hour stop at the White Mountain checkpoint. From there, it's just seventy-seven miles to the finish. One more checkpoint, appropriately called "Safety," sits fifty-five miles from White Mountain. From Safety, it's twenty-two miles to Nome and the burled arch that frame the finish line.

Throughout the years, the Iditarod has had different starts—Anchorage, Willow, even Fairbanks—but in its fifty-year history, there has only ever been one finish: Nome. Nome is central to the story of the Serum Run, the true-life race across remote territory (Alaska was not yet a state at the time) to save the lives of hundreds of children. It's an event which has enraptured Americans for a hundred years, now, and continues to inspire movies, TV shows, cartoons, and books. Even in Alaska, where heroic bouts with the weather and terrain are an everyday occurrence, the drama has become an indelible local legend. This story has been told many

A bronze statue in Wasilla depicts Balto.

times, in many ways—and still, it's worth recounting, even if it has very little to do with the modern Iditarod.

❊   ❊   ❊   ❊

IN JANUARY OF 1925, two children died of diphtheria in the remote mining town of Nome, Alaska. At the time, there was only one physician: Dr. Curtis Welch. Welch knew that the town had an insufficient supply of the serum used to treat diptheria, and predicted that the highly contagious disease would sweep through the isolated population, killing an estimated three thousand people within a matter of weeks. He put out a call for a supply of the medicine, and quickly established there were stocks of it in Anchorage. The harbor was iced in, so ships could not be used. Aviation was still in its infancy, and there were very real concerns that if the plane carrying this valuable cargo crashed, the serum would be lost as well. The only "road" into Nome was the Iditarod Trail, and the only plausible way of traveling along it was by dogsled.

The top mushers of the day were contacted, and they readily agreed to take on the perilous mission. A hundred years ago, mushers routinely traveled between towns—it was the only reliable method of transport—but these were relatively short journeys. To make things worse, it was midwinter, and the weather was particularly bad, with near-record winds and the lowest temperatures in twenty years. A decision was made by the city council to set up a relay of dog teams, working in opposite directions, which would hand off the twenty-pound packet of diphtheria antitoxin at checkpoints stationed along the route from the town of Nenana to Nulato. (The serum would be sent via train to Nenana.) Leonhard Seppala, the most renowned sled dog handler of his time, was chosen to run the relay from Nome, where he lived, to Nulato—and back. He would set off for Nulato with his dog team, led by Togo, his prized forty-eight-pound Siberian Husky, retrieve the antitoxin, then return to Nome: a 640-mile round trip, in brutal conditions.

"Wild Bill" Shannon, a former Army blacksmith was the first musher in the relay from Nenana. Shannon retrieved the package of antitoxin from the train at Nenana, then immediately set out, battling −50-degree weather and blizzard conditions. The anti-toxin was handed off from team to team throughout Alaska's Interior. At Shaktoolik, the medical baton was passed to Henry Ivanhoff. Ivanhoff pushed on; his progress was stalled, however, when his team encountered some reindeer and became entangled. Had Seppala—who had diverted course due to bad weather on the route to Nulato—not appeared from the north, the Serum Run might have ended there, outside Shaktoolik. But by pure coincidence (or divine intervention) the two teams met out on the frozen sea, near where modern Iditarod competitors run. Ivanhoff yelled out to Sepalla, "The serum! The serum! I have it here!"

With the antitoxin in hand, Seppala turned his dog team around. Facing bitter wind and chill temperatures of −85 degrees Fahrenheit, Seppala steered the team across the ice of Norton Bay. At the checkpoint in Golovin, Sepalla collapsed from exhaustion and handed the serum over to Charlie Olsen, who barely survived the perilous journey to Bluff, where he met up with the larger-than-life Norwegian musher, Gunnar Kaasen. The lead dog on Kaasen's team was a husky who would be immortalized in legend: the fearless and faithful Balto. Ironically, Balto was part of Seppala's kennel, but he had not chosen the big, black dog because he felt that Balto was too slow for this run. It was Balto nevertheless who safely guided Kaasen across the treacherous, gale-swept frontier of northern Alaska and into Nome. The courage and skill of the relay mushers and their indomitable huskies had saved the town.

Senator Clarence Dill of Washington State applauded the Serum Run on the Senate floor:

> *The Indian natives of the country volunteered their services for quick relays; the records I have just mentioned were made by Indian drivers with teams of mongrel dogs. Of course the last part of the trip was made exciting and was the more fierce because of the storm and wind that swept across the Bering Sea and coast. But we should always remember there were in the successful carrying of this anti-toxin the unknown drivers and the unknown dogs that made the success of the trip possible, and they deserve equal credit for the victory won. We who live in a climate such as we have in the United States cannot possibly realize what that trip meant. It is a trip of 650 miles which made regularly by mail trains, takes twenty-five to thirty days. By use of relay teams, they covered that in five and a half days. It is an accomplishment that will be talked about in Alaska, not only through this winter, but for many years to come. The heroic deeds of these men and the dogs have caught the imagination of the entire world and are worthy of a mighty pen and an eloquent tongue.*

The Serum Run inflamed the popular imagination. But along the way, a lot of important information was lost. Despite the efforts of Senator Dill and others to emphasize that the Serum Run was an example of teamwork—and that many of the people working on that team were Alaska Natives—it would be Balto and the Norwegian-born Kaasen who reaped the fame and rewards of "saving" Nome from the epidemic. Attempts to rebalance the record and give other participants credit tend to concentrate on Togo and Seppala (played by Willem Dafoe in the 2019 Disney movie *Togo*), rather than any of the Indigenous participants.

Nowhere was this sanitized narrative more profitable than at the box office. Just a few weeks after the Serum Run to Nome, Kaasen, Balto, and twelve other dogs took a steamship to Seattle, and from there to Los Angeles, where they'd been invited to feature in the movie short *Balto's Race to Nome*. The Hollywood producer Sol Lesser evidently understood that this was a real-life story that—with a little dramatic license—would appeal to cinema audiences. He may also have had an eye on the box office success of Hal Roach's adaptation of *The Call of the Wild*, a big hit two years before. Kaasen and Balto were swept along in a huge publicity drive for the short, which at one point saw Balto being honored by the mayor of Los Angeles at an event where the hero dog was accompanied by Mary Pickford, then one of America's most popular movie stars. In New York City people were so enthralled by Balto's bravery that a statue of the dog was paid for by public subscription and displayed prominently in Central Park, where it still resides today. I have seen the statue: it shows a husky in all its pride and splendor. Balto's tail is raised and curled over his back. His head held high, he wears a noble expression on his face. The nameplate briefly describes the dog's daring labors in that life-versus-death race. Only his name is mentioned.

Kaasen eventually got word that Seppala and the other mushers were angry with him for taking all the credit for the Serum Run. When he returned to his home in Nome after the press tour, he learned that the town was bitterly divided between those who hailed him as a hero and those who thought he'd seized all the glory. Leonhard Seppala himself split the difference: he recognized Kaasen's achievement, but resented the fact that his and (particularly) Togo's contribution had been overshadowed. The following year, Seppala would take Togo on his own long promotional tour of the United States. 'Wild Bill' Shannon also found his way to the lower 48 to boast of his role.

When Kaasen returned to Alaska, he had not brought Balto and the other dogs with him. Instead, he left them in the care of his promoter, who had promptly sold them to a sideshow. Some of the dogs were sold on, others died, the rest were left pitifully shackled together in a shed. While visiting Los Angeles in early 1926, the owner of an Ohio construction company, George Kimble, saw Balto and six other dogs living in these squalid conditions and organized a public appeal through the Cleveland *Plain Dealer*. Within ten days, the $2,000 asking price had been reached. The dogs were taken to Cleveland and, once their health was restored, they pulled a wheeled sled along the route of a downtown victory parade. The former teammates then took up residence at the Cleveland Brookside Park Zoo, where Balto died of natural causes on March 14, 1933, and was stuffed. He has been on display at the Cleveland Museum of Natural History ever since. After nearly a hundred years, his black fur has faded to a very dark brown.

Many of the place-names in accounts of the 1925 Serum Run are familiar to people following the later stages of the Iditarod, but despite what many articles and press releases suggest, the modern race has never been an attempt to reconstruct the route taken. The originators of the Iditarod have gone as far as to deny that the Serum Run was an inspiration for the creation of the race—at all. The connection isn't historic, but the thrilling events of the Serum Run and the Iditarod race both evoke the same image: a musher being pulled through a blizzard by a pack of huskies, racing as fast as physically possible through conditions so extreme that no machine would make it. Rugged individualism, tuned to nature, a human being bonded with a team of fearless dogs.

CHAPTER 23

NOME

THE LAST STAGE IS A STRAIGHTFORWARD SHOT ALONG NORTON
Sound, a mere twenty-two miles from the last checkpoint,
Safety. A few miles from the finish, the competitors don
their race bibs and official numbers. These are not usually worn
during the race, but everyone wants to look their best as they pass
under the finish. Mushers will often put new booties on the dogs,
not out of necessity, but as part of the ceremony.

The dogs come loping into town, passing under the Burled
Arch, the huge, rough-hewn slab of Alaskan spruce that serves
as a finish line. A large banner hangs above. The streets are lined
with cheering throngs of spectators. Bunting and flags drape the
buildings facing the course. Each finisher's name is broadcast
through a loudspeaker. If the finish line seems understated now,
it's worth saying that during the running of the 1973 Iditarod
the end of the 1,049-mile race had been marked by a volunteer
pouring a packet of Kool-Aid across main street to make a red
line in the ice. Unimpressed by this, one of the competitors, a
logger named Richard "Red Fox" Olson, created an arch from
a piece of spruce, and burned the words "End of Iditarod Dog
Race," "1049 Miles," "Anchorage," and "Nome" into it. It made
its debut in 1975. The original was damaged in 1999 when it was
lowered at the end of the race. A lumberjack by the name of Jim
Skogstand constructed a new arch with "End of the Iditarod Sled
Dog Race" emblazoned on it. (Notably, the original arch did not

contain the word "sled.") The original arch can be found in the Nome Recreational Center.

By the time the middle of the pack crosses the finish, it has been hours—maybe even days—since the winners were crowned, their photos taken below a giant banner, with the mushers holding trophies and the leads adorned with garlands of yellow roses. Once a team is across the line, the race judge officially congratulates them, and if they're an Iditarod rookie, they are awarded a belt buckle. I have seen the treasured award. It is not impressive. It is made of bronze, a little larger than a regular cowboy buckle, but less ostentatious. For every musher who has ever received one, it is among their most treasured possessions. How could it not be? In that small medallion lies the memories of a thousand miles of epic small victories and crushing small defeats.

Often, when the huskies arrive at a checkpoint stop, they're panting and tired. They are looking forward to a nice hot meal and some warm straw. But their attitude is totally different when they arrive at the finish. Their eyes are alive with excitement. Their trot is crisper and prouder. Their tails are pointed smartly behind their backs. In their hearts, they know that they have completed something grand. The musher waves to the appreciative audience. Amongst the cheers, the huskies often start yelping in unison, saluting the crowd with their own huskies' song. As soon as the dogs stop, the race official goes up and down the team, making sure that the microchip transponders agree with the numbers recorded prior to the start. This is done to prevent cheating, to ensure no one has substituted a fresh dog for a tired one. I can't see how that would be done easily. During the checkpoints, the teams are monitored 24/7. In the wilderness, I am not sure how a person could hike in with a new dog, locate a team, meet up with them unseen, and make a switch. I guess with some persistence and ingenuity it could be done, but the planning would have to resemble something from *Ocean's Eleven*.

Still, rules are rules, and each microchip is noted and compared against the Race List. A post-race urine sample is collected to ensure against doping.

The canine finishers have the same look as runners who've completed a marathon. They are elated and tired. Looking into the eyes of the huskies on the team, I know beyond empirical evidence that each dog feels the same satisfaction as their human counterparts. They're relishing this moment, too, sensing the excitement in the crowd. I would even go so far to say they feel proud. The veterinarians are still required to perform one last physical. The dogs are relaxed. They are sore, but a well-earned soreness. Several are already dozing by the time I get to their exam. Usually the musher's own backup team is there as well, helping to bed the dogs down for one more night. From here, they will go home, be it a few hours or a few days away.

The Iditarod Banquet in Nome takes place about a day after the final musher—the winner of "The Red Lantern," as it's come to be known—has crossed the finish line. It's a time for everyone to get together. The residents of Nome bring in trays and trays of food. The awards are handed out. In addition to the overall winner's award, there are smaller prizes to be given out. There is the Gold Coast Award for the first musher to reach Unalakleet, the Most Improved Musher Award, the Sportsmanship Award, even the Golden Clipboard Award given to the most outstanding checkpoint, and the Golden Stethoscope Award presented to the veterinarian who was most helpful on the trail. The atmosphere is casual. It is a time to catch up with the mushers I've met throughout the race. I can relax a little as well, and enjoy their stories of endurance, of late-night wilderness campfires where their only company is the huskies, of wonderfully awful coffee in the morning. Of runners hissing along in powder or greeting the sunrise cresting a hill.

Hyperbole has already crept into our tales. Winter nights were much colder; injuries treated, far more serious. Hungry and tired, the food was the best, the worst we'd ever had. All is told with a smile. Because now is good. Now we are finished. The teams will soon all head back to Anchorage, then all go their separate ways. For some, it will just be a short skip to the heart of Alaska. For others, it will be a whole other odyssey, from layover to layover until they reach their home halfway across the globe. This race is over. For many, another race is on the horizon; the Yukon Quest, the Beargrease, or one of many others around the world. Then there's the Iditarod. This year is over, but by the time they board a plane to their final destination, next year's race is already being planned.

As the festivities go on, and the partygoers party, the huskies stretch out on a bed of straw to rest. Granted, there'll be at least one volunteer who takes it upon themselves to give them a much-appreciated massage, but their adventure is over. For now. In a few days' time, they'll fly back to Anchorage to reunite with friends that had to leave the race early.

WILD DOG, FIRST FRIEND

THE STORY GOES THAT ONCE, A LONG TIME AGO, IN A PLACE THAT PROB-ably looked much like Alaska does now, a wolf saw a fire. He was cold; the fire appeared warm and inviting. An aroma of meat wafted over. His pack had warned him never to interact with humans because they were dangerous and unpredictable, but he was tired and hungry, so he placed his tail between his legs and crept humbly to the fire's edge.

Once, a long time ago, a hunter sat by his fire and cooked his dinner. He sat and warmed his hands by the flames. He was alone. There was no one to share his fire, no one to share his dinner. Then he noticed a wolf lying at the edge of the firelight. His friends had told him never to interact with wolves. They were dangerous and unpredictable. He was lonely, and the wolf looked like he might be good company, so he threw a piece of meat in its direction. The wolf gratefully ate the meal. And so their destinies were forever linked.

The wild calls. Once you've answered the call, you're bound to answer it again and again. At home, you'll quickly forget the discomforts. What you'll remember, instead, are the truly poignant parts: the shared comradeship between colleagues experiencing a difficult situation together; the warmth of a fire after being in core-chilling cold; the taste of food when you're extremely hungry; the moments of solitude and beauty; the blurring of the lines between man and nature; the satisfaction of a job well done. Like

It's all about
the dogs.

many of the mushers and dogs, I found that the lure of the Iditarod is irresistible. At the end of the event, I'm exhausted. My muscles are sore, and I have that dazed, unfocused feeling that follows from sleep deprivation, though I'm not as sleep-deprived as the mushers, I'm sure. But in a way, I also feel replenished. I know I'll return—to provide care, to be captivated by the beauty of the Arctic, to marvel at these mushers and their dogs as they pit themselves against other teams and against the challenge that is Alaska's Iditarod, to endure.

My first Iditarod was in 2012, when then twenty-five-year-old Dallas Seavey completed the course in a little over nine days, becoming the youngest musher ever to win. Also competing that year were Dallas's father, Mitch, and his grandfather, Dan, both past Iditarod champions. Of the sixty-six teams that started in Anchorage, fifty-four ultimately made it to Nome. For the veterinary team, too, it was a triumph. No serious injuries were reported, and all the dogs we treated were returned safely to their owners. It was an unforgettable experience, both personally and professionally. I felt spirited again. I had played a critical role in a world-renowned event; I had slept outside in subzero weather; I had drunk from glacial waters. I've now volunteered at more than ten Iditarods. Each year has been different, and yet the same. Maybe it's extravagant of me to say, but I feel a kinship with those early Arctic explorers, and with that first friend, too.

Ultimately, it's all about the dogs. What is there to say about the adventurous spirit of human and canine? It is presumptuous to think that we're the only species capable of experiencing and enjoying adventure. Play behavior is exhibited all around the animal kingdom. Dolphins are known to surf for amusement. Hawks spiral up and down air columns, sometimes seeking prey, but also, ornithologists believe, for fun. Who's to say that our closest companions for millennia haven't adopted our passion for fun and adventure, that dogs capable of love can't also experience the joy and pride of conquering a quest? As a veterinarian and lifelong lover of animals, it has always frustrated me that some people look down on the idea animals have an interior life resembling that of humans. My experience at the Iditarod has shown me that huskies experience love, fear, happiness, sadness, and maybe even hope. Some say that we shouldn't have events like the Iditarod—that huskies shouldn't be allowed to run with abandon through the wilderness, that their lives should be a gray existence of sleeping indoors on a bed and exercising only when their human owners are willing to take them on a leash around the neighborhood. Personally, I know thousands of huskies who would emphatically disagree.

At some point during my first Iditarod, someone handed me a business-card-sized note that read, "If the dogs had voices, they would give you a resounding howl of thanks." I appreciated the sentiment. But they do have voices: I hear them in every lick to the face on a cold night, every grin as they speed past, every nuzzle eager to be petted. In turn, I thank them, for their joy, their exuberance, and their love.

ACKNOWLEDGMENTS

FIRST, I WOULD LIKE TO THANK LANCE PARKIN FOR HIS expertise, insight, wisdom, and tireless help with this book. Many thanks, too, to my amazing editor Haley Bracken at Liveright, without whose guidance this book would not be possible. And a huge thank you to my agent, Jane Dystel, of Dystel, Goderich and Bourret, for taking a chance on a first-time author.

Thank you to Stu Nelson DVM, chief veterinarian of the Iditarod, for his deep and passionate commitment for the health of the Iditarod dogs—and also to his assistant, JoAnn Potts, and all the Iditarod veterinarians I have had the pleasure of working with all these years. On a personal note, I'd like to thank my lovely sister, Melinda Morgan Rae, and her wonderful partner, Scotty Wright, as well as my brother, Scott David Morgan, and his beautiful wife, Laura Persinger Morgan.

Thank you to my foster family, The Fosters: Tom, Kathryn, Josh, and Mitch. Thank you to Mr. Robert Deter and Ms. Marilyn Deter for your love, and for raising an amazing daughter. Most of all, thank you to my incredible wife and best friend, Kristine Ann Deter Morgan, and to our talented son, Spencer Ryan Morgan, for your encouragement and support. And thank you to my father, Norman Lee Morgan, who read the entire 600-page manuscript *before* it was edited.

Finally, thank you Mom, Nancy Ellen Rae. Whatever talents I may have as a writer came directly from you.

ILLUSTRATION CREDITS

ABOUT THE AUTHOR

DR. LEE MORGAN took a roundabout path to a veterinary career. Growing up by Ohio farmland, he graduated from Northwestern High School. He majored in biology and chemistry at Case Western Reserve University in Cleveland and ran for the legendary track coach, Bill Sudeck. He is a brother of Phi Gamma Delta fraternity.

As a sophomore, he landed an internship studying cognitive abilities in dolphins and spent eight months at the Kewalo Basin Marine Mammal Laboratory in Hawaii. That led to a job after graduation with Marine Animal Productions, training dolphins and sea lions for summertime shows and working with the animals in Mississippi during the offseason. This, in turn, led to a master's degree in marine science at the College of William and Mary in Virginia. During his master's research, he crossed paths frequently with Bob George, a veterinarian who worked with sea creatures and maintained a typical small-animal practice.

Working with this veterinarian—who had this huge base of knowledge while being able to treat dogs, cats, horses, sea turtles, dolphins, and anything else—had a profound impact on his career path and inspired him to attend veterinary school at the University of Wisconsin-Madison.

He has been owner of Georgetown Veterinary Hospital in Washington, DC, for over twenty years. He has served as a trail veterinarian for the Iditarod since 2012. He has also worked as a trail veterinarian for the Finnmarkslopet Sled Dog race held in northern Norway. He has worked on veterinary-related projects for NASA, the United States Navy, and National Geographic.

He lives and works with his wife, Kris; Lucy-Dog, who serves as the clinic's official "Greeter-Dog;" and Daisy the cat, who does not do much of anything. Lee and Kris are the proud parents of their phenomenal son, Spencer Ryan Morgan.